新 완전절친
TOEIC 베이직 RC

개정판

정주영 · 이의걸 · 글로벌어학연구소 공저

개정 3판 1쇄 발행 2018년 3월 5일
4쇄 발행 2021년 12월 10일

지은이 정주영 · 이의걸 · 글로벌어학연구소

펴낸곳 ㈜글로벌21
출판등록 2019년 1월 3일
주소 서울시 강남구 논현로76길 24
전화 02)6365-5169 팩스 02)6365-5179
www.global21.co.kr

ISBN 978-89-8233-308-8 13740

- 이 책에 실린 모든 내용, 디자인, 편집 구성의 저작권은 ㈜글로벌21과 지은이에게 있습니다.
  허락 없이 복제하거나 다른 매체에 옮겨 실을 수 없습니다.
- 본 도서는 『야금야금 공부해 한 번에 고득점 토익 베이직 RC』를 토익 신유형에 맞게 개정한 도서입니다.
- 잘못된 책은 구입하신 곳에서 바꿔 드립니다.

머리말 Prologue

우리는 유년 시절부터 대학생이 되기까지, 그리고 대학을 졸업하고 취직하기까지, 심지어 직장 내에서 승진이나 직무 적성 시험 통과를 위해서도 영어 학습에 적지 않은 비용과 시간을 투자해 오고 있습니다.

토익 시험 또한 대학 입시나 취업, 고시 준비, 직장 내에서의 영어 능력을 평가하는 척도로 여겨져 대학생, 성인은 물론 심지어 중·고등학생까지도 응시하고 있는 현실입니다. 최근 몇 년간 추이를 볼 때, 토익 응시생 수는 연인원 2백만 명 이상을 유지하고 있고 새로운 스피킹 시험들이 그 자리를 대체해 감에도 불구하고 여전히 토익 고득점을 향한 수험생들의 열기는 식지 않고 있습니다.

이에 부응하여, 서점가에는 수많은 토익 수험서와 기초 학습서들이 자리를 차지하고 수험생들의 선택을 기다리고 있으나, 지나치게 복잡한 이론으로 무장한 수험서들이 많은 것도 사실입니다. 이는 토익 입문자들에게 부담이 되고 오히려 학습 능률을 떨어뜨리는 부작용을 낳을 수 있습니다.

이에, 우리 필자들은 다년간 토익 강의와 집필에 몸담아 온 경험을 살려 불필요하고 장황한 해설과 군더더기 요소들을 과감히 없앰과 동시에 오직 신경향 문제 분석을 통한 출제 핵심 포인트와 풍부한 출제 예상 문제를 집중적으로 학습함으로써 짧은 기간 내에 토익 고득점에 이르도록 하는, **완전절친 TOEIC 베이직 LC/RC 개정판**을 새롭게 펴내게 되었습니다.

특히, 기본적인 출제 유형 분석과 풀이 전략에 더하여 토익 입문자들을 위한 가이드 역할을 할 수 있도록 기출 토익에서 빈출되는 필수 어휘, 관용 표현, 패턴 예문은 물론 다양한 비즈니스 상황 및 실생활과 연계된 대화문과 지문을 다룸으로써 단순히 과거 출제 패턴만을 답습하는 것이 아닌, 다가올 시험에 적극적으로 대처할 수 있는 기본기를 갖출 수 있도록 하였습니다.

완전절친 TOEIC 베이직 LC/RC 개정판으로 토익에 입문하는 수험생 여러분들이 이 책에 수록된 핵심 포인트와 문제 풀이 전략을 차근차근 익히고 기초학습과 실전문제 풀이를 병행해 나간다면 분명, 단기간에 높은 토익 점수를 얻게 될 것을 믿어 의심치 않으며 모쪼록 이 책이 수험생 여러분이 뜻하는 목표를 달성하는 데 큰 도움이 되기를 기대합니다.

차례 Contents

이 책의 구성과 특징　　　　　　　　　　　　　　　　006
TOEIC 소개　　　　　　　　　　　　　　　　　　　008
학습 캘린더　　　　　　　　　　　　　　　　　　　010

PART 5 & 6

Unit 01 ● 문장의 구성 요소　　　　　　　　　　　014
Unit 02 ● 문장의 5형식　　　　　　　　　　　　　024
Unit 03 ● 주어와 동사의 수 일치　　　　　　　　　034
Unit 04 ● 능동태와 수동태　　　　　　　　　　　　044
Unit 05 ● 시제　　　　　　　　　　　　　　　　　054
Unit 06 ● 명사　　　　　　　　　　　　　　　　　066
Unit 07 ● 대명사　　　　　　　　　　　　　　　　078
Unit 08 ● 형용사　　　　　　　　　　　　　　　　090
Unit 09 ● 부사　　　　　　　　　　　　　　　　　100
Unit 10 ● 전치사　　　　　　　　　　　　　　　　110
Unit 11 ● 등위·상관접속사와 접속부사　　　　　　122
Unit 12 ● to부정사　　　　　　　　　　　　　　　132
Unit 13 ● 동명사　　　　　　　　　　　　　　　　144
Unit 14 ● 분사　　　　　　　　　　　　　　　　　154
Unit 15 ● 명사절 접속사　　　　　　　　　　　　　166
Unit 16 ● 형용사절 접속사　　　　　　　　　　　　176
Unit 17 ● 부사절 접속사　　　　　　　　　　　　　186
Unit 18 ● 비교 구문　　　　　　　　　　　　　　　196
Unit 19 ● 가정법과 도치　　　　　　　　　　　　　206

PART 7

Unit 01	주제와 목적	218
Unit 02	구체적 정보	223
Unit 03	NOT/ TRUE	228
Unit 04	추론	233
Unit 05	동의어	238
Unit 06	편지와 이메일	243
Unit 07	광고	248
Unit 08	공지	253
Unit 09	회람	258
Unit 10	안내문	263
Unit 11	기사	268
Unit 12	송장과 양식	273
Unit 13	초대장	278
Unit 14	편지·이메일 연계 지문	283
Unit 15	광고 연계 지문	289
Unit 16	알림 연계 지문	295
Unit 17	기사 연계 지문	301
Unit 18	기타 연계 지문	307
Unit 19	고득점을 위한 독해 연습	313

Final Test   322

이 책의 구성과 특징

개념을 알면 문법이 보인다!

Grammar 유형 소개 및 개념 정리

신토익 학습에 필수적인 문법 사항에 대한 개념을 이해할 수 있도록 하였습니다. 무작정 외우는 방식을 지양하고 기출 시험과 신경향을 연계하여 체계적이고 실용적인 문법 학습을 할 수 있도록 합니다.

Grammar Point 정리 + Practice

빈출 유형과 출제 패턴에 따른 필수 문법 사항들을 정리, 실제 시험과 연계된 핵심 포인트를 제시하고 문장 내에서의 기능과 활용 패턴을 예문과 함께 이해할 수 있도록 하였습니다. Practice를 통해서는 문법 학습에 대한 이해도를 점검해 볼 수 있도록 합니다.

Vocabulary 기출 어휘 정리 + Practice

매 Unit마다 토익 필수 어휘를 품사별로 제시, 반복 학습을 통해 구문이나 문장을 정확히 이해하고 빠르게 문제를 풀 수 있는 실력을 갖추도록 합니다. 어휘 파악 유형 Practice로 어휘 학습 정도와 수준을 점검해 볼 수 있도록 합니다.

Actual Test

기출 시험의 출제 유형 및 신경향으로 구성한 Part 5, 6 Actual Test를 통해 해당 Unit의 문법 학습 수준을 점검하고 실제 시험 대비 적응력을 키울 수 있도록 합니다.

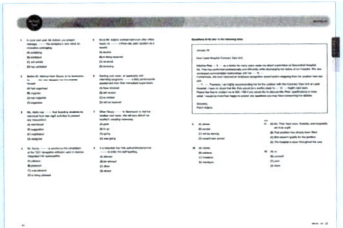

독해는 필요한 부분만 **빠르고 정확하게**!

출제 유형과 풀이 전략
Unit별로 Part 7에 나오는 독해 출제 유형과 신유형에 대한 학습 전략, 풀이 요령 등을 수록하였습니다. 시험장에서는 핵심 내용만을 빠르고 정확하게 파악하여 정답을 찾을 수 있도록 방법을 알려 줍니다.

Sample Test와 문제 분석
앞서 제시한 출제 유형, 학습 전략, 풀이 요령을 보다 알기 쉽게 이해할 수 있도록 Sample Test와 문제 분석을 통해 문제를 다루고 해결하는 과정을 보여 줍니다.

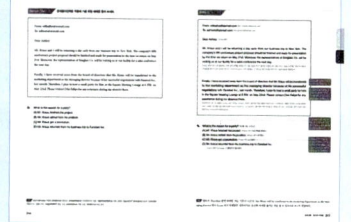

Practice와 Actual Test
Practice를 통해 앞서 배운 문제 공략법으로 독해 풀이 연습을 해봅니다. 다음으로, 실제 출제 유형에 신경향을 반영한 Part 7 Actual Test로 더욱 심도 있는 지문 이해와 속독속해 및 실력 점검을 할 수 있도록 하였습니다.

미리보는 토익, **Final Test**!

Final Test
실제 시험과 같은 출제 분야, 유형, 난이도의 모의고사를 권말에 수록, 실전처럼 풀어봄으로써 자신의 학업 성취도를 파악함과 동시에 새롭게 바뀌는 토익 시험에 대비할 수 있도록 합니다.

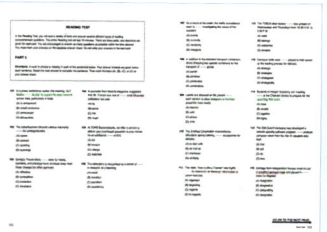

TOEIC 소개

토익이란?

TOEIC(Test of English for International Communication)은 영어가 모국어가 아닌 사람들을 대상으로 언어 본래의 기능인 커뮤니케이션 능력에 중점을 두고 일상생활, 또는 국제업무 등에 필요한 실용영어 능력을 평가하는 시험입니다. 1979년 미국 ETS(Educational Testing Service)에 의해 개발된 이래 전 세계 150개 국가 14,000개의 기관에서 승진 또는 해외파견 인원선발 등의 목적으로 널리 활용되고 있으며 우리나라에는 1982년 도입되었습니다. 현재 전 세계적으로 해마다 약 600만 명 이상이 응시하고 있습니다.

토익 시험의 구성

구성	Part	Part별 출제 내용		문항 수	제한 시간	배점
Listening Comprehension	1	사진 묘사		6	45분	495점
	2	질의 응답		25		
	3	짧은 대화		39	100	
	4	설명문		30		
Reading Comprehension	5	단문 공란 메우기(문법/어휘)		30	75분	495점
	6	장문 공란 메우기		16		
	7	독해	단일 지문	29	100	
			이중 지문	10		
			삼중 지문	15		
Total		7개 파트		200문항	120분	990점

토익 시험 출제 분야

TOEIC 시험에서는 주로 일상생활과 회사 업무 등에서 사용되는 어휘, 표현, 대화, 문장들을 다루며, 크게는 다음과 같은 분야와 관련된 문제들이 출제됩니다.

- ▶ **전문적인 비즈니스** | 계약, 협상, 마케팅, 세일즈, 비즈니스 계획, 회의
- ▶ **제조** | 공장 관리, 조립 라인, 품질 관리
- ▶ **금융과 예산** | 은행, 투자, 세금, 회계, 청구
- ▶ **개발** | 연구, 제품 개발
- ▶ **사무실** | 임원 회의, 위원 회의, 편지, 메모, 전화, 팩스, e-mail, 사무 장비와 가구
- ▶ **인사** | 구인, 채용, 퇴직, 급여, 승진, 취업 지원과 자기 소개
- ▶ **주택/기업 부동산** | 건축, 설계서, 구입과 임대, 전기와 가스 서비스
- ▶ **여행** | 기차, 비행기, 택시, 버스, 배, 유람선, 티켓, 일정, 역과 공항 안내, 자동차 렌트, 호텔, 예약, 연기와 취소

토익 시험 접수

TOEIC 시험은 인터넷으로만 접수가 가능합니다. 한국토익위원회 사이트(www.toeic.co.kr)에서 시험 일정 및 접수 기간 등 세부 내용을 확인할 수 있습니다.

토익 시험장 지참 준비물

▶ **신분증** | 반드시 규정된 신분증(주민등록증, 운전면허증, 기간 만료 전의 여권, 공무원증 등)을 지참해야 합니다. 신분증이 없으면 시험을 볼 수 없습니다.
▶ **필기구** | 연필, 지우개 (볼펜이나 사인펜은 사용할 수 없음)
▶ **시계** | 아날로그 손목시계 (전자식 시계는 사용할 수 없음)

토익 시험 시간표

[오전 9:30 시험의 경우]
▶ 09:30 ~ 09:39 | 입실(9:40 이후에는 입실 불가)
▶ 09:40 ~ 09:45 | 답안지 작성 관련 오리엔테이션
▶ 09:45 ~ 09:50 | 휴식
▶ 09:50 ~ 10:05 | 신분증 확인
▶ 10:05 ~ 10:10 | 문제지 배부 및 파본 확인
▶ 10:10 ~ 10:55 | 듣기 평가 (Listening Comprehension)
▶ 10:55 ~ 12:10 | 독해 평가 (Reading Comprehension)

토익 시험 성적 확인

정기시험 성적은 시험일로부터 약 5일 후 인터넷 홈페이지를 통해 확인할 수 있습니다. 단, 특별시험 성적은 시험일로부터 약 2주 내외에 확인할 수 있습니다. TOEIC 성적표는 우편으로 수령하거나 온라인으로 발급받을 수 있습니다. 우편 수령 시 성적 발표 후 약 7~10일 정도가 소요되며, 온라인으로 발급받을 경우 자신의 토익 성적 유효 기간 내에 홈페이지에 접속하여 직접 출력할 수 있습니다. (TOEIC 성적은 해당 시험 시행일로부터 2년 간 유효)

출처 : www.toeic.co.kr

학습 캘린더

유닛별 학습캘린더

● 목표 점수와 학습 시작일, 완료일을 정한 뒤, 각 Unit별로 학습 날짜를 정해 학습해 보세요. 하나의 Unit을 하루에 끝내기 어려울 경우, Unit당 학습 기간을 정하는 것도 좋습니다.

목표 점수	점
학습 시작일	년 월 일
학습 완료일	년 월 일

	학습 내용	학습 날짜		학습 내용	학습 날짜
Part 5&6	Unit 01	/	Part 7	Unit 01	/
	Unit 02	/		Unit 02	/
	Unit 03	/		Unit 03	/
	Unit 04	/		Unit 04	/
	Unit 05	/		Unit 05	/
	Unit 06	/		Unit 06	/
	Unit 07	/		Unit 07	/
	Unit 08	/		Unit 08	/
	Unit 09	/		Unit 09	/
	Unit 10	/		Unit 10	/
	Unit 11	/		Unit 11	/
	Unit 12	/		Unit 12	/
	Unit 13	/		Unit 13	/
	Unit 14	/		Unit 14	/
	Unit 15	/		Unit 15	/
	Unit 16	/		Unit 16	/
	Unit 17	/		Unit 17	/
	Unit 18	/		Unit 18	/
	Unit 19	/		Unit 19	/
				Final Test	/

월별 학습캘린더

● 목표 점수와 학습 시작일, 완료일을 정한 뒤, 스스로 일정을 계획해서 학습해 보세요. 8주에 걸쳐 모든 Unit을 학습하는 방법, 또는 4주에 걸쳐 모든 Unit을 학습한 뒤 나머지 4주 동안 복습하는 방법이 있습니다.

목표 점수	점					
학습 시작일	년		월		일	
학습 완료일	년		월		일	

월	화	수	목	금	토	일

Unit 01	문장의 구성 요소	Unit 11	등위·상관접속사와 접속부사
Unit 02	문장의 5형식	Unit 12	to부정사
Unit 03	주어와 동사의 수 일치	Unit 13	동명사
Unit 04	능동태와 수동태	Unit 14	분사
Unit 05	시제	Unit 15	명사절 접속사
Unit 06	명사	Unit 16	형용사절 접속사
Unit 07	대명사	Unit 17	부사절 접속사
Unit 08	형용사	Unit 18	비교구문
Unit 09	부사	Unit 19	가정법과 도치
Unit 10	전치사		

Part 5&6

Part 5-6

Unit 01 문장의 구성 요소

영어에서도 문장이 성립되려면 최소한의 필수 구성 요소인 주어와 동사가 있어야만 합니다. 실제 토익 시험에서는 주어가 될 수 있는 것, 주어가 될 수 없는 것, 동사가 될 수 있는 것, 동사가 될 수 없는 것, 가주어나 진주어를 묻는 유형의 문제가 출제되고 있습니다.

주어와 동사

주어는 동작이나 상태의 주체를 나타내는 말이고 동사는 주어의 동작이나 상태를 나타내는 말입니다. '나는 걷는다.'라는 문장에서 걷는 동작의 주체인 '나는'이 문장의 주어이고 주어의 동작인 '걷는다'가 동사입니다. 이렇게 최소한 주어 하나와 동사 하나가 문장을 구성하는 필수 요소이며 두 요소 중 하나라도 빠지면 문장이 될 수 없습니다.

I walk. 나는 걷는다.
　주어 동사

People run. 사람들은 달린다.
　주어　　동사

목적어와 보어, 수식어

항상 '주어+동사'로 된 문장만을 쓸 수는 없겠지요. 그래서 더 길고 다양한 문장을 만들기 위해 목적어, 보어, 수식어 같은 다른 문장 구성 요소가 필요합니다.

목적어는 주어가 하는 동작의 대상이 되는 말입니다.

I love her. 나는 그녀를 사랑한다.

보어는 주어나 목적어의 성질이나 상태를 보충 설명해주는 말입니다.

She is pretty. 그녀는 예쁘다.
She is a singer. 그녀는 노래하는 사람이다.

수식어는 앞의 문장 구성 요소를 제외한 나머지 부분으로 다른 문장 요소나 문장 전체를 수식해 의미를 더해주는 말입니다.

She sings well. 그녀는 노래를 잘한다.
She is a good singer. 그녀는 노래를 잘하는 사람이다.

주어의 종류

주어가 될 수 있는 것은 명사와 대명사 또는 명사 어구(to부정사, 동명사, 명사절)입니다.

<u>Profits</u> decreased. 수익이 줄었다.
  명사

<u>He</u> arrived. 그가 도착했다.
대명사

<u>Reading comics</u> is my pastime. 만화를 읽는 것이 내 취미다.
   동명사

 동사의 종류

동사의 종류는 보통 be동사, 조동사, 일반동사로 나눕니다.

- **be동사** '~이다, 있다'라는 의미로 주어의 상태를 나타내는 동사입니다. 시제와 인칭에 따라 형태가 다르므로 변화형을 잘 알고 있어야 합니다.

	현재 시제	과거 시제
1인칭	I am We are	I was We were
2인칭	You are	You were
3인칭	He/She/It is They are	He/She/It was They were

- **조동사** 동사를 보조해 의미를 보충해주는 말로 will/would, can/could, may/might, must, should 등이 있습니다. 토익 시험에서는 여러 조동사의 뜻을 구분하는 문제는 출제되지 않습니다. 조동사 뒤에는 반드시 동사원형이 와야 한다는 요점을 기억하는 것이 중요합니다.

- **일반동사** be동사와 조동사를 제외한 동사로 전체 동사의 90% 이상을 차지합니다.

1 시험에 반드시 나오는 주어 유형

주어 자리에 올 수 있는 것

문장의 주어로는 명사, 대명사 그리고 명사에 상응하는 to부정사, 동명사, 명사구, 명사절이 사용될 수 있습니다. 명사절은 접속사 that/if/whether/what/how/who/when 등이 이끄는 절입니다.

<u>The staff</u> attended a reception. 직원들이 연회에 참석했다.
　명사

<u>They</u> have an excellent reputation. 그들은 평판이 아주 좋다.
　대명사

<u>Learning new skills</u> is very important. 새로운 기술을 배우는 것은 매우 중요하다.
　　동명사

<u>To implement changes</u> is the top priority. 변화를 실행하는 것이 최우선 과제다.
　　to부정사

<u>What I like</u> is Dr. Jay's paper. 내가 좋아하는 것은 Jay 박사의 논문이다.
　명사절

가주어와 진주어

▶ 가주어 it

주어인 to부정사구나 명사절이 길 때에는 주어 자리에 가주어 it을 대신 넣고 긴 주어를 문장 뒤로 보냅니다. 가주어 it은 아무런 의미가 없으므로 해석하지 않습니다. 이때 문장의 진짜 주어인 to부정사구나 명사절을 진주어라고 합니다.

It is the policy <u>to check the background of all job applicants</u>. 모든 지원자들의 배경을 조사하는 것이 방침이다.
　　　　　　　진주어 (to부정사)

It is important <u>that the patients receive proper care</u>. 환자들이 적절한 치료를 받는 것이 중요하다.
　　　　　　진주어 (명사절)

It is not determined <u>whether the picnic will be held</u>. 야유회가 열릴지는 결정되지 않았다.
　　　　　　　진주어 (명사절)

▶ 가주어 there

'There+동사(be동사, remain, exist 등)+명사' 구문에서 there는 가주어 역할을 합니다. 이때 동사의 수는 진주어인 다음 명사에 일치시켜야 합니다. 가주어 there는 아무런 의미가 없으므로 해석하지 않습니다.

There (is / **are**) <u>a sales tax</u> on all items. 모든 품목에는 판매세가 있다.
　　　　　　진주어

There (remain / **remains**) <u>some difficulties</u> to overcome. 극복해야 할 난제들이 남아 있다.
　　　　　　　진주어

Practice

정답 및 해설 p.4

A. 괄호에서 적절한 것을 고르세요.

1 The (cancel / cancellation) of the contract with Leetig Construction would eliminate some of the profit.

2 The (attractive / attractions) of Flora Town draw the attention of many visitors and travelers every year.

3 (That / If) Julibee Company's stock has been climbing is evidence that business has become successful.

4 It is not recommended (to use / using) machines without proper authorization or supervision.

B. 빈칸에 가장 적절한 것을 고르세요.

5 Mr. Parker was given responsibility of the project after ------- gave his presentation with unmoved confidence.
(A) he
(B) his
(C) him
(D) himself

6 Now that our proposal is approved by our sponsors, ------- is clear that our project will be completed smoothly.
(A) there
(B) it
(C) that
(D) any

7 ------- high standards of service will be our priority for the next six months.
(A) Maintain
(B) Maintains
(C) Maintaining
(D) Maintained

8 ------- are many places to visit in Whitewest Valley such as the mountain trails and the nearby waterfall.
(A) There
(B) It
(C) You
(D) They

어휘 1 contract 계약, 계약서 eliminate 제거하다, 없애다 profit 이익, 수익 2 draw 끌다, 잡아끌다 attention 관심, 주목 visitor 방문객 traveler 여행자 3 stock 주식 climb 오르다 evidence 증거 4 recommend 권장하다 proper 적절한 authorization 허가, 인가 supervision 감독 5 responsibility 책임, 의무 unmoved 확고한 confidence 자신감 6 proposal 제안, 계획 approve 승인하다 sponsor 광고주, 스폰서 clear 분명한 complete 완료하다, 끝마치다 smoothly 순조롭게 7 priority 우선순위 8 mountain trail 등산로 nearby 가까운 waterfall 폭포

2 시험에 반드시 나오는 동사 유형

동사 자리에 올 수 있는 것

▶ **be동사** 주어의 인칭, 수, 시제에 따라 am, are, is, was, were로 형태가 변합니다.

We (is / are) proud to announce the opening of our new gallery.
새로운 갤러리의 개장을 발표하게 되어 자랑스럽습니다.

▶ **조동사** 조동사 will/would, can/could, may/might, should, must 뒤에는 동사원형이 와야 합니다.

We will (return / to return) your money as long as you return your merchandise.
상품을 반납하시면 돈을 돌려드리겠습니다.

The Museum of Natural History will (be closed / closes) for six months.
자연사 박물관이 6개월 동안 문을 닫게 될 것이다.

★ 조동사로 사용되는 do는 뒤에 동사원형이 나오며 부정문, 의문문을 만들거나 일반동사를 강조합니다.

She doesn't smoke. 그녀는 담배를 피우지 않는다. [부정문]
Do you like the book? 그 책을 좋아하나요? [의문문]
I do love her. 나는 그녀를 정말 사랑한다. [강조]

▶ **일반동사** be동사와 조동사를 제외한 나머지 동사들

I need your account number. 당신의 계좌번호가 필요합니다.
The boss approved the project. 사장이 그 프로젝트를 승인했다.

▶ **명령문** 주어를 생략하고 동사원형을 사용합니다. 이때 please를 앞에 붙여 주면 부탁의 의미가 됩니다.

(Please) Take the time to review the report. 시간을 내어 보고서를 검토해 보세요.

동사 자리에 올 수 없는 것

▶ **to부정사와 동명사는 문장의 동사가 될 수 없습니다.**

Most employees (to commute / commuting / commute) to work by bicycle.
대부분의 직원들은 자전거로 통근한다.

▶ **명사나 형용사도 문장의 동사 자리에 올 수 없습니다.**

Mr. Lee (preference / prefers) to do business with a young group.
Lee 씨는 젊은 그룹과 함께 일하는 것을 선호한다.

TTC company (continues / continual) to be Setcom's most important client.
TTC 사는 계속 Setcom의 가장 중요한 고객이 될 것이다.

Practice

정답 및 해설 p.5

A. 괄호에서 적절한 것을 고르세요.

1. If you cannot solve a problem at work, you should (reporting / report) it to your manager or supervisor.

2. The computer programmer (to notify / notifies) the user of the required update.

3. In the upcoming staff meeting, team manager Josie Thorpe (reviewing / will review) team members' suggestions.

4. Weather reporters (predict / predicting) that there will be heavy snowfall in the beginning of December.

B. 빈칸에 가장 적절한 것을 고르세요.

5. Although Polo Bakery is best known for its custom-designed wedding cakes, it also ------- in children's birthday parties.
   (A) specializes
   (B) specialization
   (C) specialty
   (D) specializing

6. Please ------- your shoes in front of the door before entering the house.
   (A) to leave
   (B) leaves
   (C) leaving
   (D) leave

7. The plan must be tested and approved before it can ------- in the field.
   (A) has implemented
   (B) be implemented
   (C) implementing
   (D) implementation

8. Supermarkets always store vegetables and fruits at low temperature so that they do not -------.
   (A) deteriorates
   (B) deteriorate
   (C) deteriorating
   (D) to deteriorate

어휘 ¹solve 해결하다 problem 문제, 과제 report 보고하다 supervisor 관리자 ²notify 통지하다 required 요구되는, 필수의 ³review 검토하다 upcoming 다가오는 suggestion 제안(서) ⁴predict 예측하다 snowfall 강설(량) ⁵custom-designed 고객 맞춤형의 specialize 전문으로 하다 ⁶leave 놓아두다 ⁷field 현장 implement 시행하다 ⁸store 저장하다 vegetable 채소 low 낮은 temperature 온도, 기온 deteriorate 나빠지다, 악화되다

Unit 01 : 문장의 구성 요소

3 반드시 알아야 하는 기출 동사 어휘 ❶

- [ ] **expand**
  확대하다, 확장하다
  - expand its client base 고객층을 확대하다
  - expand our current facility 현재 시설을 확장하다

- [ ] **place**
  놓다, (명령·주문 등을) 하다
  - place purse over lap 핸드백을 무릎 위에 올려놓다
  - place an order 주문을 하다

- [ ] **resume**
  다시 시작하다[되다]
  - The game resumed. 경기가 다시 시작되었다.
  - resume operation 가동을 재개하다

- [ ] **schedule**
  일정을 잡다, 예정하다
  - schedule an interview 인터뷰 일정을 잡다
  - Construction is scheduled to begin. 공사가 시작될 예정이다.

- [ ] **consist**
  (~로) 이루어져 있다, (~에) 있다
  - Happiness consists in giving. 행복은 주는 데 있다.
  - The hotel consists of 176 rooms. 그 호텔은 176개의 객실로 이루어져 있다.

- [ ] **reduce**
  줄이다, 축소하다
  - reduce tax liability 세액을 줄이다
  - reduce the production time 제조 시간을 줄이다

- [ ] **open**
  열다, 개장하다
  - decide to open a new office 새 사무실을 열기로 결정하다
  - will officially open 공식적으로 문을 열 것이다

- [ ] **postpone**
  연기하다, 미루다
  - The concert is postponed due to bad weather. 날씨가 나빠 콘서트가 연기되었다.
  - The meeting will be postponed. 회의가 연기될 것이다.

- [ ] **announce**
  발표하다, 선언하다
  - announce a new policy 새 정책을 발표하다
  - finally announce a merger 마침내 합병을 선언하다

- [ ] **accept**
  받다, 받아들이다
  - He will accept the offer. 그는 제안을 받아들일 것이다.
  - accept the full-time position 정규직을 수락하다

- [ ] **express**
  표현하다, 나타내다
  - express respect 경의를 표하다
  - Words fail to express how I felt. 내가 느낀 감정을 말로 표현할 수 없다.

- [ ] **direct**
  향하게 하다, 보내다, (길을) 알려 주다
  - Please direct any questions to me. 아무 질문이나 보내주세요.
  - Could you direct me to the library? 도서관으로 가는 길을 알려 주시겠어요?

- [ ] **discourage**
  의욕을 꺾다, 좌절시키다
  - discourage theft 도난을 방지하다
  - incentives to discourage employees from early retirement
    직원들의 조기 퇴직을 억제하기 위한 유인책

- [ ] **lead**
  안내하다, 이끌다, ~으로 이어지다
  - lead to a new career 새로운 경력으로 이어지다
  - lead a discussion 토론을 이끌다

- [ ] **equip**
  (장비·능력을) 갖추다, 갖추게 하다
  - The kitchen is equipped with energy-efficient appliances.
    주방에는 에너지 절약형 가전제품이 갖추어져 있다
  - be equipped to study in college 대학에서 공부할 능력을 갖추다.

Practice

정답 및 해설 p.6

A. 괄호에서 적절한 것을 고르세요.

1. The traffic control department (placed / settled) speed limit signs on the new highways to ensure the safety of all drivers.

2. The conference will (assemble / resume) as soon as the speaker returns from a short break.

3. Professor Forester has (scheduled / served) the next session on British History for May 16.

4. Taking public transportation significantly (reduces / retrieves) the emission of air pollutants.

B. 빈칸에 가장 적절한 것을 고르세요.

5. Chairman Peter Nichols ------- concerns about the unstable budget.
   (A) focused
   (B) appeared
   (C) applied
   (D) expressed

6. The organization is ------- donations for aiding the survivors of the recent disaster.
   (A) proceeding
   (B) competing
   (C) accepting
   (D) electing

7. Owing to a heavy snowstorm, the flight schedule has been ------- until further notice.
   (A) programmed
   (B) defined
   (C) classified
   (D) postponed

8. JRR Housing Co. ------- newly constructed facilities with several appliances for convenience.
   (A) assembles
   (B) equips
   (C) invests
   (D) attributes

어휘 1 traffic 교통 department 부서 speed limit 속도 제한 ensure 보장하다 2 conference 총회, 회담 break (짧은) 휴식 3 professor 교수 session 수업 (시간) 4 public transportation 대중교통 significantly 상당히, 대폭 emission 배출 pollutant 오염물질 5 chairman 회장 concern 걱정, 우려 unstable 불안정한 budget 예산 6 organization 단체, 기관 donation 기부(금) aid 돕다, 지원하다 survivor 생존자 recent 최근의 disaster 재난, 재해 7 snowstorm 눈보라 flight 비행, 항공편 8 construct 건설하다 facility 시설, 설비 appliance 가전제품 convenience 편리, 편의

Unit 01 : 문장의 구성 요소 21

Actual Test

1. It is important ------- all workers follow safety rules when operating machines inside the factory.
   (A) it
   (B) that
   (C) there
   (D) to

2. Mr. Grant will ------- early tomorrow morning if his flight has not been delayed.
   (A) arriving
   (B) arrival
   (C) arrive
   (D) arrived

3. The main server board for LAN connections and surveillance at DDT Company ------- twenty-four hours a day.
   (A) operators
   (B) operating
   (C) operates
   (D) operation

4. The payment for this month does not ------- any bonus or overtime pay.
   (A) including
   (B) included
   (C) include
   (D) includes

5. If you have problems with the electrical system, please ------- to our maintenance personnel.
   (A) speak
   (B) spoke
   (C) speaks
   (D) to speak

6. There are many quality ------- that all appliances must pass before they are launched.
   (A) checkable
   (B) checks
   (C) checked
   (D) check

7. ------- to errors that appear in the report should be e-mailed to FishPermit@dnr.gov.
   (A) Correcting
   (B) Corrections
   (C) Correct
   (D) Corrected

8. Bob Irwin indicates that there ------- certainly more women than men who prefer to wear clothes for style than for comfort.
   (A) are
   (B) is
   (C) been
   (D) being

22

Questions 9-12 refer to the following notice.

The --- 9. --- of the laundry room at Glen Hills Apartment Complex is restricted to residents of the complex.

This facility --- 10. --- six washing machines and six dryers that are available for use 24 hours a day.

Since we cannot monitor the facility at all times, we ask for your cooperation in keeping it well-maintained. If you find that any machine is malfunctioning, please call our maintenance department at 555-0162. --- 11. ---. In most cases, a technician will repair the machine within 48 hours of --- 12. --- your call. Thank you for your cooperation.

9. (A) use
    (B) used
    (C) useful
    (D) uses

10. (A) including
    (B) includes
    (C) included
    (D) to include

NEW
11. (A) Be sure to provide the machine number when reporting the problem to help the technician respond promptly.
    (B) Maintenance department is on the first floor of the building.
    (C) You'd better drop by the maintenance department in person as we are short-staffed.
    (D) It is prohibited from operating the washing machine after midnight.

12. (A) receive
    (B) receives
    (C) be received
    (D) receiving

Unit 02 문장의 5형식

Part 5-6

영어 문장을 구성하는 방식은 총 5가지가 있는데, 이를 5형식이라고 합니다. 복잡하게 보이지만 각 형식에 맞는 대표적인 동사만 알면 쉽게 익힐 수 있습니다. 실제 토익 시험에서는 2, 4, 5형식이 가장 많이 출제됩니다. 2형식과 5형식 동사의 보어 형태, 대표적인 4형식 동사, 4형식 동사의 수동태 변화, 이 세 가지가 주로 출제되는 유형입니다.

1형식 문형: 주어+자동사

- 주어와 동사만으로 완전한 문장입니다.
- 1형식 동사 뒤에는 목적어나 보어가 필요 없습니다. 앞뒤에 수식어(부사, 전치사구, to부정사, 부사절)가 붙어 문장이 얼마든지 길어질 수 있습니다.

The train arrived. 열차가 도착했다.
　주어　　　동사

He works hard. 그는 열심히 일한다.
주어　동사　　부사

2형식 문형: 주어+자동사+보어

- 주어와 동사만으로는 불완전해 보어가 필요한 문장입니다.
- 보어 자리에는 형용사나 명사가 옵니다.

They are happy. 그들은 행복하다.
주어　동사　보어 (형용사)

Peter became a lawyer. Peter는 변호사가 되었다.
주어　　　동사　　　보어 (명사)

3형식 문형: 주어+타동사+목적어

- 주어와 동사 다음에 목적어를 필요로 하는 문장입니다.
- 1, 2형식 동사를 제외한 대부분의 동사는 목적어가 필요한 3형식 동사(타동사)입니다.

He loves her. 그는 그녀를 사랑한다.
주어　동사　목적어

She bought a travel book. 그녀는 여행서를 샀다.
주어　　동사　　　　목적어

4형식 문형: 주어+수여동사+간접목적어+직접목적어

- 동사 다음에 두 개의 목적어가 필요한 문장입니다.
- 간접목적어는 '~에게'라고 해석하며 직접목적어는 '~을/를'이라고 해석합니다.

He gave his friend a book. 그는 친구에게 책을 주었다.
주어 동사   간접목적어 직접목적어

The company offers Ms. Lyn a good salary. 그 회사는 Lyn 씨에게 괜찮은 급여를 제공한다.
　　주어　　　　동사　　간접목적어　　직접목적어

- 4형식 문형은 간접목적어 또는 직접목적어를 주어로 해서 2가지 수동태 문장이 가능합니다.

They awarded James the prize. 그들은 James에게 상을 주었다.
주어   동사   간접목적어 직접목적어

→ James was (awarded / awarding) the prize (by them). James는 상을 받았다.

★ 동사 뒤에 목적어 the prize가 있어 능동태인 awarding을 정답으로 고르기 쉽지만 간접목적어가 주어로 나온 수동태에서도 목적어가 뒤따라 나올 수 있습니다. 따라서 이런 문제는 문장 의미를 해석해 풀어야 합니다. 상을 받았다는 의미가 적절하므로 수동태인 awarded가 정답입니다.

5형식 문형: 주어+타동사+목적어+목적격 보어

- 목적어 다음에 목적어의 상태나 동작을 보충 설명하는 목적격 보어가 필요한 문장입니다.
- 목적어와 목적격 보어는 주어와 동사의 관계로 생각할 수 있습니다.

He makes me happy. 그는 나를 행복하게 해요.
주어 동사 목적어 목적격 보어

She kept the door open. 그녀는 문을 계속 열어 두었다.
주어 동사   목적어   목적격 보어

1 시험에 반드시 나오는 1, 2형식 문형

● 1형식 문형: 주어+자동사

▶ **자주 쓰이는 1형식 동사**

go 가다	come 오다	arrive 도착하다	work 일하다	exist 존재하다
last 지속되다	rise 오르다	decline 감소하다	proceed 진행하다	occur 발생하다
appear 나타나다	deal 다루다	succeed 성공하다	specialize 전문으로 하다	

▶ **1형식 동사 주위에 빈칸이 있으면 부사가 정답입니다.**

The workers worked (~~diligent~~ / diligently) throughout the day. 직원들은 하루 온종일 부지런히 일했다.

▶ **1형식 동사는 뒤에 목적어를 바로 쓸 수 없으므로 뒤에 전치사가 오고 목적어가 와야 합니다.**

She deals (~~her~~ / with her) client's requests efficiently. 그녀는 고객의 요청을 효과적으로 다룬다.

● 2형식 문형: 주어+자동사+보어(형용사/전치사구/동명사/to부정사)

▶ **자주 쓰이는 2형식 동사**

be ~이다	become ~이 되다	remain 남다	stay 머물다	seem ~인 것 같다
look ~처럼 보이다	feel ~라고 느끼다	sound ~처럼 들리다		

▶ **2형식 동사의 보어로 형용사나 명사가 오는데, 토익에서는 형용사가 정답으로 자주 출제됩니다.**

New products are becoming (profitable / ~~profitably~~) in many countries. 신상품은 많은 나라에서 이윤을 내고 있다.
                                      형용사   부사

▶ **be동사(is, are, was, were)와 형용사 사이에 올 수 있는 것은 부사입니다.**

Hampshire is (~~easy~~ / easily) accessible by train. Hampshire는 열차로 쉽게 접근할 수 있다.
                    형용사   부사

▶ **remain+형용사(여전히 ~이다), remain to+동사원형(아직 ~해야 한다) 구조가 자주 출제됩니다.**

The final result remains to be seen. 최종 결과는 두고 봐야 한다.
It remains to be seen (~~that~~ / whether) the campaign will be successful. 그 캠페인이 성공할지는 두고 봐야 한다.

★ It remains to be seen whether+절(~하게 될지 두고 봐야 한다)의 형태로 명사절 접속사인 whether를 넣는 문제도 자주 출제되니 꼭 기억하세요.

Practice

A. 괄호에서 적절한 것을 고르세요.

1. Real estate agents are worried that potential buyers will be discouraged as property prices are rising (steady / steadily) over time.

2. Whether the adjustments will be made today or delayed until further notice, the result remains (to be / have been) seen.

3. Workers in the production line have been (extreme / extremely) busy trying to meet the deadline for the shipment that is due next week.

4. If the mattress becomes (dirt / dirty), treat it with the correct cleaner.

B. 빈칸에 가장 적절한 것을 고르세요.

5. The nutrients found in fruits and vegetables are ------- for the development of our bodies as they provide the necessary vitamins and minerals.
   (A) essential
   (B) essentially
   (C) essence
   (D) essences

6. Chittenden County Transportation Authority is ------- to return to negotiations with the union.
   (A) ready
   (B) readier
   (C) readily
   (D) readiness

7. The Prime Minister just ------- from Washington and is planning to hold a press conference regarding the Free Trade Agreement.
   (A) sent
   (B) arrived
   (C) delayed
   (D) examined

8. The Grand Waterpark is not ------- for any lost or stolen items; therefore, one must be careful not to leave personal belongings unattended.
   (A) responsible
   (B) responsibleness
   (C) responsibly
   (D) responsibility

어휘 1 real estate agent 부동산 중개업자 worried 우려하는 potential 가능성 있는, 잠재적인 discouraged 낙담한 property 재산, 부동산 2 adjustment 조정, 수정 delay 연기하다, 지연시키다 further 더 이상의 notice 공지, 통보 3 meet the deadline 기한을 맞추다 shipment 선적(물), 발송(물) 4 treat 다루다 correct 맞는, 적절한 5 nutrient 영양소 development 발달, 발전 provide 공급하다 necessary 필요한 6 transportation 교통 authority 당국 union 노조 7 Prime Minister 총리, 수상 press conference 기자회견 regarding ~에 관해 8 stolen 도난당한 belongings 소지품 unattended 방치된

2 시험에 반드시 나오는 3, 4, 5형식 문형

3형식 문형: 주어+타동사+목적어(명사/대명사/동명사/to부정사/부사절)

▶ 1, 2형식 동사를 제외한 일반동사의 대부분이 목적어가 필요한 3형식 동사입니다.

Ace Electronics has developed a (system / systemic) in cooperation with Star Software.
                                                              명사   형용사

Ace 전자는 Star 소프트웨어와 협력해 시스템을 개발해왔다.

4형식 문형: 주어+타동사+간접목적어+직접목적어

▶ 자주 쓰이는 4형식 동사 ★ 4형식 동사는 모두 3형식 동사로도 사용될 수 있습니다.

give ~에게 ~을 주다	offer ~에게 ~을 제공하다	bring ~에게 ~을 가져오다	
send ~에게 ~을 보내다	award ~에게 ~을 수여하다	grant ~에게 ~을 주다	assign ~에게 ~을 할당하다
charge ~에게 ~을 부과하다	issue ~에게 ~을 발급하다	win ~에게 ~을 가져오다	

▶ 4형식 문형에서는 동사 다음에 목적어가 두 개 와야 합니다.

We (offer / submit) our clients various solutions. 우리는 고객들에게 다양한 솔루션을 제공한다.
                       간접목적어   직접목적어

5형식 문형: 주어+동사+목적어+목적격 보어(형용사/분사/to부정사/명사)

▶ 형용사, 분사를 목적격 보어로 취하는 5형식 동사

make 만들다	keep 유지하다	find 찾다, 알아내다	consider 여기다, 생각하다
call 부르다	leave 놔두다	deem 간주하다	

They keep the area clean. 그들은 그 구역을 깨끗하게 유지합니다.
주어 동사   목적어   목적격 보어 (형용사)

▶ to부정사를 목적격 보어로 취하는 5형식 동사

ask 부탁하다	request 요청하다	expect 기대하다	encourage 격려하다
enable 가능하게 하다	allow 허락하다	permit 허락하다	

I ask you to attend the meeting. 당신에게 회의에 참석해주실 것을 부탁드립니다.
주어 동사 목적어   목적격 보어

▶ 명사를 목적격 보어로 취하는 5형식 동사

call A B A를 B로 부르다	consider A B A를 B로 간주하다	appoint A B A를 B로 임명하다	elect A B A를 B로 선출하다

They call me Dr. Jekyll. 사람들이 나를 Jekyll 박사라고 부른다.
주어 동사 목적어 목적격 보어

Practice

정답 및 해설 p.12

A. 괄호에서 적절한 것을 고르세요.

1. My assistant will (allow / send) you a list of deserving candidates for the promotion.

2. The premium membership card (grants / indicates) you full access to all our facilities.

3. The travel package includes (transportation / to transport) costs and a personal tour guide.

4. I would like to encourage you (considered / to consider) reading the newspaper rather than watching television.

B. 빈칸에 가장 적절한 것을 고르세요.

5. Anyone who wants to ------- in the annual marathon should register beforehand.
   (A) complete
   (B) attend
   (C) participate
   (D) release

6. Everyone who attended community service at the healthcare center ------- a letter of appreciation last week.
   (A) was sending
   (B) would send
   (C) will send
   (D) was sent

7. MRT computers will ------- machines to perform faster and smoother operations.
   (A) inhibit
   (B) prefer
   (C) enable
   (D) keep

8. The new AAC model ------- customers to make multiple phone calls at once for the price of one call.
   (A) allows
   (B) promotes
   (C) accepts
   (D) gives

어휘 1 assistant 조수, 보좌관 deserving 자격이 있는 candidate 후보 promotion 승진 2 access 접근, 이용 facility 시설 3 include 포함하다 personal 개인적인 4 encourage 권하다, 장려하다 5 annual 매년의, 연례의 register 등록하다 beforehand 미리, 사전에 6 attend 참가하다 community 지역사회 healthcare center 보건소 appreciation 감사 7 perform 실행하다 operation 작동, 작업 8 multiple 여러 개의 at once 한 번에

Unit 02 : 문장의 5형식   29

3 반드시 알아야 하는 기출 동사 어휘 ❷

- [ ] **reserve**
  예약하다, 보유하다
  - **reserve** a place 장소를 예약하다
  - **reserve** the right to claim damages 손해배상을 청구할 권리가 있다

- [ ] **encounter**
  마주치다, 부닥치다
  - **encounter** many difficulties 많은 어려움을 만나다
  - **encounter** problems 문제들에 부닥치다

- [ ] **focus**
  초점을 맞추다, 집중하다
  - **focus** on educational issues 교육 문제들에 초점을 맞추다
  - **focus** on strategies 전략들에 집중하다

- [ ] **sign**
  서명하다, 사인하다
  - **sign** the statement 명세서에 사인하다
  - **sign** an official offer 공식 제안서에 서명하다

- [ ] **organize**
  조직하다, 설립하다
  - **organize** a small business 소기업을 설립하다
  - **organize** a medical conference 의학 총회를 조직하다

- [ ] **inspect**
  검사하다, 점검하다
  - **inspect** rental cars 렌터카를 점검하다
  - be thoroughly **inspected** 철저하게 점검을 받다

- [ ] **enlarge**
  확대하다, 확장하다
  - **enlarge** the sales divisions 영업부를 확대하다
  - **enlarge** a sea port 항구를 확장하다

- [ ] **accommodate**
  수용하다, 받아들이다
  - **accommodate** more than 500 guests 500여 명의 손님을 수용하다
  - **accommodate** your individual needs 여러분의 개인적인 요구를 받아들이다

- [ ] **refute**
  반박하다
  - **refute** the competitor's claim 경쟁사의 주장을 반박하다
  - **refute** such criticism 이러한 비난을 반박하다

- [ ] **possess**
  소유하다, 갖고 있다
  - **possess** a valid driver's license 유효한 운전 면허증을 가지고 있다
  - **possess** at least five years of experience 적어도 5년 정도의 경험이 있다

- [ ] **protect**
  보호하다, 보존하다
  - **protect** the company's property 회사의 자산을 보호하다
  - **protect** the product's freshness 제품의 신선함을 보존하다

- [ ] **respond**
  ~에 대답하다, 응답하다
  - Please **respond** no later than Tuesday. 늦어도 화요일까지는 답변해 주세요.
  - **respond** to all inquiries 모든 문의에 답하다

- [ ] **promote**
  승진시키다, 홍보하다
  - He has been **promoted**. 그는 승진했다.
  - **promote** great nature photography 멋진 자연 사진을 홍보하다

- [ ] **conceive**
  생각해 내다, 구상하다
  - **conceive** the plot 줄거리를 생각해 내다
  - **conceive** the idea 아이디어를 생각해 내다

- [ ] **gain**
  얻다
  - **gain** the necessary experience 필요한 경험을 얻다
  - **gain** national recognition 전국적 인지도를 얻다

Practice

정답 및 해설 p.14

A. 괄호에서 적절한 것을 고르세요.

1. Patients who (require / encounter) problems with receiving the MiaGel treatment are encouraged to consult with their doctors before continuing treatment.

2. Refunds for products are only available to clients who (sign / offer) a legitimate contract.

3. Scuba divers who plan to instruct students must (possess / specify) a valid master certification.

4. If you wish to (decide / reserve) a seat for Dr. Lanting's lecture, please contact the main office.

B. 빈칸에 가장 적절한 것을 고르세요.

5. Ms. Wilson is in charge of ------- various social events for students at Oakland Junior High.
   (A) applying
   (B) organizing
   (C) bridging
   (D) correcting

6. Musician Kirk Reese ------- the lyrics for his latest acoustic album, *Infinite Sky*, during a hot air balloon experience in England.
   (A) lectured
   (B) conceived
   (C) resembled
   (D) motivated

7. Employees specializing in data communications are required to sign a confidentiality agreement to ------- sensitive intellectual property.
   (A) prevent
   (B) impress
   (C) silence
   (D) protect

8. Mr. Grant has been ------- to the position of Industry Analyst of the Owl Company and will now be under the direct command of Captain Winters.
   (A) registered
   (B) promoted
   (C) pleased
   (D) increased

어휘 ¹patient 환자 treatment 치료 encourage 격려하다, 장려하다 consult 상의하다, 상담하다 ²refund 환불 product 제품, 생산물 available 이용할 수 있는 legitimate 합법적인 ³plan 계획하다 instruct 가르치다, 지시하다 valid 유효한 ⁴lecture 강연 contact 연락하다 ⁵in charge of ~의 책임을 맡고 있는 various 다양한 junior high 중학교 ⁶lyric 가사 latest 최신의 experience 경험 ⁷employee 직원 specialize in ~을 전문으로 하다 confidentiality 기밀 sensitive 민감한 intellectual property 지적 재산 ⁸industry 산업, 업계 analyst 분석가 direct 직접적인 command 지휘, 관할

1. Mr. Raffeto ------- the task of deciding which project should be presented this month.
   (A) gives
   (B) was given
   (C) to be given
   (D) is giving

2. Despite being given only a short time for practice, the orchestra's performance was -------.
   (A) succeed
   (B) success
   (C) successful
   (D) successfully

3. When out of ideas for new furniture designs, Ms. Ocean finds it ------- to ask her colleagues for suggestions.
   (A) help
   (B) helps
   (C) to help
   (D) helpful

4. The company scheduled a meeting with the agenda of planning events to keep its customers -------.
   (A) satisfaction
   (B) satisfy
   (C) satisfyingly
   (D) satisfied

5. Children must learn to be ------- when handling dangerous objects.
   (A) cautious
   (B) caution
   (C) cautiously
   (D) cautiousness

6. The recent 1.2 version that was revised due to unexpected errors will replace the ------- version.
   (A) exist
   (B) existing
   (C) exists
   (D) existed

7. Kelly Palmer will stay ------- to complete the remaining pages of the essay.
   (A) late
   (B) lately
   (C) lateness
   (D) latest

8. Each of the components must be sufficiently independent to be considered -------.
   (A) individual
   (B) individually
   (C) individualism
   (D) individualist

Questions 9-12 refer to the following letter.

Dear Mr. Olson,

I am writing to you to --- 9. --- that MG Insurance Co. entered into a partnership with PEK Company last week on December 3.

It will be our pleasure to work --- 10. --- to serve you, our clients, using a better and more thorough approach.

We are still in the process of merging; therefore, fortunately, no unnecessary changes will be made to your personal accounts. However, you can expect the merger to be completed within the next four months. --- 11. ---.

Furthermore, if you wish to learn more about any of our new offers, please feel free to contact us at 555-0110 or visit our new website at www.mgpekunited.org. Thank you for continuing to allow --- 12. --- to serve you. We look forward to working with you in the future.

Sincerely,
Patrick Elens
Senior Managing Director
MGPEK United Co.

9 (A) result
   (B) remain
   (C) announce
   (D) determine

10 (A) nearly
   (B) certainly
   (C) together
   (D) unless

NEW
11 (A) After four months, we are no longer able to do business with you.
   (B) We request that you review the enclosed brochure regarding the changes in our new policies.
   (C) Because of the considerable change, we need to hire about ten new employees.
   (D) Most customers are disappointed with the merger.

12 (A) us
   (B) our
   (C) we
   (D) ourselves

Unit 03 주어와 동사의 수 일치

Part 5-6

주어와 동사의 수가 일치하는 것을 '수 일치'라고 합니다. 다시 말하면 주어가 단수이면 동사도 단수, 주어가 복수이면 동사도 복수가 되어야 한다는 말입니다. 토익에서는 주어 뒤에 길게 수식어를 붙여 동사의 주어를 혼동시키는 방식의 문제가 자주 출제되고 있습니다. 수식어 거품을 잘 제거해야 하는데, 반복적으로 연습하다 보면 어렵지 않게 숙달할 수 있습니다. 난이도가 비교적 낮은 유형이지만 꾸준히 출제되고 있습니다.

단수 주어+단수 동사

동사의 단수형

	be동사	have	일반동사
현재	is	has	동사원형+e, es
과거	was	had	동사원형+ed, 불규칙 과거형

Your bag is too heavy. 당신의 가방은 너무 무거워요.
단수 주어

The library has many books. 도서관에는 책들이 많다.
단수 주어

The report was ready for publication. 보고서가 발간될 준비가 되어 있다.
단수 주어

Eugene had a talent. Eugene은 재능이 있었다.
단수 주어

복수 주어+복수 동사

동사의 복수형

	be동사	have	일반동사
현재	are	have	동사원형
과거	were	had	동사원형+ed, 불규칙 과거형

Your bags are too heavy. 당신의 가방들은 너무 무거워요.
복수 주어

The libraries have many books. 도서관들에는 책들이 많다.
복수 주어

The reports were ready for publication. 보고서들이 발간될 준비가 되어 있었다.
복수 주어

They had talents. 그들은 재능들이 있었다.
복수 주어

주어와 동사 사이의 수식어구 함정

주어 뒤에 전치사구, 관계사절, 분사구, to부정사구 등의 수식어를 집어넣어 주어와 동사를 멀리 떨어뜨려 놓고 수 일치를 묻는 문제에서 의외로 많은 수험자가 실수를 합니다. 수식어는 아무리 길어도 동사의 수에 전혀 영향을 주지 않으므로 주어 다음의 수식어를 제외하고 동사를 파악하는 연습을 하는 것이 중요합니다.

The increase shown on this month's utility bills (is / ~~are~~) due to the high consumption of electricity
　단수 주어　　　　　　　분사 수식어
in the summer. 이번 달 공과금에 나와 있는 인상분은 여름철의 높은 전기 소비량으로 인한 것이다.

★ 동사 바로 앞의 bills를 주어로 착각하면 복수 동사 are를 정답으로 고르기 쉽습니다. 이 문장의 주어는 The increase로 단수이고 bills는 수식어의 일부일 뿐입니다.

A welcome reception for the newly hired employees (is / ~~are~~) scheduled for Monday at 2 p.m.
　단수 주어　　　　　　전치사 수식어
신입 직원들을 위한 환영회가 월요일 오후 2시로 예정되어 있습니다.

★ 동사 바로 앞의 employees를 주어로 착각하면 복수 동사 are를 정답으로 고르기 쉽습니다. 이 문장의 주어는 A welcome reception으로 단수이고 employees는 수식어의 일부일 뿐입니다.

Those who do not remember the past (are / ~~is~~) doomed to repeat it. 과거를 기억하지 않는 사람들은 그것을 반복할 운명이다.
　주어　　　　　수식어구

★ 빈칸 앞의 past를 주어로 착각하기 쉽습니다.

1 시험에 반드시 나오는 단수 주어와 단수 동사의 수 일치

 단수 주어+단수 동사

The firm (**is** / ~~are~~) looking for a financial planner. 회사는 재무설계사를 구하고 있다.
　가산명사

Mr. Morris (~~approve~~ / **approves**) of the construction of a new stadium. Morris 씨는 새 스타디움의 건설에 찬성한다.
　대명사

Customer information (**is** / ~~are~~) readily accessible online. 고객 정보는 온라인으로 손쉽게 접근이 가능하다.
　불가산명사 (항상 단수 취급)

 every/each/another/much/a little/little+(단수 명사)+단수 동사

Every security officer (**is** / ~~are~~) entitled to free beverages while on duty. 모든 경비원은 근무 중에 무료 음료를 마실 자격이 있다.
Another factor (**is** / ~~are~~) the current market price. 또 하나의 요인은 현행 시장 가격이다.
Little (**has** / ~~have~~) been written about the kingdom. 그 왕국에 관해 쓰여진 글은 거의 없다.
★ 최근에 much와 little만을 주어로 하여 단수 동사를 고르게 하는 문제가 자주 출제되고 있습니다.

 the number of/one of the/each of the+복수 명사+단수 동사

The number of prizes (**is** / ~~are~~) strictly limited. 상의 수는 엄격히 제한되어 있다.
★ a number of+복수 명사+복수 동사와 반드시 구별해야 합니다.

Each of the candidates (**has** / ~~have~~) strengths in specific areas. 후보들 각자는 특정 분야에서 강점을 갖고 있다.

 to부정사/동명사/명사절+단수 동사

Taking photographs (**is** / ~~are~~) prohibited during the performance. 공연 중에 사진을 찍는 것은 금지되어 있다.
　　동명사
That Hues Corporation's sales has increased sharply (**is** / ~~are~~) not surprising. Hues 주식회사의 매출이 급증한 것은 놀랍지 않다.
　　　　　명사절

주어와 동사 사이의 수식어

A five-acre park in the mountains (**is** / ~~are~~) open to the travelers. 5에이커 면적의 산속 공원이 여행자들에게 개방되어 있다.
★ 빈칸 앞의 mountains는 수식어의 일부이므로 동사의 수와 상관이 없습니다.

The installation of new systems (**is** / ~~are~~) scheduled to start at 10:00 a.m. 새 시스템의 설치가 오전 10시에 시작될 예정이다.
★ 빈칸 앞의 systems는 수식어의 일부이므로 동사의 수와 상관이 없습니다.

Practice

정답 및 해설 p.19

A. 괄호에서 적절한 것을 고르세요.

1. Each of the discussions at the conference room (relate / relates) to the international market.

2. The reconstruction (plan / plans) is being implemented steadily at the park and will be completed by June 4.

3. The number of people exercising in the gym (has / have) risen dramatically over the last five years.

4. Setting realistic ambitions (is / are) a great step toward building personal motivation.

B. 빈칸에 가장 적절한 것을 고르세요.

5. One of the most interesting topics at the recent convention ------- how to increase profit through property investment.
   (A) was
   (B) were
   (C) being
   (D) been

6. Much of the recent increase in the sales of men's pants ------- attributable to the rising popularity of Delware's designs.
   (A) has
   (B) have
   (C) is
   (D) are

7. Unfortunately, our supply of loanable funds ------- currently depleted; however, we expect to receive fresh supply soon.
   (A) is
   (B) are
   (C) being
   (D) to be

8. Maintaining the sanitation of public bathrooms, which are used by hundreds of people, ------- been very difficult.
   (A) is
   (B) are
   (C) has
   (D) have

어휘 ¹ discussion 논의 relate to ~와 관련이 있다 ² reconstruction 재건축, 복원 implement 시행하다 steadily 꾸준히 complete 완료하다 ³ gym 체육관 dramatically 극적으로 ⁴ realistic 현실적인 ambition 야망, 포부 personal 개인의 motivation 동기 부여, 자극 ⁵ recent 최근의 convention 집회, 대회 profit 이익 investment 투자 ⁶ attributable ~에 원인이 있는 popularity 인기, 유행 ⁷ unfortunately 불운하게도 supply 공급(량) loanable funds 대부자금 currently 현재는 depleted 고갈된 ⁸ sanitation 위생설비

Unit 03 : 주어와 동사의 수 일치 37

2 시험에 반드시 나오는 복수 주어와 복수 동사의 수 일치

● 복수 주어+복수 동사

The meeting rooms (is / are) available only in the mornings. 회의실들은 오전에만 이용 가능하다.
Colleagues (has / have) described him as an energetic member. 동료들은 그를 정력적인 멤버로 묘사해왔다.
She and I (has / have) been close acquaintances for many years. 그녀와 나는 여러 해 동안 친하게 알고 지내왔다.

● many/a few/few+복수 동사

Most attendees were satisfied with the seminar, but a few (was / were) disappointed.
대부분의 참가자들은 그 세미나에 만족했지만 몇 명은 실망했다.

● several/a number[variety/series/selection] of+복수 명사+복수 동사

A number of obstacles (is / are) preventing the acquisition. 많은 장애물들이 인수를 막고 있다.
★ The number of+복수 명사+단수 동사와 반드시 구별해야 합니다.

Several companies (need / needs) security guards for their facilities. 몇몇 회사들은 자사 시설을 지킬 경비원이 필요하다.

● some/most/all/half+of the+단수[복수] 명사+단수[복수] 동사

Most of the message (indicates / indicate) that the customer is frustrated.
메시지의 대부분은 고객이 불만스러워하고 있음을 보여준다.
All of the evidence (has / have) been considered carefully. 모든 증거는 신중하게 고려되었다.
Some of the books (was / were) out of print. 그 책들의 일부는 절판되었다.
Half of the employees (commutes / commute) to work by subway. 직원들의 절반이 지하철로 통근한다.

● 주어와 동사 사이의 수식어구

The needs for using alternative energy (is / are) increasingly emphasized. 대체 에너지 이용의 필요성이 점점 강조되고 있다.
　주어　　　　　수식어구
★ 빈칸 앞의 energy를 주어로 착각하기 쉽습니다.

All computers in the school (were / was) damaged because of the fire. 그 학교의 모든 컴퓨터들은 화재 때문에 손상되었다.
　주어　　　　수식어구
★ 빈칸 앞의 school을 주어로 착각하기 쉽습니다.

Practice

정답 및 해설 p.20

A. 괄호에서 적절한 것을 고르세요.

1 The nurses (has / have) the obligation of repeatedly attending to patients that need special care.

2 First-class (seats / seat) for Saturday night's football game are being sold until tomorrow.

3 Most of the food (supply / supplies) are stored in the warehouse under optimum temperature to prevent contamination.

4 A series of errors (was / were) highlighted by software programmers during the trial test.

B. 빈칸에 가장 적절한 것을 고르세요.

5 We offer a large selection of breakfast items that ------- homemade muffins, bagels, and omelets.
   (A) include
   (B) includes
   (C) inclusion
   (D) are included

6 The leftovers in the refrigerator ------- to be eaten or tossed away soon.
   (A) need
   (B) needing
   (C) needs
   (D) to need

7 A ------- of colors were used in this painting to express a unique and flashy art style.
   (A) unity
   (B) connection
   (C) variety
   (D) division

8 People planning to travel abroad ------- required to hold a valid passport for clearance.
   (A) is
   (B) are
   (C) being
   (D) been

어휘 1 obligation 의무, 책임 repeatedly 반복해서 attend to 돌보다, 시중들다 3 warehouse 창고 optimum 최적의 prevent 막다, 방지하다 contamination 오염 4 a series of 일련의 highlight 강조하다 trial 시험적인 5 a large selection of 정선된 많은 6 leftover 남은 음식 refrigerator 냉장고 toss away 버리다 7 express 표현하다, 나타내다 flashy 현란한 8 travel abroad 해외로 여행하다 valid 유효한 clearance 출입국 수속

3 반드시 알아야 하는 기출 동사 어휘 ❸

- [ ] **provide**
  제공하다, 공급하다
  - provide the best service 최고의 서비스를 제공하다
  - provide them with food 그들에게 식량을 공급하다

- [ ] **assess**
  평가하다, 산정하다
  - assess their strengths and weaknesses 그들의 강점과 약점을 평가하다
  - assess the amount of compensation 보상액을 산정하다

- [ ] **inform**
  알리다, 통지하다
  - I'll inform you immediately. 즉시 알려드리겠습니다.
  - inform you of some changes 당신에게 변경 사항들을 알려주다

- [ ] **base**
  기초로 하다, 본거지로 삼다
  - be based on a popular comic book 인기 만화를 바탕으로 하다
  - The company is based in London. 그 회사는 런던에 본사가 있다.

- [ ] **negotiate**
  협상하다, 성사시키다
  - refuse to negotiate with terrorists 테러범들과 협상하기를 거부하다
  - negotiate contracts with our suppliers 우리 공급업체들과 계약을 성사시키다

- [ ] **write**
  쓰다, 편지하다
  - write a news article in the local newspaper 지역 신문에 기사를 쓰다
  - She wrote to him in Swiss. 그녀는 스위스에 있는 그에게 편지했다.

- [ ] **administer**
  관리[운영]하다, 집행하다
  - administer public affairs 공무를 집행하다
  - be administered by the audit department 회계감사부에 의해 운영되다

- [ ] **limit**
  제한하다
  - This course is limited to 30 people. 이 강좌는 인원이 30명으로 제한되어 있다.
  - Human abilities are limited. 인간 능력에는 한계가 있다.

- [ ] **offer**
  제공하다, 제안하다
  - He offers excellent prices. 그는 탁월한 가격을 제공한다.
  - I've been offered a much better position. 훨씬 나은 자리를 제의받았어요.

- [ ] **take place**
  발생하다, (행사가) 열리다
  - The Olympics take place every four years. 올림픽은 4년마다 열린다.
  - The accident took place at the crossroads. 그 사고는 교차로에서 발생했다.

- [ ] **restrict**
  제한하다, 통제하다
  - Having pets restricts your freedom. 애완동물이 있으면 자유를 제한받는다.
  - Traffic is restricted in that area. 그 지역에서 교통이 통제되고 있다.

- [ ] **specialize**
  전공하다, 전문으로 하다
  - specialize in chemistry 화학을 전공하다
  - The restaurant specializes in seafood. 그 식당은 해산물 요리를 전문으로 한다.

- [ ] **anticipate**
  예측하다, 예상하다
  - anticipate the increased demands 수요 증가를 예측하다
  - It was earlier than we had anticipated. 그것은 우리가 예상한 것보다 빨랐다.

- [ ] **simplify**
  단순화하다, 간소화하다
  - simplify the concept 그 개념을 단순화하다
  - simplify the visa application 비자 신청을 간소화하다

- [ ] **follow**
  따르다, 지키다
  - She beckoned him to follow her. 그녀는 그에게 자기를 따라오라고 손짓했다.
  - follow the instructions 지시사항을 따르다

Practice

A. 괄호에서 적절한 것을 고르세요.

1. Please do not forget to (inform / confirm) the director that we need those scripts by tomorrow.

2. Public transportation modes, such as subways, (provide / commute) citizens with access to remote areas of the city in a short amount of time.

3. Jet Blue Airlines (travels / offers) free use of airport lounges to its VIP passengers.

4. The cultural festival for Kenton High School will (put together / take place) next Friday from 9 a.m. to 6 p.m.

B. 빈칸에 가장 적절한 것을 고르세요.

5. The representatives of both companies began ------- product prices.
   (A) negotiating
   (B) suggesting
   (C) endorsing
   (D) assigning

6. The efforts to ------- the manufacturing process in the Tokyo plant should lower the production costs.
   (A) contact
   (B) simplify
   (C) overweigh
   (D) progress

7. The number of applicants accepted for this season's recruitment will be ------- to a maximum of twelve people.
   (A) started
   (B) limited
   (C) remained
   (D) asserted

8. Dr. Tony, who is a psychiatrist, ------- in the study and treatment of patients with mental disorders.
   (A) considers
   (B) measures
   (C) specializes
   (D) receives

어휘 ¹director 감독, 연출가 script 각본, 대본 ²public transportation 대중교통 mode 양식, 방식 access 접근 (수단) remote 멀리 떨어진, 외딴 area 지역 ³passenger 승객 ⁴cultural festival 문화제 ⁵representative 대표 ⁶effort 노력 process 과정 lower 낮추다 production cost 생산비 ⁷applicant 지원자 accept 받아주다 recruitment 모집, 충원 ⁸psychiatrist 정신과 의사 treatment 치료 mental disorder 정신장애

Actual Test

1. The events that ------- organized by the management involve activities for promoting teamwork.
   (A) having
   (B) have
   (C) are
   (D) be

2. ------- for the Service Training Seminar have been sent to all employees in the service department.
   (A) Invite
   (B) Invitation
   (C) Invitations
   (D) To invite

3. Boosting market sales and profitable income ------- a challenge to Naudi Company.
   (A) pose
   (B) is posed
   (C) posing
   (D) has posed

4. Most of the comic strips drawn by Renny Cortez ------- very funny and dramatic.
   (A) be
   (B) is
   (C) are
   (D) been

5. In an effort to maintain productivity in the factory, one of the directors ------- a more strict working schedule.
   (A) implement
   (B) is implementing
   (C) implementing
   (D) is implemented

6. What should take priority ------- customer satisfaction.
   (A) is
   (B) are
   (C) have
   (D) has been

7. Each of the samples ------- examined at the laboratory last week, but we have not yet found the corresponding match.
   (A) is
   (B) are
   (C) was
   (D) were

8. Use the polaroid camera sparingly because the instant film that it requires ------- very expensive.
   (A) are
   (B) is
   (C) been
   (D) being

Questions 9-12 refer to the following letter.

Dear Ms. Wong,

Thank you for your recent visit to Say Beauty Shop. We at Say Beauty --- 9. --- opinions from valued customers, such as yourself, to improve the services we provide.

Please be so kind as to take a moment and fill out the enclosed survey related to your shopping experience at Say Beauty. Once you take the survey, you will be entered in a special --- 10. --- to win a $200 gift certificate redeemable in exchange for any item on sale. --- 11. ---.

Thank you for your --- 12.--- and we hope to see you again soon.

Best Wishes,

Jamie Badger
General Manager

9   (A) solicits
    (B) soliciting
    (C) are soliciting
    (D) has solicited

10 (A) raffling
    (B) raffle
    (C) raffled
    (D) raffles

NEW

11 (A) We accept only credit cards.
    (B) It will be very helpful for us to find ways to serve you better in the future.
    (C) This survey is intended for our regular customers.
    (D) You need to buy over $500.

12 (A) referral
    (B) purchase
    (C) advertising
    (D) cooperation

Unit 04 능동태와 수동태

Part 5-6

능동태는 주어가 동작의 주체가 되는 문장을 말하고 수동태는 주어가 동작의 대상이 되는 문장을 말합니다. 따라서 능동태 동사는 '~하다'로 해석하고 수동태 동사는 '~되다, 당하다'라고 해석합니다. 토익에서는 능동태와 수동태 문제가 중간 난이도에 속하며 1, 2형식 문장의 수동태 여부, 4, 5형식 문장의 수동태 형식 등이 자주 출제되고 있습니다. 반복적으로 문제를 풀다 보면 어렵지 않게 정리할 수 있습니다. 꾸준히 출제되고 있는 중요한 유형입니다.

능동태를 수동태로

'주어+동사+목적어' 형태의 능동태 문장에서 목적어가 주어 자리로 가면서 동사의 형태가 'be+p.p.(과거분사)'로 바뀐 문장을 수동태라고 합니다. 능동태 문장의 주어는 수동태 문장에서 보통 'by+목적격' 형태로 바뀝니다.

[능동태] John builds a house. John이 집을 짓는다.
주어   동사   목적어

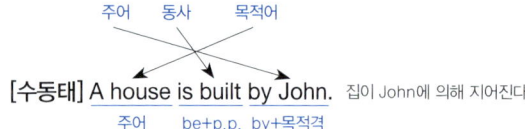

[수동태] A house is built by John. 집이 John에 의해 지어진다.
주어   be+p.p. by+목적격

수동태를 만들 수 없는 1, 2형식 문장

기본적으로 문장에 목적어가 있어야 그 목적어가 수동태의 주어가 될 수 있는데, 1형식과 2형식 문장에는 원래 목적어가 없으므로 수동태를 만들 수 없습니다. 따라서 1, 2형식 동사의 수동형이 문제에 나오면 무조건 오답입니다.

1형식 동사: go, come, rise, exist, look, increase
2형식 동사: be, become, keep, remain, stay, seem, appear

He (became / ~~was become~~) a doctor. 그는 의사가 되었다.
Many birds (~~have been remained~~ / have remained) on the island. 많은 새들이 그 섬에 남아 있다.

수동태의 형태

수동태의 기본 형태는 'be+p.p.'입니다. 주어와 시제에 따라 여러 가지 형태로 바뀔 수 있습니다. 다음 표를 통해 간단히 정리해 보겠습니다.

시제	수동태	예문
현재 과거 미래	is/am/are+p.p. was/were+p.p. will be+p.p.	The chair is fixed. 의자가 수리된다. The chair was fixed. 의자들이 수리되었다. The chair will be fixed. 의자가 수리될 것이다.
현재진행 과거진행	is/am/are+being+p.p. was/were+being+p.p.	The chair is being fixed. 의자들이 수리되고 있다. The chair was being fixed. 의자가 수리되고 있었다.
현재완료 과거완료 미래완료	has/have+been+p.p. had+been+p.p. will have+been+p.p.	The chair has been fixed. 의자가 수리되어왔다. The chair had been fixed before you sat. 당신이 앉기 전에 의자가 수리되어 있었다. The chair will have been fixed by the time you return. 당신이 돌아올 때에는 의자가 수리되어 있을 것이다.

1 시험에 반드시 나오는 능동태와 수동태 유형

능동태와 수동태의 구별

▶ 동사 뒤에 목적어가 있으면 능동태, 목적어가 없으면 수동태입니다.

[능동태] The demonstrators obstructed traffic. 시위자들이 교통을 차단했다.
         주어   동사   목적어

[수동태] Traffic was obstructed by the demonstrators. 교통이 시위자들에 의해 차단되었다.
         주어   be+p.p.   by+주체

4, 5형식 문장의 수동태

▶ **4형식**: '주어+동사+간접목적어+직접목적어' 형식의 문장은 목적어가 두 개이므로 수동태도 두 개 만들 수 있습니다. 토익에서는 간접목적어가 주어로 오는 수동태가 주로 출제됩니다.

[능동태]

The company offered Jonathan a good position. 회사는 Jonathan에게 좋은 자리를 제안했다.
   주어   동사   간접목적어   직접목적어

[간접목적어가 주어로 나온 수동태]

Jonathan was offered a good position by the company. Jonathan은 회사에 의해 좋은 자리를 제안받았다.
  주어   be+p.p.   직접목적어   by+주체

★ 수동태가 되면 뒤에 직접목적어가 남습니다.

[직접목적어가 주어로 나온 수동태]

A good position was offered to Jonathan by the company. 회사로부터 좋은 자리가 Jonathan에게 제안되었다.
     주어   be+p.p.   간접목적어   by+주체

★ 간접목적어 앞에 전치사 to를 붙여야 합니다.

▶ **5형식**: '주어+동사+목적어+목적격 보어' 형식의 문장은 수동태가 되면 뒤에 목적격 보어가 남습니다.

[능동태]

Most people consider it one of the top manufacturers in the country.
   주어   동사   목적어   목적격 보어   수식어

대부분의 사람들은 그곳을 국내 최고의 제조사 중의 하나로 여긴다.

[수동태]

It is considered one of the top manufacturers in the country by most people.
주어 be+p.p.   목적격 보어   수식어   by+주체

그곳은 대부분의 사람들에 의해 국내 최고의 제조사 중의 하나로 여겨진다.

Practice

정답 및 해설 p.26

A. 괄호에서 적절한 것을 고르세요.

1. Although James did his best, the winning prize (gives / was given) to another contestant with a higher score.

2. The non-transferable membership that we purchased is (guaranteed / guaranteeing) for six years.

3. Your account will be temporarily (locked / locking) due to the many failed attempts to log in.

4. My aunt, Susan Gardner, (was told / told) to see a therapist every week for four months after her knee surgery.

B. 빈칸에 가장 적절한 것을 고르세요.

5. Employees at Tobal Company expressed their disappointment to their CEO when they realized that nobody ------- for the past three years.
   (A) was promoting
   (B) has promoted
   (C) had been promoted
   (D) has been promoting

6. The answers to these questions ------- on page 57 of the History textbook.
   (A) can find
   (B) can be found
   (C) are finding
   (D) will be finding

7. Because our guest was a vegetarian, we ------- the location of the dinner from Rogers Ranch to the Zhao Garden restaurant.
   (A) moved
   (B) will be moved
   (C) have been moved
   (D) were moved

8. Ms. Penner is well ------- by her colleagues because of her ability to communicate in five different languages.
   (A) respects
   (B) respect
   (C) respective
   (D) respected

어휘 1 contestant (대회의) 참가자 2 non-transferable 양도할 수 없는 purchase 구입하다 guarantee 보장하다 3 temporarily 일시적으로 attempt 시도 4 therapist 치료사 surgery 수술 5 express 표현하다 disappointment 실망 realize 깨닫다 7 vegetarian 채식주의자 location 장소 8 colleague 동료 ability 능력

Unit 04 : 능동태와 수동태

2 시험에 반드시 나오는 감정동사 수동태와 수동태+전치사

감정동사의 수동태

▶ 감정을 나타내는 동사들은 주어가 감정을 느끼는 주체일 때 수동태로 사용합니다.

Customers are satisfied with our products. 고객들은 우리 제품에 만족한다.
The enterprise is interested in exploring new business opportunities. 그 기업은 새로운 사업 기회를 찾는 데 관심이 있다.

▶ 감정동사의 수동태 표현

excite → be excited 흥분되다
delight → be delighted 아주 기쁘다
interest → be interested 관심이 있다
startle → be startled 깜짝 놀라다
tire → be tired 피곤하다
frustrate → be frustrated 짜증나다

please → be pleased 기쁘다, 만족하다
satisfy → be satisfied 만족하다
surprise → be surprised 놀라다
fascinate → be fascinated 매료되다
disappoint → be disappointed 실망하다
concern → be concerned 걱정하다, 관심이 있다

수동태 동사의 주체를 나타내는 전치사+명사

▶ 일반적으로 수동태 동사의 주체는 'by+명사'로 나타냅니다.

The facility is conducted by the safety officer. 그 시설은 안전관리자에 의해 운영되고 있다.
Misuse is not covered by the manufacturer's warranty. 오남용은 제조사의 품질보증에 의해 보상받지 못한다.

▶ 그러나 동사에 따라 by 대신에 다른 전치사가 오기도 합니다.

be disappointed with ~에 실망하다
be associated with ~와 연관이 있다
be filled with ~으로 가득하다
be involved in ~에 관련되다
be related to ~와 관련이 있다
be accustomed to ~에 익숙하다
be divided into ~로 나눠지다
be surprised at ~에 놀라다

be equipped with ~을 갖추고 있다
be pleased with ~에 만족하다
be acquainted with 잘 알고 있다
be engaged in ~에 종사하다
be limited to ~로 제한되다
be dedicated to ~에 헌신하다
be worried about ~를 걱정하다
be tired of ~에 싫증나다

be satisfied with ~에 만족하다
be faced with ~에 직면하다
be interested in ~에 관심이 있다
be absorbed in ~에 몰두하다
be exposed to ~에 노출되다
be transferred to ~로 이전되다
be known for ~로 알려지다
be concerned about ~에 관심이 있다

Practice

정답 및 해설 p.27

A. 괄호에서 적절한 것을 고르세요.

1. Passengers (requests / are requested) to remove all metal objects from their bodies when going through the airport security inspection.

2. Korte City Traffic Division apologizes to the citizens who (are involving / were involved) in the recent accidents that occurred due to problems with the traffic signals.

3. This year, the graduation ceremony will be held outside the campus because the school auditorium is being renovated (by / of) City Construction.

4. Sun Media is well known (to / for) creating high-quality content and developing cross-media advertisement.

B. 빈칸에 가장 적절한 것을 고르세요.

5. The server computers of GTS Intel ------- in the EASTERN building on the third floor.
   (A) locate
   (B) locating
   (C) to locate
   (D) are located

6. Recent studies show that 47% of the employees participating in the survey ------- with their jobs.
   (A) will have satisfied
   (B) are satisfied
   (C) were satisfying
   (D) will satisfy

7. A promotion video that ------- to the company's new software is currently under production.
   (A) dedicate
   (B) had dedicated
   (C) dedication
   (D) will be dedicated

8. In case her condition worsens, patient Angie might ------- to the Intensive Care Center.
   (A) transferring
   (B) be transferred
   (C) transfers
   (D) being transferred

어휘 1 passenger 승객 remove 제거하다 object 물건 inspection 정밀 검사 2 apologize 사과하다 recent 최근의 occur 생기다, 일어나다 traffic signal 신호등 3 graduation ceremony 졸업식 auditorium 강당 renovate 개조하다 4 cross-media 매체 결합의 advertisement 광고 6 participate 참여하다 7 currently 지금 under production 생산 중인 8 in case ~하는 경우에는 worsen 악화되다

3 반드시 알아야 하는 기출 동사 어휘 ❹

☐	**expect** 기대하다, 예상하다	• It is expected to be a popular item. 그것은 인기 품목이 될 것으로 기대된다. • I didn't expect this to happen. 이런 일이 생길 줄은 예상하지 못했다.
☐	**promise** 약속하다, 가망성이 있다	• promise to boost profits 수익을 끌어올리기로 약속하다 • The dark clouds promise rain. 먹구름을 보니 비가 올 것 같다.
☐	**increase** 늘리다, 증가하다	• We have to increase funding. 우리는 자금을 늘려야 한다. • Traffic has increased by fifteen percent. 교통량이 15퍼센트 증가했다.
☐	**vote** 투표하다	• Congress voted the bill through. 의회는 투표를 해서 그 법안을 통과시켰다. • vote against spending more money 돈을 더 많이 쓰는 데 반대표를 던지다
☐	**outline** ~의 윤곽을 그리다, ~의 개요를 말하다	• be outlined in the company's handbook 회사 안내서에 간단히 적혀 있다 • outline the plot of the novel 소설의 줄거리를 대강 말해주다
☐	**conduct** 행하다, 지휘하다	• The survey is conducted on a regular basis. 설문조사는 정기적으로 실시된다. • conduct an orchestra 관현악단을 지휘하다
☐	**comply** 따르다, 승낙하다, 준수하다	• comply with the firm's new policy 회사의 새 정책을 따르다 • comply with the law 법률을 준수하다
☐	**endorse** 지지하다, 승인하다, 추천하다	• endorse the Republican candidate 공화당 후보를 지지하다 • endorse the new makeup line 새 화장품 라인을 추천하다
☐	**intend** ~할 작정이다, 의도하다	• I intend to be a musician. 나는 음악가가 될 작정이다. • I never intended to upset you. 당신을 화나게 할 의도는 없었습니다.
☐	**advise** 조언하다, 권하다, 알리다	• She advised me to take a rest. 그녀는 내게 휴식을 취할 것을 권했다. • Please advise us of any change. 변동 사항이 있으면 저희에게 알려주십시오.
☐	**complete** 완료하다, (서식을) 작성하다	• complete the training course 교육 과정을 마치다 • Please complete this registration card. 이 등록 카드를 작성해주세요.
☐	**acquire** 얻다, 습득하다, 입수하다	• acquire a foreign language 외국어를 습득하다 • The museum acquired great artworks. 그 박물관은 훌륭한 예술품들을 입수했다.
☐	**reach** ~에 도달하다, 이르다	• reach the airport on time 공항에 정시에 도착하다 • reach a conclusion 결론에 이르다
☐	**shorten** 줄이다, 단축하다	• shorten the length of the skirt 치마의 길이를 줄이다 • shorten the wait time for patients 환자들의 대기 시간을 단축하다

Practice

A. 괄호에서 적절한 것을 고르세요.

1. Citizens who are willing to (attend / vote) for candidates running for Congress must present their identification cards at the booth.

2. Eating too much junk food will definitely (finish / shorten) your lifespan.

3. Picus News (requests / promises) to report on significant current affairs and provide economic analysis for its viewers and readers.

4. The board of directors (expects / assumes) to make a firm decision regarding the establishment of the fund within a day.

B. 빈칸에 가장 적절한 것을 고르세요.

5. Those who ------- the new recycling policy must practice reducing the amount of waste to protect the environment.
   (A) endorse
   (B) persuade
   (C) thrive
   (D) realize

6. What distinguishes Grace Clinic with other facilities is that it ------- to provide equal care to everyone regardless of their ability to pay.
   (A) initiates
   (B) previews
   (C) intends
   (D) considers

7. The administrators should ------- staff members regarding any changes in the weekly reports.
   (A) recommend
   (B) advise
   (C) offer
   (D) review

8. Mr. Vanderburg recently ------- a reputation for 'God of Service' after consistently working in the field for over 11 years.
   (A) intervened
   (B) merged
   (C) determined
   (D) acquired

어휘 1 candidate 후보 congress 국회, 의회 present 제시하다 identification card 신분증 2 junk food 정크푸드 (인스턴트식품이나 패스트푸드) definitely 명확하게, 확실히 lifespan 수명 3 significant 중대한 affair 일, 사건 analysis 분석 4 firm 확고한, 굳은 establishment 설립, 확립 5 policy 정책 reduce 줄이다 waste 쓰레기 6 distinguish 구별하다 equal 같은, 동일한 regardless of ~에 상관없이 7 administrator 관리자 regarding ~에 관하여 8 reputation 평판 consistently 일관되게

Actual Test

1. The methods for operating the machine at adjustable speeds ------- in the user's manual.
   (A) summarizes
   (B) are summarizing
   (C) summarized
   (D) are summarized

2. Lark Software Company's market value ------- by Dengil Company's rising stock prices and strong financial performance.
   (A) surpassing
   (B) surpassable
   (C) to surpass
   (D) is surpassed

3. At monthly Executive Board meetings, members share and discuss those ideas and suggestions that ------- as most favorable.
   (A) are indicating
   (B) have indicated
   (C) were indicated
   (D) had been indicating

4. Whenever you are in a car, always fasten your seatbelt and ensure that it is ------- before the car begins to move.
   (A) secured
   (B) securing
   (C) securely
   (D) security

5. Owing to the upcoming Presidential Elections, classes ------- until next Monday.
   (A) have deferred
   (B) are deferring
   (C) will be deferred
   (D) have been deferring

6. All rooms in the Continental Hotel are ------- with individually controlled air conditioning, cable television, and free Internet.
   (A) equip
   (B) equipment
   (C) equipped
   (D) equipping

7. A product order form has been ------- to Ms. Guidy Parlos, the general manager of our distributor in Italy.
   (A) send
   (B) sends
   (C) sent
   (D) sending

8. Having not seen her for nearly four years, Lizy's grandparents were ------- by her mature appearance.
   (A) startle
   (B) startling
   (C) startled
   (D) startles

Questions 9-12 refer to the following notice.

Our RSI personal computers have been manufactured to meet specific standards. However, if any part of your computer proves to be defective --- 9. --- the given warranty period, it can be taken to an authorized and licensed RSI service center for repair or replacement at no charge. When transporting the computer over long distances, it should --- 10. --- in a sturdy box with tight packing material, such as Styrofoam, to prevent any damage that is not covered by the warranty. Please be advised that RSI Company takes no responsibility for items damaged in --- 11. ---. --- 12. ---.

If you have any questions or concerns regarding your warranty, please call 1-800-RSI-Comp.

9 (A) above
   (B) beside
   (C) except
   (D) within

10 (A) have been placed
   (B) be placed
   (C) place
   (D) be placing

11 (A) surplus
   (B) development
   (C) inventory
   (D) transit

NEW
12 (A) Packing boxes can be purchased online.
   (B) The warranty period is six months.
   (C) Therefore, be sure to pack carefully when sending it through a delivery service.
   (D) Personal computers will be out of stock soon.

Unit 05 시제

Part 5-6

특정한 행동이나 사건을 시간의 흐름에 따라 표현하기 위한 동사의 변화형을 시제라고 합니다. 학교에서는 영어의 12시제를 배우지만 토익에서는 보통 9개 시제만 출제되고 확실한 단서가 주어지므로 쉽게 해결할 수 있습니다. 현재, 과거, 미래 시제에 쓰이는 부사어와 현재완료, 과거완료, 미래완료 시제의 개념은 반드시 이해해야 합니다. 토익 시험에 꾸준히 출제되는 중요한 유형입니다.

단순 시제

특정한 시간에 발생한 일이나 상태를 나타내는 시제입니다.

▶ 현재 시제: 동사원형(+s/es)

현재의 습관이나 현재 보이는 상황, 사실, 불변의 진리를 말할 때 사용합니다.

현재를 나타내는 부사(always, usually, often 등)가 함께 자주 사용됩니다.

I often watch TV. 나는 자주 TV를 본다.

▶ 과거 시제: 동사원형+ed

과거에 일어난 일이나 과거의 동작, 상태를 말할 때 사용합니다.

과거를 나타내는 부사(yesterday, last night, ago 등)가 함께 자주 사용됩니다.

I watched TV last night. 나는 어젯밤에 TV를 보았다.
I lived in Busan. 나는 부산에서 살았다. ★ 현재는 살고 있지 않음을 알 수 있습니다.

▶ 미래 시제: will+동사원형

미래에 대한 의지, 계획, 추측을 말할 때 사용합니다.

미래를 나타내는 부사(soon, tomorrow, later, next week 등)가 함께 자주 사용됩니다.

I will watch TV later. 나는 나중에 TV를 볼 것이다.

진행 시제

특정한 시점에서 동작이 계속 진행 중임을 나타내는 시제입니다.

▶ 현재진행 시제: am/is/are -ing

현재 순간에 진행되고 있는 상황으로 '~하고 있는 중이다'라는 뜻입니다.

He is driving a car. 그는 차를 운전하고 있다.

아주 가까운 미래는 현재진행형으로 표현하기도 합니다.

Are you coming tomorrow? 내일 오니?

▶ **과거진행 시제: was/were -ing**

과거의 어느 시점을 설명할 때, 뭔가 진행되고 있던 상황을 표현합니다.

He was driving a car. 그는 차를 운전하고 있었다.

▶ **미래진행 시제: will be -ing**

미래의 어느 시점에서 진행되고 있을 일을 말합니다.

He will be driving a car. 그는 차를 운전할 것이다.

완료 시제

특정한 시점보다 앞선 시점부터 발생한 일이나 상태가 특정한 시점까지 계속됨을 나타내는 시제입니다.

▶ **현재완료 시제: have/has p.p.**

과거부터 시작되어 현재까지 계속되는 일을 말합니다.

He has worked for five years. 그는 5년째 일해왔다.
I have lived in Busan. 나는 부산에 살고 있다. ★ 현재도 계속 살고 있음을 알 수 있습니다.

▶ **과거완료 시제: had p.p.**

과거 시점이 있고 그 과거보다 더 이전에 일어난 일을 말합니다.

He had worked for five years before he resigned. 그는 퇴사하기 전에 5년 동안 일했었다.

▶ **미래완료 시제: will have p.p.**

미래의 어느 시점에서 끝날 일을 말합니다.

미래완료를 나타내는 부사와 함께 사용합니다(by the time, by+미래 시점).

He will have worked for five years by the end of this month. 그는 이달 말이면 5년째 일하게 될 것이다.

1 시험에 반드시 나오는 단순 시제

● 현재 시제

> regularly 정기적으로 usually 보통 always 항상 currently 현재
> often 자주 still 여전히 every day/week/month 매일/주/월

▶ 일반적인 사실이나 반복되는 일을 나타냅니다. 현재 시제와 함께 쓰이는 부사를 알아야 합니다.

Ms. Rose travels regularly for business. Rose 씨는 사업차 정기적으로 여행을 한다.
The rooms are currently unavailable. 그 방들은 현재 이용할 수 없다.

▶ 시간 · 조건의 부사절에서는 미래 시제 대신에 현재 시제를 사용합니다.

I will tell him the truth when he arrives. 그가 도착하면 그에게 사실을 말할 것이다.
If she comes tomorrow, I'll propose to her. 그녀가 내일 온다면 나는 그녀에게 청혼할 것이다.

● 과거 시제

> in+과거 연도 ago ~ 전에 yesterday 어제
> last week/month/year 지난주/달/해

▶ 과거에 발생한 일이나 상태를 나타냅니다. 과거 시제와 함께 쓰이는 부사를 알아야 합니다.

Last week, sales associates attended the seminar. 지난주에 영업사원들이 세미나에 참석했다.
JC company began 20 years ago as a small business. JC 사는 20년 전에 작은 업체로 시작했다.

● 미래 시제

> tomorrow 내일 soon/shortly 곧
> next week/month/year 다음 주/달/해 later 나중에
> this (coming) Saturday 이번 토요일에

▶ 앞으로 일어날 사건이나 추측, 의지를 나타냅니다. 미래 시제와 함께 쓰이는 부사를 알아야 합니다.

Dr. Noah will complete his paper soon. Noah 박사는 논문을 곧 완성할 것이다.
The conference will be held later today. 콘퍼런스는 오늘 늦게 열릴 것이다.

● 시제 일치의 예외

> suggest 제안하다 insist 주장하다 request 요청하다
> require 요구하다 ask 부탁하다 recommend 권하다

▶ '주장, 명령, 요구, 제안' 의미의 동사 뒤에 나오는 that절에서는 수와 시제에 상관없이 동사원형을 사용합니다.

They requested that the analyst examine the data. 그들은 분석가가 데이터를 조사할 것을 요청했다.
The weather forecaster insisted that skies remain sunny. 기상캐스터는 하늘이 계속 맑을 것이라고 주장했다.

> essential 필수적인 imperative 반드시 해야 하는 necessary 필요한 important 중요한

▶ It ~ that 가주어 구문에서 '의무, 당위성'을 나타내는 형용사 뒤에 나오는 that절의 동사는 'should+동사원형'이 되어야 하는데, 대개 should를 생략하고 수와 시제에 상관없이 동사원형을 사용합니다.

It is important that the cocktail (should) be shaken first. 우선 칵테일을 흔드는 것이 중요하다.

Practice

정답 및 해설 p.34

A. 괄호에서 적절한 것을 고르세요.

1. Last month, Dr. Nelson (obtained / has obtained) the permission to examine the artifacts before they were displayed in the museum.

2. Mr. Forester, author of *Heartful Soul*, (brought / brings) inspiration to approximately two million readers last year.

3. The player that scores the most points in the Star League Playoffs next week (profile / will be profiled) in the magazine.

4. The lucky winners for the Valentines Raffle Event (will announce / will be announced) soon.

B. 빈칸에 가장 적절한 것을 고르세요.

5. Ms. Gomez ------- a new system in 2002 that enabled real-time monitoring.
   (A) create
   (B) creating
   (C) created
   (D) creates

6. It is recommended that the manager ------- the staff with procedures for closing the store.
   (A) assist
   (B) assists
   (C) assisting
   (D) assistant

7. Donami Productions ------- filming the sequel to their successful blockbuster movie this coming Friday.
   (A) began
   (B) will begin
   (C) has begun
   (D) was beginning

8. In an urgent meeting that was held earlier this morning, our Head Director, Mr. Arnold Morton, ------- that the contract had been cancelled.
   (A) is announced
   (B) would announce
   (C) announced
   (D) announces

어휘 1 obtain 얻다, 획득하다 permission 허가, 허락 examine 검사하다, 조사하다 artifact 유물 2 author 저자 inspiration 영감 approximately 대략 3 score 득점하다 profile 프로필을 알려주다 4 winner 우승자 raffle 경품 추첨 5 enable 가능하게 하다 real-time 실시간의 create 창조하다, 만들어 내다 6 recommend 권하다 procedure 절차 assist 돕다 7 film 촬영하다 sequel 속편 8 urgent 긴급한 head director 이사장 cancel 취소하다

Unit 05 : 시제 57

2 시험에 반드시 나오는 진행 시제

현재진행 시제

▶ 현재 순간에 진행되고 있는 상황을 나타냅니다.

GT Motors is introducing a new line of trucks. GT 자동차가 신형 트럭 제품군을 선보이고 있다.
The firm is looking for an accountant now. 회사는 지금 회계사를 찾고 있다.

▶ 가까운 미래를 나타낼 때 미래 시제 대신에 현재진행형을 사용하기도 합니다.

The cleaning company is coming next week to run the service.
청소 업체가 다음 주에 서비스를 하러 올 것이다.
I am calling you to inquire about the test tonight. 오늘밤에 시험에 대해 문의하려고 당신에게 전화할 것입니다.

과거진행 시제

▶ 과거의 어떤 시점에 진행되고 있던 상황을 나타냅니다.

When my friend came, I was eating lunch. 친구가 왔을 때 나는 점심을 먹고 있었다.
★ 토익 시험에는 거의 출제되지 않습니다.

미래진행 시제

▶ 미래 시제와 큰 차이가 없습니다.

Jennifer will be giving a tour of the museum tomorrow. 내일 Jennifer가 박물관을 안내해 줄 것이다.
The rest of the employees will be joining us shortly. 나머지 직원들이 곧 우리와 합류할 것이다.

진행 시제를 만들 수 없는 감정동사

like 좋아하다	please 기쁘게 하다	prefer 선호하다	hate 미워하다
want 원하다	surprise 놀라게 하다	shock 충격을 주다	believe 믿다

KG group is (pleased / pleasing) to announce the promotion of Mr. Roy.
KG 그룹은 Roy 씨의 승진을 발표하게 되어 기쁩니다.

Practice

정답 및 해설 p.35

A. 괄호에서 적절한 것을 고르세요.

1. The director of JKH Production (will be hosting / hosted) a dinner party at the Portland Lodge next Saturday at 6 p.m.

2. Certain bank loan advertisements (are receiving / receives) more attention because of their policies of slashing interest rates.

3. Mike Harrison explained his economic perspective while he (was having / has) a lunch meeting with his colleagues.

4. Walter Company (will have introduced / will be introducing) its newly designed wireless earphones next week.

B. 빈칸에 가장 적절한 것을 고르세요.

5. Currently, Belltower Association ------- for a freelance yet reliable business consultant.
   (A) has searched
   (B) was searching
   (C) is searching
   (D) will have searched

6. Donna Myers ------- on financial budget costs during the assembly next Tuesday.
   (A) was reporting
   (B) reported
   (C) will be reporting
   (D) has been reporting

7. Ms. Jess ------- to reduce her expenses significantly.
   (A) like
   (B) was liking
   (C) would like
   (D) is liking

8. I am ------- that you have agreed to appear on my show.
   (A) please
   (B) pleased
   (C) pleasing
   (D) pleasure

어휘 1 host 개최하다 2 certain 어떤 loan 대출 attention 주목 slash 삭감하다 interest rate 금리 3 perspective 견해, 관점 colleague 동료 4 introduce 소개하다 wireless 무선의 5 currently 현재, 지금 reliable 신뢰할 수 있는 search for 찾다, 구하다 6 budget cost 예산 비용 assembly 의회, 회의 7 reduce 줄이다 expense 지출 significantly 상당히, 대폭 8 appear 나타나다, 출연하다

Unit 05 : 시제   59

3 시험에 반드시 나오는 완료 시제

현재완료 시제

> for/in+기간 over[during] the past[last]+기간
> since+연도 recently/lately 최근에

▶ **과거에 시작된 일이 현재까지 지속되고 있음을 나타냅니다. 과거의 기간을 나타내는 부사어가 함께 사용됩니다.**

The student has studied hard over the past three years. 그 학생은 지난 3년간 열심히 공부해왔다.
The company has manufactured personal computers since 1985.
그 회사는 1985년부터 개인용 컴퓨터를 제조해왔다.

▶ **'Since+과거, 주어+현재완료' 형태가 많이 사용됩니다.**

Since Ms. Louis was elected as president, she has hardly been seen in her office.
Louis 씨는 회장으로 선출된 이후부터 자기 사무실에서 좀처럼 볼 수가 없다.

▶ **시간의 부사절에 현재뿐 아니라 현재완료도 사용합니다.**

After this period (has ended / ends), you will become a full-time worker.
이 기간이 끝난 후에 당신은 정식 직원이 될 것입니다.
 보통 시간의 부사절에는 현재를 사용하지만 현재완료도 사용할 수 있으므로 양쪽 모두 맞습니다.

과거완료 시제

▶ **과거의 어느 시점보다 이전에 발생한 일을 나타냅니다.**

After James had worked for 40 years, he decided to retire from the company.
James는 40년 동안 일한 후에 회사에서 은퇴하기로 결정했다.
Mr. Kent had left for the airport by the time his secretary called him.
Kent 씨는 비서가 그에게 전화를 했을 때 이미 공항으로 떠났었다.
 토익 시험에서는 'By the time+과거, 주어+과거완료' 형태로도 출제됩니다.

미래완료 시제

▶ **과거 또는 현재에 시작된 일이 미래의 어느 시점에 끝날 것을 나타냅니다.**

By the time I finish this report, I will have written over 500 pages.
내가 이 보고서를 끝마칠 무렵에는 500페이지 이상 작성했을 것이다.
 토익 시험에서는 'By the time+현재, 주어+미래완료' 형태로만 출제되고 있습니다.

Practice

정답 및 해설 p.36

A. 괄호에서 적절한 것을 고르세요.

1. Everyone who (is joined / has joined) the Photography Club during the past month will be invited to the upcoming photo exhibition.

2. Ms. Darlington (will have completed / completed) thirty years of service at the Green Cross Community Center by the time she turns sixty.

3. Popular for its cultural diversity, the United States (is receiving / has received) nearly 17 million immigrants over the past twelve years.

4. Plymetrica Electronics (has begun / had begun) inspecting the building even before the consultant approved the property clearance.

B. 빈칸에 가장 적절한 것을 고르세요.

5. By the time he gains a complete understanding of the system, Mr. Theodore ------- on the test machines for three consecutive days.
   (A) will have worked
   (B) has been working
   (C) was working
   (D) works

6. The updated versions for the advanced device achieved perfection a week earlier than we -------.
   (A) anticipate
   (B) are anticipating
   (C) were anticipated
   (D) had anticipated

7. Numerous investment agencies ------- about the vacant building on Rossi Avenue before Oxbridge Central Group purchased it.
   (A) inquiring
   (B) had inquired
   (C) would be inquiring
   (D) will have inquired

8. Jeremy Craigs ------- as a part of the Genova University board of directors for almost 20 years by the time he retires.
   (A) been served
   (B) had served
   (C) has served
   (D) will have served

어휘 1 upcoming 다가오는, 곧 있을 exhibition 전시회 2 complete 끝내다, 완전한 turn (나이·시기가) 되다 3 diversity 다양성 immigrant 이민자 4 property 부동산 clearance 정리, 처분 5 gain 얻다 understanding 이해하다 consecutive 연속되는 6 advanced 고급의 achieve 성취하다 perfection 완벽, 완전 anticipate 예상하다 7 numerous 수많은 agency 기관 vacant 비어 있는 8 board of directors 이사회 retire 은퇴하다, 퇴직하다

Unit 05 : 시제   61

4 반드시 알아야 하는 기출 동사 어휘 ❺

☐ **substitute** 대체하다, 대신하다	• substitute olive oil for butter 버터를 올리브유로 대체하다 • She will substitute for me. 그녀가 내 역할을 대신할 것이다.
☐ **prohibit** 금지하다, 못하게 하다	• Parking on this street is prohibited. 이 거리에는 주차가 금지되어 있다. • Time prohibits me from asking questions. 시간 관계상 질문을 할 수 없다.
☐ **analyze** 분석하다	• analyze the business climate 사업 환경을 분석하다 • analyze a vast amount of information 방대한 양의 정보를 분석하다
☐ **extend** 연장하다, 늘리다	• extend the warranty period to two years 품질보증 기간을 2년으로 연장하다 • extend the life expectancy to 80 years 기대 수명을 80세까지 늘리다
☐ **develop** 발전시키다, 개발하다	• develop new packaging ideas 새로운 포장 아이디어를 개발하다 • develop good relationships 좋은 관계를 발전시키다
☐ **repair** 수리하다, 바로잡다	• This computer needs to be repaired. 이 컴퓨터는 수리가 필요하다. • repair errors in the program 프로그램의 오류를 바로잡다
☐ **deliberate** 숙고하다, 심의하다	• He deliberated for a full hour. 그는 꼬박 한 시간 동안 숙고했다. • They are deliberating whether to pass that law. 그들은 그 법률을 통과시킬지 여부를 심의 중이다.
☐ **recognize** 알아보다, 인정하다	• He hardly recognized his old friend. 그는 옛 친구를 거의 알아보지 못했다. • be recognized as a leading company 대표적인 기업으로 인정받다
☐ **outfit** (복장·장비를) 갖추어 주다	• The car is outfitted with special options. 그 차에는 특별 옵션들이 장착되어 있다. • He outfitted himself for travel. 그는 여행 장비를 갖추었다.
☐ **specify** 명시하다, 지정하다	• specify the amount of money 금액을 명시하다 • specify a password 암호를 지정하다
☐ **consult** 상담[상의]하다, 참조하다, 찾아보다	• You should consult your doctor. 의사의 진찰을 받아야 합니다. • consult the manual 설명서를 참조하다
☐ **consider** 고려하다, 여기다	• consider the possibility of relocation 이전 가능성을 고려하다 • consider it (to be) a great honor 그것을 커다란 영광으로 여기다
☐ **purchase** 구입하다, (희생의 대가로) 얻다	• You can purchase tickets online. 온라인으로 티켓을 구입하실 수 있습니다. • His success was dearly purchased. 그의 성공은 큰 희생을 치르고 얻은 것이다.
☐ **forward** 보내다, 전달하다, 진행시키다	• forward a catalog to a customer 고객에게 카탈로그를 보내다 • forward a plan 계획을 추진하다
☐ **investigate** 조사하다, 수사하다	• investigate the recent problems 최근의 문제들을 조사하다 • He has been investigated by the police. 그는 경찰의 수사를 받아왔다.

Practice

A. 괄호에서 적절한 것을 고르세요.

1. Smoking should be (persuaded / prohibited) in public places because secondhand smoke is harmful to others.

2. Seven brave civilians were (recognized / advocated) for their efforts in saving a group of people who were trapped underground as a result of an earthquake.

3. Please (consult / inquire) Mr. Baker's memo dated October 14 to determine the time of your next appointment.

4. Local supermarkets will be (extending / reaching) its hours until midnight due to the holiday season.

B. 빈칸에 가장 적절한 것을 고르세요.

5. Undergraduates who are ------- studying in this graduate school should attend tomorrow's presentation.
   (A) considering
   (B) accompanying
   (C) transforming
   (D) concerning

6. CTS Vision Inc. has recently ------- a new state-of-the-art eyeglasses, fit for comfort and daily use.
   (A) based
   (B) thought
   (C) resulted
   (D) developed

7. Final tests and medical data must be further ------- before deciding to perform surgery.
   (A) supervised
   (B) required
   (C) analyzed
   (D) vacated

8. Since smartphones have become a popular trend, simple cellular phones are no longer ------- at many retail stores.
   (A) purchased
   (B) handed
   (C) gained
   (D) paid

어휘 1 public place 공공장소 secondhand smoke 간접흡연 harmful 해로운 2 civilian 일반 시민, 민간인 effort 노력 trap 가두다 underground 땅속에 as a result of ~의 결과로 earthquake 지진 3 determine 결정하다 appointment 약속, 예약 4 local 지역의, 지방의 midnight 자정 due to ~로 인해 5 undergraduate 학부생 graduate school 대학원 attend 참석하다 6 state-of-the-art 최첨단의 comfort 편안함 7 further 더 깊이 perform surgery 외과 수술을 하다 8 no longer 더 이상 ~ 않다 retail store 소매점

1. In June next year, Mr. Edison, our project manager, ------- the company's new robot for innovative packaging.
   (A) exhibiting
   (B) exhibited
   (C) will exhibit
   (D) has exhibited

2. Before Mr. Markus hired Stacey at his bookstore, he ------- the new releases into the shelves himself.
   (A) had organized
   (B) organize
   (C) can organize
   (D) organizes

3. Ms. Hollin has ------- that boarding students be restricted from late night activities to prevent any misconduct.
   (A) mentioned
   (B) suggested
   (C) negotiated
   (D) assigned

4. Mr. Sonny ------- to announce the completion of the T337 navigation software used in devices integrated into automobiles.
   (A) pleases
   (B) pleasant
   (C) was pleased
   (D) is being pleased

5. Since Mr. Adams worked hard even after office hours, he ------- a three-day paid vacation as a reward.
   (A) receive
   (B) is being received
   (C) received
   (D) receiving

6. Starting next week, all applicants with internship programs ------- a daily performance assessment from their immediate supervisors.
   (A) have received
   (B) will receive
   (C) to receive
   (D) will be received

7. When Tanya ------- to Vancouver to visit her families next week, she will also attend her brother's wedding ceremony.
   (A) goes
   (B) to go
   (C) going
   (D) was going

8. It is essential that only authorized personnel ------- to enter the staff building.
   (A) allowed
   (B) be allowed
   (C) allow
   (D) allows

Questions 9-12 refer to the following letter.

January 29

Dear Leafe Hospital Coronary Care Unit,

Katalina Pots --- 9. --- as a doctor for many years under my direct supervision at Gesundheit Hospital. Ms. Pots has performed professionally and efficiently while discharging her duties at our hospital. She also developed commendable relationships with her --- 10. ---.
Furthermore, she even received an employee recognition award before resigning from her position here last year.
--- 11. ---. Therefore, I am highly recommending her for the position with the Coronary Care Unit at Leafe Hospital. I have no doubt that Ms. Pots would be a worthy asset to --- 12. --- health care team.
Please feel free to contact me at 555-1196 if you would like to discuss Ms. Pots' qualifications in more detail. I would be more than happy to answer any questions you may have concerning her abilities.

Sincerely,
Patch Adams

9 (A) serves
   (B) served
   (C) will be serving
   (D) would have served

10 (A) clients
   (B) patients
   (C) investors
   (D) members

NEW
11 (A) Ms. Pots' hard work, flexibility, and hospitality are truly a gift.
   (B) That position has already been filled.
   (C) She doesn't qualify for the position.
   (D) The hospital is open throughout the year.

12 (A) us
   (B) yourself
   (C) your
   (D) them

Unit 06 명사

Part 5-6

사람이나 사물의 이름을 명사라고 합니다. 토익에서는 명사가 와야 하는 자리, 가산명사와 불가산명사, 사람 명사와 사물 명사의 종류 등이 주로 출제됩니다. 토익에서 꾸준히 출제되고 있는 중요한 유형입니다.

명사의 형태

명사의 형태는 무척 다양하지만 특정한 형태의 어미가 있는 명사들도 많습니다. 대표적인 명사 어미들은 -ion, -tion, -sion, -ty, -ness, -ance, -ence, -ment입니다.

-ion	region 지역	union 연합
-tion	nation 국가	condition 조건
-sion	decision 결정	television 텔레비전
-ty	beauty 아름다움	sincerity 성실
-ness	happiness 행복	business 사업
-ance	distance 거리	assistance 도움
-ence	experience 경험	diligence 근면
-ment	payment 지급	movement 움직임

가산명사와 불가산명사

대부분의 명사는 수를 셀 수 있지만 형태가 일정하지 않은 물질이나 눈에 보이지 않는 추상적인 개념처럼 셀 수 없는 명사들도 있습니다. 그래서 셀 수 있는 명사를 **가산명사**, 셀 수 없는 명사를 **불가산명사**라고 부릅니다.

가산명사	cup 컵	student 학생	book 책
	boy 소년	phone 전화기	umbrella 우산
불가산명사	water 물	milk 우유	sugar 설탕
	love 사랑	beauty 아름다움	Sidney 시드니 (이름)
	funding 자금	spending 지출	accounting 회계

명사의 단수를 복수로 만드는 방법

영어에서는 명사의 단수와 복수를 엄격하게 구분해 표현합니다. 단수 형태를 복수 형태로 만드는 일반적인 방법은 다음과 같습니다.

대부분의 명사, 모음+o로 끝나는 명사	끝에 s를 붙입니다.	book 책 → books 책들 tree 나무 → trees 나무들 chair 의자 → chairs 의자들 video 비디오 → videos 비디오들
-s, -sh, -ch, -x, 자음+o로 끝나는 명사	끝에 es를 붙입니다.	bus 버스 → buses 버스들 brush 붓 → brushes 붓들 bench 벤치 → benches 벤치들 box 상자 → boxes 상자들 tomato 토마토 → tomatoes 토마토들
자음+y로 끝나는 명사	y를 i로 고치고 es를 붙입니다.	baby 아기 → babies 아기들 city 도시 → cities 도시들 story 이야기 → stories 이야기들
-f, -fe로 끝나는 명사	f, fe를 v로 고치고 es를 붙입니다.	leaf 나뭇잎 → leaves 나뭇잎들 wolf 늑대 → wolves 늑대들 wife 아내 → wives 아내들 knife 칼 → knives 칼들
불규칙하게 변하는 명사	불규칙하게 변하므로 변화형을 하나씩 익혀야 합니다.	child 아이 → children 아이들 man 남자 → men 남자들 woman 여자 → women 여자들 tooth 이 → teeth 이들 foot 발 → feet 발들 mouse 쥐 → mice 쥐들
단수와 복수 형태가 같은 명사	형태가 변하지 않습니다.	fish 물고기 → fish 물고기들 salmon 연어 → salmon 연어들 sheep 양 → sheep 양들 deer 사슴 → deer 사슴들 species 종(種) → species 종들 means 수단 → means 수단들

1 시험에 반드시 나오는 명사 자리

명사가 와야 하는 자리

▶ 주어

The (schedule / ~~scheduled~~) for the construction project is hanging on the wall.
그 건설 프로젝트를 위한 일정표가 벽에 걸려 있다.

The (changes / ~~changing~~) are small but will have impact on our productivity.
그 변화들은 작았지만 우리의 생산성에 영향을 미치게 될 것이다.

▶ 관사+명사

It is the (responsibility / ~~responsible~~) of event planner to set up equipment.
장비를 설치하는 것은 행사 기획자의 책임이다.

The staff had to ask a (~~technical~~ / technician) to fix it. 직원들은 기술자에게 그것을 고쳐 달라고 부탁해야 했다.

▶ 소유격+명사

A second job can add to your (~~qualify~~ / qualifications). 부업은 당신의 자격요건을 늘려줄 수 있습니다.

We recommend that you visit one of our authorized (~~dealing~~ / dealers).
저희는 당신이 저희의 공인 판매점 중의 한 곳을 방문하시기를 권합니다.

▶ 타동사+명사

Please contact Mr. Ken if you have not received (information / ~~informative~~). 정보를 받지 못하셨다면 Ken 씨에게 연락하십시오.

Companies need to provide (training / ~~trained~~) to new employees. 회사들은 신입 직원들에게 교육을 제공할 필요가 있다.

★ training은 -ing 형태의 불가산명사입니다.

▶ 형용사+명사

After repeated requests by local (~~residential~~ / residents), the gym was opened to the community.
지역 주민들의 요청이 거듭된 후에 그 체육관이 지역사회에 문을 열었다.

Mr. Armstrong has made a significant (~~contribute~~ / contribution) to the American economy.
Armstrong 씨는 미국 경제에 지대한 공헌을 해왔다.

▶ 전치사+명사

Mr. Jordan called earlier today for (~~confirming~~ / confirmation).
Jordan 씨는 확인을 위해 오늘 일찍 전화했다.

Street food vendors are offering finger food in (~~respond~~ / response) to customer demands.
음식 노점상들은 고객의 요구에 부응해 손으로 집어 먹는 음식을 제공하고 있다.

Practice

정답 및 해설 p.43

A. 괄호에서 적절한 것을 고르세요.

1. The (popularity / popular) of Oriental medicine has drawn positive responses from patients, particularly from Western countries.

2. Mr. Geronimo will be the guest speaker in this year's (convene / convention) in Austin, Texas.

3. To ensure public order, the security department has confirmed the (implementation / implement) of the plan to install surveillance cameras.

4. All visitors carrying proper authorization have received (approval / approving) to enter the main facility.

B. 빈칸에 가장 적절한 것을 고르세요.

5. Mr. Nash has reported that ------- related to the rental of commercial property are too costly.
   (A) expended
   (B) expensively
   (C) expensive
   (D) expenses

6. To assist you in deciding on your -------, our real estate agent Mr. Lambert will be available during office hours.
   (A) reside
   (B) resident
   (C) residential
   (D) residence

7. Once you acquire a housing loan, the financial ------- will deal with you on a regular basis.
   (A) institution
   (B) institutional
   (C) institutionally
   (D) institutionalize

8. After a year of -------, the Silver Sky building project was ceased due to a lack of resources and budget.
   (A) constructive
   (B) constructor
   (C) construction
   (D) constructed

어휘 1 Oriental 동양의 medicine 의학 positive 긍정적인 2 convention 컨벤션, 집회 3 confirm 확정하다 surveillance 감시 implementation 이행, 실행 4 authorization 허가[인가]증 5 commercial 상업적인 property [prɑ́pərti] 재산, 부동산 6 assist 돕다 real estate agent 부동산 중개인 available 만날 수 있는 7 acquire 얻다 on a regular basis 정기적으로 8 cease 중단하다 resource 자원 budget [bʌ́dʒit] 예산

2 시험에 반드시 나오는 복합명사와 불가산명사

복합명사

▶ 복합명사는 2개 이상의 명사들이 결합된 것입니다. 다음은 대표적인 복합명사들입니다.

customer satisfaction 고객 만족	job opening 일자리, 구인	account information 계좌 정보
job description 직무 내용	site supervisor 현장 감독	attendance record 출석률
work environment 근무 환경	travel expense 여행 경비	telephone conversation 전화 통화
training session 교육 시간	facility regulation 시설 규정	safety regulation 안전 규정
interest rate 금리	meal preference 식사 기호	security reason 보안상의 이유
keynote address 기조연설	delivery schedule 배송 일정	support worker 지원 인력

▶ 복합명사에서 앞의 명사는 대개 단수로 사용되지만 복수로 사용되는 예외적인 경우도 있습니다.

savings account 예금 계좌	awards ceremony 시상식	awards banquet 시상식 연회
sales department 영업부	customs office 세관	sales representative 영업 직원

불가산명사

▶ 의미가 비슷한 가산명사와 불가산명사

가산명사	불가산명사	가산명사	불가산명사
plan 계획	planning 기획	approach 접근 방식	access 접근, 열람, 출입
survey 설문조사	research 연구, 조사	alternative 대안	alternation 교대
cloth 옷감, 천	clothing 의류	description 묘사, 설명	information 정보
permit 허가증	permission 허가	receipt 영수증	receipt 수령, 인수
estimate 견적서	estimation 견적		

▶ 반드시 알아야 하는 불가산명사

advice 충고	consent 승낙, 허락	luggage 수하물	assistance 도움
merchandise 상품	employment 고용	knowledge 지식	equipment 장비
furniture 가구	machinery 기계류	weather 날씨	money 돈
confusion 혼란	experience 경험	progress 발전	wealth 부

▶ 항상 복수로 쓰는 명사

scissors 가위	goods 상품	belongings 소지품	valuables 귀중품
earnings 소득	customs 세관	surroundings 환경	savings 저축, 예금

Practice

정답 및 해설 p.44

A. 괄호에서 적절한 것을 고르세요.

1. Since the district is heavily crowded with cars, new development plan for a public parking (structure / structures) has been proposed.

2. Mr. Jenkyl was nominated as a site (supervisory / supervisor) after working in the construction industry for three and a half years.

3. Several university students apply for various job (opening / openings) offered by the school internship programs to gain personal experience.

4. Some hotels ask their customers to specify their meal (prefers / preferences) upon room reservations to enable attentive service.

B. 빈칸에 가장 적절한 것을 고르세요.

5. A session will be held tomorrow on facility ------- and guidelines for the newly recruited staff members.
   (A) will regulate
   (B) regulated
   (C) is regulating
   (D) regulations

6. Justin Seaborn decided to become a sales ------- after realizing his gifts in social communication and presentation.
   (A) representative
   (B) represent
   (C) representation
   (D) represented

7. Technical manager, Courtney Lawrence advised all the staff members to update their computer firewall and anti-virus programs for ------- reasons.
   (A) secured
   (B) secures
   (C) securely
   (D) security

8. In case the printers do not work, please ask our staff for -------.
   (A) assistant
   (B) assist
   (C) assistance
   (D) assisted

어휘 1 district 지구, 구역 be heavily crowded with ~으로 무척 혼잡하다 2 nominate 지명하다, 임명하다 3 job opening 일자리 internship 인턴사원 근무 4 specify 명확히 말하다 reservation 예약 attentive 주의 깊은, 세심한 5 session 수업 (시간) guideline 지침 recruit 모집하다 6 gift 재능 communication 의사소통 presentation 발표, 설명 7 advise 조언하다, 권고하다 firewall 방화벽 8 in case ~할 경우에는

Unit 06 : 명사

3 시험에 반드시 나오는 사람 명사와 사물 명사

사람 명사와 사물 명사

▶ **사람 명사와 사물 명사의 구분**

빈칸에 들어갈 적절한 명사를 고르는 문제의 보기로 사람 명사와 사물 명사가 함께 출제됩니다. 다음 명사들은 반드시 알아야 합니다.

사람 명사	사물 명사	사람 명사	사물 명사
applicant 지원자	application 지원서	supervisor 감독자	supervision 감독
recipient 수령인	receipt 수령, 영수증	complier 순응자	compliance 순종
architect 건축가	architecture 건축	representative 대표, 담당자	representation 표시, 대리
professional 전문가	profession 직업	distributor 배급[유통]업자	distribution 배급, 유통
accountant 회계사	account 계좌	assistant 조수	assistance 도움
retailer 소매상	retail 소매	author 작가	authorization 공인
attendant 참석자	attendance 참석	advisor 고문	advice 조언, 충고
inspector 조사관	inspection 조사	photographer 사진가	photography 사진술
consultant 상담자	consultation 상담	director 이사, 감독	direction 방향, 지시
performer 수행자, 공연자	performance 수행, 공연	visitor 방문자	visit 방문
packager 포장업자	package 포장, 소포		

All+복수 명사

All (~~analyst~~ / analysts) should attend the meeting.
모든 분석가들은 회의에 참석해야 한다.

All (~~item~~ / items) are shipped within 48 hours.
모든 상품은 48시간 이내에 발송된다.

Practice

정답 및 해설 p.45

A. 괄호에서 적절한 것을 고르세요.

1. Many lawyers are willing to provide a free one-hour (consultants / consultation) for first-time clients.

2. Machinery must be imported in full (compliance / complier) with national law and customary policy.

3. Wealthy people often look to hire (architecture / architects) to design and build custom homes.

4. Secondhand (retails / retailers) tend to care less about the quality of the products and more about the price at which they are selling products.

B. 빈칸에 가장 적절한 것을 고르세요.

5. Employers have the habit of thoroughly examining résumés to find a qualified ------- for an important position.
   (A) apply
   (B) applied
   (C) application
   (D) applicant

6. Mr. Matthews and his team of skilled ------- are known for their quality work and timely results.
   (A) profession
   (B) professions
   (C) professional
   (D) professionals

7. The administrators are in ------- of the suggestions and will make a decision by tomorrow.
   (A) receiving
   (B) to receive
   (C) receipt
   (D) recipient

8. All ------- imported through shipment must go through customs investigation for legal approval and release.
   (A) packager
   (B) packages
   (C) packaged
   (D) package

어휘 ¹willing to 기꺼이 ~하다 first-time 첫 번째의 ²machinery 기계류 import 수입하다 customary 관습상의 ³hire 고용하다 custom 주문 제작의, 맞춤의 ⁴secondhand 중고품의 tend to ~하는 경향이 있다 ⁵thoroughly 철저하게 examine 조사하다 résumé 이력서 qualified 자격 있는, 적임인 ⁶skilled 숙련된 timely 적시의, 때맞춘 ⁷administrator 행정관, 관리자 ⁸shipment 선적, 발송 investigation 조사 release 방출

4 반드시 알아야 하는 기출 명사 어휘 ❶

☐ **permit** 허가(증)	• The city issues the building permit. 시에서 건축 허가증을 발급한다. • The parking permit must be signed. 주차 허가증에 서명해야만 한다.	
☐ **equipment** 장비, 설비	• the laboratory's safety equipment 실험실의 안전 장비 • a factory with state-of-the-art equipment 최첨단 설비를 갖춘 공장	
☐ **acceleration** 가속, 가속도	• an acceleration in job losses 가속화되는 실업 • the acceleration of gravity 중력 가속도	
☐ **capability** 능력, 역량	• beyond the scope of human capability 인간 능력의 범위를 넘어서는 • increase the manufacturing capability 제조 역량을 늘리다	
☐ **agenda** 의제, 안건	• The agenda is on the board. 의제가 심의 중에 있다. • push an agenda 안건을 밀어붙이다	
☐ **sequence** 순서, 연속	• a sequence of never-ending changes 끝없는 변화의 연속 • be performed in a particular sequence 특정한 순서대로 수행되다	
☐ **suggestion** 제안, 암시	• collect suggestions from residents 주민들의 제안들을 수집하다 • remove the pain by the power of suggestion 암시의 힘으로 통증을 제거하다	
☐ **inquiry** 문의, 조회	• inquiries about lost luggage 분실한 수하물에 대한 문의 • I'm calling in regard to your inquiry. 문의하신 내용과 관련해 전화 드립니다.	
☐ **confidence** 신뢰, 자신감	• maintain public confidence in the judiciary 사법부에 대한 대중의 신뢰를 유지하다 • She is lacking in confidence. 그녀는 자신감이 없다.	
☐ **consideration** 고려, 배려	• take into consideration the candidate's qualifications 후보의 자질을 고려하다 • show enough consideration for other people 다른 사람들을 충분히 배려하다	
☐ **expertise** 전문 기술	• mechanical expertise 기계에 관한 전문 지식 • my area of expertise 내 전문 분야	
☐ **passion** 격정, 열정	• a speech full of passion 격정으로 가득한 연설 • have a passion for serving customers 고객을 접대하는 데 열정이 있다	
☐ **congestion** 밀집, 혼잡	• congestion of population 인구 밀집 • reduce highway congestion 고속도로의 혼잡을 줄이다	
☐ **access** 접근, 출입, 열람	• be denied access to the information 그 정보에 대한 접근을 거부당하다 • He gave me free access to all the files. 그는 모든 파일을 자유롭게 열람하게 해주었다.	
☐ **reception** 리셉션, 축하 연회	• a wedding reception 결혼 피로연 • a welcome reception 환영회	

Practice

정답 및 해설 p.47

A. 괄호에서 적절한 것을 고르세요.

1. (Properties / Inquiries) about lost items found can be made by calling the front desk during office hours.

2. The additional workforce has significantly increased manufacturing (qualification / capability).

3. Employees and visitors entering the power plants are required to wear safety (equipment / construction).

4. The instructors will give the student drivers their learner (permits / garages) after conducting proper evaluation.

B. 빈칸에 가장 적절한 것을 고르세요.

5. The community's annual holiday ------- will be held at the Lantern Hotel tomorrow from 5 p.m.
   (A) invitation
   (B) reception
   (C) deposit
   (D) appointment

6. Participants will be provided with a basic outline of the ------- of the day's events in a few minutes.
   (A) admission
   (B) sequence
   (C) inventory
   (D) version

7. Workers using public transportation should be careful to avoid routes with severe traffic ------- because it can disrupt their schedules.
   (A) climates
   (B) kilometers
   (C) congestion
   (D) direction

8. The committee is preparing a survey to collect ------- from staff members regarding the company's renovated facility.
   (A) suggestions
   (B) attendees
   (C) successes
   (D) competitors

어휘 1 office hours 근무 시간 2 additional 추가의 workforce 인력 significantly 상당히, 대폭 manufacturing 제조의 3 power plant 발전소
4 instructor 강사 conduct 실시하다, 수행하다 evaluation 평가 5 community 지역 사회 6 participant 참가자 outline 윤곽, 개요
7 transportation 교통수단 severe 심한, 혹독한 disrupt 와해시키다, 중단시키다 8 committee 위원회 collect 수집하다, 모으다

1. ------- for the loss of benefits of employees may be covered by the contract stated.
   (A) Compensation
   (B) Compensates
   (C) Compensatory
   (D) Compensated

2. Bill Carter was admired by superiors for his ------- and perseverance at the workplace.
   (A) adapt
   (B) adaptable
   (C) adaptability
   (D) adapts

3. Mr. Harley Macbee, general manager of Blight Company will be overseeing ------- with domestic and foreign distributors.
   (A) negotiate
   (B) negotiates
   (C) negotiations
   (D) negotiated

4. Certain university professors encourage students to read books for -------, rather than solely reading for assignment purposes.
   (A) pleasurable
   (B) pleasure
   (C) pleased
   (D) pleasant

5. Customers who purchase the Body-Fit exercise machine will be given free ------- to a four-hour training video from the Web site.
   (A) accessing
   (B) accessed
   (C) access
   (D) accesses

6. The executive ------- at Wheeler Enterprise will be attending the conference next Friday.
   (A) directing
   (B) director
   (C) directed
   (D) direction

7. ------- to the Shinzo Lab Center are prohibited from taking photos within the facility.
   (A) To visit
   (B) Visit
   (C) Visiting
   (D) Visitors

8. Under all -------, participants must demonstrate fair play and exercise friendly sportsmanship during matches.
   (A) circumstances
   (B) circumstantial
   (C) circumstantially
   (D) circumstance

Questions 9-12 refer to the following advertisement.

Phens Corporation is one of the leading --- 9. --- of top-selling canned goods in the country.
Once in contract, we offer the lowest prices on canned goods for annual supply, with discounts of 8 percent or more, depending on your negotiated agreement. In addition to these reasonable --- 10. ---, we provide a variety of canned goods from poultry to fresh fruit.
We supply canned goods to over 200 mega markets. Regardless of the number of orders, you will receive --- 11. --- a single bill for the contract deposit of shipping and delivery.
To obtain a complete list of the canned goods available or to place an order, please visit www.phencorp.org. --- 12. ---.

9 (A) distributing
   (B) distributors
   (C) distributed
   (D) distribution

10 (A) request
   (B) attempts
   (C) goals
   (D) rates

11 (A) only
   (B) either
   (C) even
   (D) until

NEW

12 (A) All canned goods are pretty expensive.
   (B) We are looking forward to doing business with you in the near future.
   (C) This offer is valid only for loyal customers.
   (D) We don't charge for shipping.

Unit 07 대명사

Part 5-6

대명사는 말 그대로 '명사를 대신하는 말'입니다. 영어에서는 일단 한 번 말한 명사는 다시 사용하지 않고 대명사로 대신해 말합니다. 사람을 대신하는 것은 인칭대명사, 명확하지 않은 것을 대신하는 것은 부정대명사, 사람이나 사물을 가리키는 것은 지시대명사, 주어 자신이 동사의 대상이 되는 것은 재귀대명사라고 합니다. 토익에서는 인칭대명사가 가장 많이 출제되고, 난이도는 가장 낮은 유형에 속하는데 최근 들어서는 부정대명사도 아주 많이 출제되고 있고, 난이도도 높은 편이라서 반드시 정리를 해야 고득점이 가능합니다.

인칭대명사

사람과 사물을 가리키는 인칭대명사는 가장 많이 사용되는 대명사입니다. 인칭대명사는 시험에 반드시 출제되므로 숙지하고 있어야 합니다.

격		주격	소유격	목적격	소유대명사	재귀대명사
인칭		은/는, 이/가	~의	~을/를, ~에게	~의 것	자신
1인칭	나	I	my	me	mine	myself
	우리	we	our	us	ours	ourselves
2인칭	당신	you	your	you	yours	yourself
	당신들					yourselves
3인칭	그	he	his	him	his	himself
	그녀	she	her	her	hers	herself
	그것	it	its	it	-	itself
	그들, 그것들	they	their	them	theirs	themselves

부정대명사

정해지지 않은 것을 가리킵니다. 최근 들어 시험에서 비중 있게 다루어지고 있습니다.

one another the other others the others other	other는 형용사 역할을 하므로 뒤에 반드시 명사가 와야 합니다. others는 대명사 역할을 하므로 뒤에 반드시 복수 동사가 와야 합니다.
each other one another	가장 많이 출제되고 있습니다. 주어 자리에 절대 올 수 없고 전치사나 동사의 목적어 자리에만 올 수 있습니다.
any anyone anybody	주어 자리에 올 수 있습니다. 의미 구별(어떤, 누구, 누구라도)이 중요합니다. anyone 뒤에는 of가 붙을 수 없습니다.
no one none nobody	주어 자리에 올 수 있습니다. no one 뒤에는 of가 붙을 수 없습니다.
few little many	few, little, many가 단독으로 대명사로 사용될 수 있습니다. few, many 뒤에는 복수 동사, little 뒤에는 단수 동사가 와야 합니다.
some somebody	주어 자리에 사용될 수 있습니다. 뒤에 단수/복수 동사 모두 올 수 있습니다.

지시대명사

'이것'과 '저것'을 구별하여 가리킵니다.

> this 이것, 이 사람 → these 이것들, 이 사람들   that 저것, 저 사람 → those 저것들, 저 사람들

- this와 that은 단수 동사 앞에 사용하고 these와 those는 복수 동사 앞에 사용합니다. this와 that의 차이를 묻거나 these와 those의 차이를 묻는 문제는 토익에 출제되지 않습니다.

  This is an urgent problem. 이것은 긴급한 문제다.   **These are** my books. 이것들은 내 책들이다.
  That is the newest model. 저것은 최신 모델이다.   **Those are** useful. 저것들은 유용하다.

- 지시대명사 this/that/these/those는 지시형용사로도 사용됩니다. 지시형용사 뒤에는 명사가 옵니다.

  These computers are amazing. 이 컴퓨터들은 놀랍다.
  지시형용사   명사

1 시험에 반드시 나오는 대명사

인칭대명사

▶ **주격** 뒤에 동사가 옵니다. 수식을 하거나 받지 않고 반드시 단독으로 사용됩니다.

After you finish reviewing the manual, put it in the cabinet. 안내서 검토가 끝나면 캐비닛 안에 넣으세요.
Although Dr. Larry is a newcomer, he has already become an asset to the hospital.
Larry 박사는 새로 왔음에도 불구하고 이미 병원에서 중요한 인물이 되었다.

▶ **목적격** 앞에 동사나 전치사가 옵니다. 수식을 하거나 받지 않고 반드시 단독으로 사용됩니다.

Analysts use the latest technology to help them reach their goals.
분석가들은 최신 과학기술을 이용해 그들이 자기 목표를 달성하도록 도와준다.
Mr. William completes work assigned to him quickly. William 씨는 자신에게 할당된 일을 빨리 끝마친다.

▶ **소유격** 명사의 범위를 나타내는 한정사 기능을 하므로 뒤에 명사가 꼭 와야 합니다.

Teachers can make their classes more effective with visual aids. 교사들은 시각 보조물로 수업을 더 효율적으로 만들 수 있다.

재귀대명사

▶ **재귀대명사** 주어와 목적어가 동일할 때 사용합니다.

The nurse has committed herself to caring for patients. 그 간호사는 환자들을 보살피는 데 전념했다.

▶ **강조 용법의 재귀대명사** 주어 바로 뒤나 완전한 문장 끝에 위치하며 생략 가능합니다.

We ourselves cooked our meals for two days. 이틀 동안 우리는 직접 식사를 만들었다.
The manager decided to train new sales employees himself. 과장은 신입 영업직원들을 직접 교육하기로 결정했다.

▶ **재귀대명사의 관용표현**

Daniel prefers working by himself. Daniel은 혼자 일하는 것을 선호한다.
The interns are asked to develop a new product for themselves. 인턴들은 그들 스스로를 위한 신상품을 개발하도록 요구받았다.

소유대명사

▶ **이중 소유격** 한정사+명사+of+소유대명사

She has been a close colleague of mine for two years. 그녀는 2년째 나의 가까운 동료이다.
★ 한정사는 두 개 겹쳐서 쓰지 않고(a my close colleague) 이중소유격을 사용합니다.

▶ **보어**

We will offer our opinions, but the final choice is yours. 우리가 의견들을 제시하겠지만 최종 선택은 당신 것입니다.
= your choice

Practice

정답 및 해설 p.51

A. 괄호에서 적절한 것을 고르세요.

1. Students wishing to change course schedules should first contact (them / their) professors to obtain approvals.

2. When approaching the check-in counter at the airport, (yourself / you) should present your personal identification.

3. Several volunteers will follow Mr. Sawyer to assist (his / him) with the preparations for the next experiment.

4. Entomologist George Bosh was explaining why spiders do not get caught on (their / theirs) webs.

B. 빈칸에 가장 적절한 것을 고르세요.

5. To ensure that ------- assignment is not lost in or deleted from the hard disk, I will save a separate file on a portable USB drive.
   (A) my
   (B) I
   (C) me
   (D) mine

6. During the recent Visual Arts Convention, Ms. Sophie Foster was highly complimented by many art fans for ------- creativity.
   (A) she
   (B) herself
   (C) hers
   (D) her

7. Since Brian Song is the supervisor, all customer complaints should be reported to -------.
   (A) he
   (B) his
   (C) himself
   (D) him

8. James and Tony will retire from the company and open a store by -------.
   (A) them
   (B) themselves
   (C) theirs
   (D) their

어휘 1 approval 승인, 동의 2 approach ~에 접근하다 identification 신분증 3 volunteer 자원봉사자 preparation 준비 experiment 실험 4 entomologist 곤충학자 5 ensure 확실히 ~하게 하다 assignment 과제, 임무 portable 휴대용의 6 convention 컨벤션, 집회 compliment 칭찬하다 7 supervisor 관리자 complaint 불평, 불만 8 retire 퇴직하다

2 시험에 반드시 나오는 부정대명사

부정대명사

▶ **one, the other** 가리키는 대상이 둘일 때 사용합니다.

There are two umbrellas: one is blue and the other is red. 우산 두 개가 있다. 하나는 빨간색이고 다른 하나는 파란색이다.

▶ **one, another, the others/others** 가리키는 대상이 셋 이상일 때 사용합니다. 여러 개 중의 하나는 one, 또 다른 하나는 another, 다른 몇 개는 others, 나머지 전부는 the others를 사용합니다.

There are five umbrellas: one is blue and another is red and the others are white.
우산 다섯 개가 있다. 하나는 파란색, 다른 하나는 빨간색이고 다른 것들은 모두 흰색이다.

There are many umbrellas: one is blue and another is red and others are white.
우산 여러 개가 있다. 하나는 파란색, 다른 하나는 빨간색이고 다른 것들은 흰색이다.

▶ **each other, one another** 주어 자리에 올 수 없으며 전치사나 동사의 목적으로 사용됩니다.

(One another / Anyone) who is interested in ~ ~에 관심 있는 사람은 누구나
(No one / Each other) registered for ~ 아무도 ~에 등록하지 않았다
communicate with each other 서로 의사소통하다
help each other 서로 돕다
meet one another 서로 만나다

수를 나타내는 부정대명사

▶ **anyone[anybody], no one[nobody], none** 주어 자리에 사용할 수 있으며 뒤에 단수 동사가 옵니다.

Anyone who has read the book 그 책을 읽은 사람은 누구나
No one / Nobody is permitted to enter this area. 아무도 이 구역에 들어가는 것이 허락되지 않는다.

▶ **most, some, neither**

most/some of the + 복수 명사/불가산명사
neither of the + 복수 명사

▶ **few, little, many**

Invitations were sent to all members, but few will be able to attend.
초청장이 모든 회원에게 발송되었지만 소수만 참석할 수 있을 것이다.

Little has been written about the incident. 그 사건에 대해 기록된 것은 거의 없다.

Many are called, but few are chosen. 부름 받은 자는 많으나 선정된 자는 적으니라.

Practice

정답 및 해설 p.52

A. 괄호에서 적절한 것을 고르세요.

1. In addition, they can communicate with (one another / each) through the discussion forums.

2. (Nobody / Any) has run faster than Bart Philips at the Sports Festival's 500-meter sprint.

3. Due to the difference in time zone, (most / almost) of the phone calls with the Winston Company in Los Angeles are held at night.

4. If (one another / no one) participates in the session until Friday, I will permanently disband the group without warning.

B. 빈칸에 가장 적절한 것을 고르세요.

5. ------- has been mentioned about Mr. Spooker's visit to Cambodia, so we do not know whether the negotiation went smoothly or not.
   (A) Little
   (B) Who
   (C) Few
   (D) Any

6. ------- who has heard Mr. Raymond's piano performance would know why he was considered one of the most influential musicians of all time.
   (A) Some
   (B) These
   (C) You
   (D) Anyone

7. We are currently experiencing technical problems; therefore, we apologize for ------- inconvenience caused by the server.
   (A) both
   (B) any
   (C) many
   (D) these

8. ------- of the results showed significant association with the report.
   (A) Whichever
   (B) Each other
   (C) Anywhere
   (D) Neither

어휘 1 in addition 게다가, 이밖에도 forum 공개 토론회, 포럼 2 sprint 단거리 경주 3 due to ~으로 인해 4 participate 참가하다 permanently 영구히 disband 해체하다 5 negotiation 협상, 교섭 6 performance 공연 influential 영향력 있는 7 technical 기술적인 inconvenience 불편 8 significant 중요한, 중대한 association 연관성

Unit 07 : 대명사 83

3 시험에 반드시 나오는 지시대명사

지시대명사

▶ **this/these와 that/those**

this/that은 앞에 나온 단수 명사를 대신하며 these/those는 복수 명사를 대신합니다. that/those는 뒤에 'of+명사'가 수식어로 자주 붙습니다. this와 these는 수식어가 붙을 수 없습니다.

Nagoya's weather is comparable to (that / those) of Busan. 나고야의 날씨는 부산의 날씨와 비슷하다.

The benefit packages are not good when measured against (those / that) of our rival companies.
이 복지 혜택들은 경쟁사들의 혜택들과 비교 평가해 볼 때 좋은 것이 아니다.

▶ **those**

뒤에 관계대명사절, 과거분사, 현재분사가 붙어 '~하는 사람들'이라는 의미가 됩니다.

Those who work after 7 p.m. will receive the overtime rate for those hours.
오후 7시 이후에 일하는 사람들은 그 시간들만큼 추가근무 수당을 받을 것이다.
★ Anyone who works와 구별해야 합니다.

Those interested in relocating should submit a plan to Mr. Kelley by June 3.
전근에 관심 있는 사람들은 6월 3일까지 Kelley 씨에게 계획안을 제출해야 한다.

Those planning to study in New Zealand must apply for a student visa.
뉴질랜드에서 공부하려고 계획 중인 사람들은 학생 비자를 신청해야만 한다.

지시형용사

지시대명사가 명사 앞에 와서 '이 ~, 저 ~'로 해석될 경우 지시형용사라고 합니다.

▶ **this, that+단수 명사**

this[that] campaign 이[저] 캠페인   that[this] matter 저[이] 문제

▶ **these, those+복수 명사**

these[those] forms 이[저] 양식들   those[these] packaging materials 저[이] 포장재들

Practice

정답 및 해설 p.53

A. 괄호에서 적절한 것을 고르세요.

1. In 2013, the profits decreased by two million dollars from (that / those) of the previous year.

2. (These / This) two materials have features that are quite different from each other.

3. Many tourist sites have now been made more accessible because (whose / these) attractions enable foreigners to enjoy and experience the local culture.

4. The basic design of the truck is very similar to (that / those) of earlier models.

B. 빈칸에 가장 적절한 것을 고르세요.

5. ------- who wish to obtain more information about the workshop that is being held this week on Friday should speak with Mr. Farlin.
   (A) Anybody
   (B) Another
   (C) Those
   (D) Each

6. ------- documents which were found in the cabinet are outdated, but the information may be useful for future references.
   (A) Them
   (B) Theirs
   (C) That
   (D) These

7. Applicants should be developing self-confidence and the skills that would reflect a strong personality, as ------- are the qualities that will impress employers.
   (A) them
   (B) their own
   (C) these
   (D) that

8. Our graduates will be successful in various professional careers, including ------- outside of traditional chemical engineering fields.
   (A) that
   (B) them
   (C) those
   (D) theirs

어휘 1 decrease 감소하다, 줄어들다 previous 이전의, 앞선 2 material 재료, 소재 feature 특징 3 accessible 접근할 수 있는 attraction 명소 4 similar 비슷한, 유사한 5 obtain 얻다 6 document 문서, 서류 outdated 구식의, 낡은 reference 참조, 참고 7 applicant 지원자, 신청자 self-confidence 자신감 reflect 반영하다 8 various 다양한, 여러 가지의 chemical engineering 화학 공학

4 반드시 알아야 하는 기출 명사 어휘 ❷

☐ **process**
과정, 공정
- the ageing process 노화 과정
- the process of making cheese 치즈 제조 공정

☐ **identification**
신원 확인, 신분증
- the identification of the crash victims 추락사고 희생자들의 신원 확인
- Please make sure your identification is visible. 신분증이 보이도록 해주세요.

☐ **selection**
구색, 선택, 취급
- The catalog offers a wide selection of items.
  그 카탈로그는 광범위한 품목을 폭넓게 취급한다.
- a limited selection of home furniture 제한적인 가구 선택

☐ **branch**
지점, 지부
- all branches of the company 회사의 모든 지점들
- managers from all branches 전 지점에서 온 관리자들

☐ **presence**
존재, 출석
- She didn't notice my presence. 그녀는 내가 있는 것을 알아차리지 못했다.
- The queen graced the occasion with her presence.
  여왕이 참석해 그 자리를 빛내주었다.

☐ **defect**
결함, 결점
- physical defects in the materials 재료의 물리적 결함
- due to a manufacturing defect 제조상의 결함으로 인해

☐ **development**
발전, 개발
- recent development in the industry 최근 업계의 발전
- the first stage of development 개발 첫 단계

☐ **component**
구성 요소, 성분, 부품
- a central component of the economy 경제의 중심 요소
- major components in smartphones 스마트폰의 주요 부품들

☐ **study**
공부, 학문, 연구
- This book is suitable for independent study. 이 책은 자습용으로 적합하다.
- solutions tested in the study 연구에서 검증된 해법들

☐ **deadline**
최종 기한, 마감 시간
- finish the proposal by the deadline 마감 시간까지 제안서를 끝내다
- the deadline for submitting materials 자료 제출의 최종 기한

☐ **supervision**
감독, 지휘
- receive close supervision 철저한 감독을 받다
- Children are under the supervision of their parents.
  아이들은 부모의 지도를 받는다.

☐ **result**
결과
- summarize the results of the research 연구 결과를 요약하다
- as a result of his hard work 그가 열심히 일한 결과로

☐ **response**
응답, 반응
- look forward to your prompt response 당신의 신속한 답장을 고대하다
- in response to customer demand 고객의 요구에 부응하여

☐ **distribution**
분배, 배급
- a fair distribution of funding 자금의 공정한 분배
- the distribution of food to the refugees 난민들에 대한 식량 배급

☐ **charge**
요금, 대금
- an additional charge 추가 요금
- Delivery is free of charge. 배송은 무료입니다.

Practice

정답 및 해설 p.54

A. 괄호에서 적절한 것을 고르세요.

1. Dr. Willow will present a speech on the (development / recruitment) of a new medicine for stabilizing the blood pressure of critically ill patients.

2. More than 10% of water bottles tested in the (subject / study) were found to contain bacteria.

3. Consultants regularly visit our factory to evaluate the efficiency of our manufacturing (demand / process).

4. Due to the New Year's holiday, all the (residences / branches) of Bysler Bank will remain closed until Monday, January 3.

B. 빈칸에 가장 적절한 것을 고르세요.

5. The research division of Westpole Institute is now under the ------- of Mr. Aaron Hong.
   (A) prediction
   (B) supervision
   (C) indication
   (D) completion

6. Pegasa Engineering Group is developing an alternative energy ------- plan for better efficiency.
   (A) distraction
   (B) assortment
   (C) fragment
   (D) distribution

7. When entering the security department, your ------- is required for opening certain doors.
   (A) decision
   (B) reservation
   (C) identification
   (D) interruption

8. The board of directors approved the ------- of the company's monthly financial plan.
   (A) makers
   (B) spaces
   (C) times
   (D) results

어휘 1 stabilize 안정시키다 critically ill 위독한 2 bacteria 박테리아, 세균 3 regularly 정기적으로 evaluate 평가하다 efficiency 능률, 효율 4 due to ~ 때문에 5 research 연구, 조사 division 부문, 부 institute 연구소 6 alternative energy 대체 에너지 7 security 안전, 보안 require 필요로 하다 8 approve 승인하다 financial 재정의, 재무의

Unit 07 : 대명사 **87**

Actual Test

1 Athletes who feel exhausted from intensive exercises often reward ------- with delicious food to regain their strength and motivation.
(A) they
(B) them
(C) theirs
(D) themselves

2 Mr. Perry, the project manager, conducts frequent checks to evaluate whether all his team members are performing ------- duties adequately.
(A) they
(B) them
(C) their
(D) theirs

3 After ------- listen to the announcement, please tell me the details about the course.
(A) you
(B) your
(C) yours
(D) yourself

4 If you have any ideas or suggestions for the new interior designs, please send ------- to Mr. Nixon.
(A) him
(B) there
(C) them
(D) what

5 ------- is allowed to enter the tunnel without Eric's permission, even the police.
(A) Few
(B) Some
(C) One another
(D) No one

6 ------- can apply for the job at the new department as long as their qualifications for the position are suitable.
(A) Anybody
(B) Yourself
(C) Whose
(D) Their

7 ------- wishing to attend the annual holiday event must contact Ms. Priscilla by Tuesday, November 15.
(A) Them
(B) My
(C) Anyone
(D) Whomever

8 Although program designers usually work separately, weekly scheduled meetings enable them to collaborate with -------.
(A) the same
(B) this
(C) each other
(D) much

88

Questions 9-12 refer to the following advertisement.

Do you find modern architecture interesting? If you want to know more about --- 9. ---, architect Jerald Hadgen will tell you all that you want to know at an open lecture at Lakeshire University on Friday, August 10.

Over the past few years, Mr. Hadgen has been writing a --- 10. --- column in *Dezeen Magazine*. He is also the author of the best seller *Dreaming of that Home* and has made guest appearances on several television programs in Australia and New Zealand.

The lecture is a part of a --- 11. --- sponsored by the director of Lakeshire University. The lecture will be held in the Meeting Hall, which is located in the second building of Lakeshire University, at 2 p.m. Although the lecture is free for students, faculty, and staff, all other visitors will have to pay $10 each for admission to this lecture. --- 12. ---.

9 (A) them
   (B) those
   (C) it
   (D) itself

10 (A) respect
   (B) respects
   (C) respectfully
   (D) respected

11 (A) host
   (B) series
   (C) museum
   (D) concert

NEW
12 (A) Complimentary breakfast is available in the lobby.
   (B) Tuition fees are $20 for participants.
   (C) If you'd like to make a reservation, please call 555-1479.
   (D) Books are available at any bookstores throughout the country.

Unit 08 형용사

Part 5-6

명사의 상태나 성질을 나타내는 말을 형용사라고 합니다. 형용사는 명사를 위해 있는 품사라고 말할 정도로 항상 명사를 수식하거나 묘사합니다. 한 단어로 된 형용사뿐만 아니라 여러 단어로 구성된 형용사구와 형용사절도 명사를 수식할 수 있으며 이것들을 모두 형용사어라고 부릅니다. 형용사의 위치 문제는 난이도가 낮은 편이지만 요즘은 난이도가 약간 높은 분사 형용사, 수량 형용사, 혼동 형용사가 많이 출제되고 있으므로 대비를 해야 합니다.

형용사의 형태

형용사의 형태는 무척 다양하지만 가장 대표적인 형용사 어미는 -able, -tive, -sive, -ous, -tic, -less, -ful, -y입니다.

-able	reliable 믿을 만한	desirable 바람직한
-tive	positive 긍정적인	negative 부정적인
-sive	expensive 비싼	defensive 방어적인
-ous	various 다양한	glorious 영광스러운
-tic	dramatic 극적인	realistic 현실적인
-less	careless 부주의한	useless 쓸모없는
-ful	successful 성공적인	beautiful 아름다운
-y	busy 바쁜	easy 쉬운

명사+ly → 형용사

형용사에 -ly를 붙이면 부사(sadly, smoothly 등)가 되지만 명사에 -ly를 붙이면 형용사가 됩니다.

friendly 우호적인   timely 적시의   lovely 사랑스러운   costly 값비싼
weekly 매주의   yearly 매년의   monthly 매월의   orderly 질서정연한

friendly relations 우호적인 관계
a timely rain 때맞춰 내리는 비

형용사의 용법

▶ 한정적 용법

형용사가 명사를 앞에서 직접 수식하는 경우 명사의 성격을 한정해 준다고 해서 형용사의 한정적 용법이라고 합니다.

The island is famous for its beautiful beaches. 그 섬은 아름다운 해변으로 유명하다.
a big room 큰 방
the difficult case 어려운 사건

▶ 서술적 용법

형용사가 be동사나 불완전자동사(2형식 동사) 뒤의 주격 보어나 5형식 동사의 목적격 보어로 사용되어 주어나 목적어의 상태를 보충 설명하는 것을 형용사의 서술적 용법이라고 합니다. afraid(두려운), alive(살아 있는), alone(혼자의, 고독한), asleep(잠든), aware(알고 있는)과 같은 형용사는 서술적 용법으로만 사용됩니다.

The room is big. 그 방은 크다.
　　　　　주격 보어
The task is difficult. 그 업무는 어렵다.
　　　　　　주격 보어
The man is alone in the boat. 남자가 홀로 배를 타고 있다.
　　　　　주격 보어
Sunshine on my shoulder makes me happy. 어깨에 내리쬐는 햇빛이 나를 행복하게 만든다.
　　　　　　　　　　　　　　　　목적격 보어
I found the movie boring. 그 영화는 따분했다.
　　　　　　　　목적격 보어

1 시험에 반드시 나오는 형용사 자리와 분사형 형용사

● 형용사가 와야 하는 자리

▶ be동사/become+형용사

Effective interpersonal communication is (vital / ~~vitally~~) for success. 효과적인 대인 커뮤니케이션은 성공을 위해 필수적이다.

Students are (responsible / ~~responsibility~~) for familiarizing themselves with the school regulations.
학생들은 교칙을 숙지해야 할 책임이 있다.

A total ban on smoking in cafés will become (effective / ~~effectively~~) starting from tomorrow.
카페에서의 전면 흡연 금지가 내일부터 시행된다.

▶ 형용사+명사

Many duty free shops offer (~~excellency~~ / excellent) prices for various products.
많은 면세점들은 다양한 제품에 우수한 가격을 제시한다.

Psychologists believe that exposure to classical music during early childhood has a (beneficial / ~~benefits~~) effect on mental development. 심리학자들은 유아기에 클래식 음악에 노출되는 것이 정신 발달에 유익한 효과가 있다고 믿는다.

▶ be동사+부사+형용사

The site inspector was highly (~~critic~~ / critical) of the railways' poor safety record.
현장 조사관은 선로의 부실한 안전 기록을 호되게 비판했다.

▶ 5형식 문형의 목적격 보어 keep/make/find/consider/call/leave+목적어+목적격 보어(형용사)

Please keep our kitchen area (pleasant / ~~pleasing~~) and clean. 주방을 쾌적하고 깨끗하게 유지하세요.

We will make the house (safe / ~~safely~~). 우리는 집을 안전하게 만들겠습니다.

● 분사형 형용사

▶ -ing 형용사

existing 존재하는	incoming 들어오는	inviting 매력적인	promising 유망한
demanding 까다로운	growing 성장하는	remaining 남아 있는	lasting 지속적인
leading 선도하는	overwhelming 압도적인	encouraging 고무적인	outstanding 뛰어난, 미납된

the remaining work 나머지 일   an outstanding customer service 뛰어난 고객 서비스

▶ -ed 형용사

detailed 세부적인	discounted 할인된	damaged 손상된	limited 제한된
designated 지정된	distinguished 유명한, 저명한	written 서면의	dedicated 헌신적인
crowded 붐비는	accomplished 뛰어난	unexpected 예기치 않은	required 필수의

a written confirmation 서면 확인   distinguished companies 이름난 회사들

Practice

정답 및 해설 p.59

A. 괄호에서 적절한 것을 고르세요.

1. If the office has shared equipment, such as printers and scanners, they need to be easily (accessible / accessing) to everyone who needs to use them.

2. The team of experts will verify whether the product from Liaro Jewelry is (authentic / authenticity).

3. One trade group claims that it has found (statistical / statistically) evidence that outdoor team-building exercises significantly increase cooperation and trust.

4. Ms. Webber's (enthusiastic / enthusiasm) support for the Masterson high school volleyball team gave the team confidence and boosted their morale.

B. 빈칸에 가장 적절한 것을 고르세요.

5. The new Watie Jet Skis are easy to control, highly ------- and capable of speeds exceeding 65mph.
   (A) maneuver
   (B) maneuverable
   (C) maneuverability
   (D) to maneuver

6. If two or more species share many DNA sequences, it is ------- that they are at least closely related.
   (A) like
   (B) likely
   (C) likened
   (D) likelihood

7. The measures proposed by Mr. Harper included the ------- approval of direct foreign investment in high-priority industries.
   (A) prompt
   (B) prompts
   (C) promptly
   (D) promptness

8. In 2013, an unusual orange tide appeared in the ------- waters of Nigeria.
   (A) coasts
   (B) coaster
   (C) coastal
   (D) coastlines

어휘 1 share 공유하다 equipment 장비 2 expert 전문가 verify 확인하다 3 trade 무역 claim 주장하다 evidence 증거 cooperation 협력, 협동 4 confidence 자신감 boost 끌어올리다 morale 사기, 의욕 5 control 조종하다 capable 할 수 있는 exceed 초과하다 6 species 종(種) sequence 순서, 서열 closely 긴밀히 related 관련된 7 measure 대책 propose 제안하다 approval 승인 investment 투자 high-priority 높은 우선순위의 8 tide 조수 appear 나타나다

2 시험에 반드시 나오는 수량 형용사와 혼동하기 쉬운 형용사

수량 형용사

▶ **each/every/another+단수 가산명사**

each room 각각의 방   each candidate 각 지원자   each package 각각의 소포
every catalog 모든 목록   every member 모든 회원   every month 매달
another day 다른 날   another reason 다른 이유   another opportunity 또 하나의 기회

★ every, another 뒤에 둘 이상의 수 표현이 있을 경우 복수 명사와 함께 사용할 수 있습니다.

every three years 3년마다   another two months 2개월 더

▶ **several/many/numerous/various/a series of/few/a few+복수 가산명사**

several topics 몇 가지 주제   several contractors 몇몇 계약자들   several awards 몇 개의 상
a few days 며칠   a few questions 몇 가지 질문   a few letters 몇 통의 편지
a series of outdoor concerts 연속되는 야외 공연   a series of afternoon seminars 연속되는 오후 세미나

▶ **much/little/a little/a large amount of+불가산명사(단수)**

little change 변동이 거의 없음   little demand 수요가 거의 없음   a little assistance 약간의 도움
a large amount of glass 다량의 유리   a large amount of money 거액의 돈

▶ **some은 주로 긍정문에 사용되며 복수 명사와 불가산명사를 수식합니다.**

I have some questions. 나는 몇 가지 질문이 있다.
some purchase (X), some contracts (O), some information (O)

▶ **any는 주로 부정문, 조건문, 의문문에 사용되며 단수·복수 명사와 불가산명사를 수식합니다.**

I don't have any questions. 나는 어떤 질문도 없다.
any purchase (O), any contracts (O), any information (O)

혼동하기 쉬운 형용사

considerable 상당한	considerate 사려 깊은	confident 확신하는, 자신하는	confidential 기밀의
respectable 존경할만한	respective 각자의	informative 유익한	informed 해박한
comparable 비슷한	compared 비교되는	dependable 믿음직한	dependent 의존하는, 좌우되는
impressive 인상적인	impressed 감명을 받은	advisable 바람직한	advisory 고문의
sensible 현명한	sensitive 민감한	economic 경제의	economical 절약하는
seasonal 계절별의	seasoned 양념된	successful 성공한	successive 연속적인
reliable 믿을 수 있는	reliant 의존적인	competitive 경쟁력 있는	competent 유능한
comprehensible 이해할 수 있는	comprehensive 종합적인		

a successful candidate 당선자   five successive days 연속 5일
economic value 경제적인 가치   an economical housekeeper 알뜰한 주부

Practice

정답 및 해설 p.60

A. 괄호에서 적절한 것을 고르세요.

1. (Other / Each) department must assign a designated person for processing invoices, payrolls, cash items, and travel expenses.

2. For the first time in ten years, poverty rates have significantly fallen in (all / every) region of the country.

3. Hyperdak Electronics is so (confidential / confident) about the design and durability of its customized computers that it is providing customers with a two-year warranty.

4. With thousands of string lights, the giant Christmas tree at the Central Park makes an (impressed / impressive) visual impact.

B. 빈칸에 가장 적절한 것을 고르세요.

5. Since Justin joined the team in 2011, he has made ------- valuable contributions to the current software.
   (A) some
   (B) much
   (C) little
   (D) every

6. Dentists recommend that people change their toothbrush ------- three months or whenever the bristles begin to fray.
   (A) during
   (B) every
   (C) about
   (D) only

7. The Heinrich Association organized an ------- meeting on Thursday, March 17, with the guest attendance of Mr. Graham.
   (A) informative
   (B) informing
   (C) informed
   (D) informally

8. If Mr. Ulrich retires, it will be difficult to find a person with ------- experience and skills in financial management.
   (A) compare
   (B) comparing
   (C) compared
   (D) comparable

어휘 1 assign 맡기다, 배정하다 designate 지정하다 process 처리하다 invoice 송장, 청구서 payroll 급여 명부 expense 비용 2 poverty 가난, 빈곤 region 지역 3 durability 내구성 customized 주문 제작한 warranty 품질보증 4 giant 거대한 visual 시각적인 impact 효과 5 valuable 귀중한 contribution 기여 6 dentist 치과의사 recommend 권장하다 whenever ~할 때마다 bristle (솔의) 털 fray 닳다 7 association 협회 attendance 참석 8 retire 은퇴하다 financial 재정의, 재무의

Unit 08 : 형용사 95

3 반드시 알아야 하는 기출 명사 어휘 ❸

☐ **flexibility** 융통성, 유연성	• He shows flexibility in his attitude. 그는 융통성 있는 태도를 보인다. • offer additional flexibility 추가적인 융통성을 제공하다	
☐ **vacancy** 공석, 빈자리	• fill the vacancy in marketing 마케팅부의 공석을 채우다 • They have a vacancy in the department. 그 부서에 빈자리가 하나 있다.	
☐ **setting** 환경, 장소	• an ideal setting 이상적인 환경 • the perfect setting for a honeymoon 신혼여행을 위한 완벽한 장소	
☐ **consultation** 상담, 협의, 진찰	• complimentary fitness consultation 무료 건강 상담 • consultation hours 진료 시간	
☐ **proof** 증거, 증명	• show the proof of employment 고용 증명을 보여주다 • proof of purchase 구입 증거	
☐ **basis** 근거, 기초	• on the basis of ~을 근거로 하여 • The basis of a marriage is trust. 결혼 생활의 기초는 신뢰이다.	
☐ **incentive** 인센티브, 우대 혜택	• offer customers extra incentives 고객에게 추가 우대 혜택을 제공하다 • incentives to encourage employees 직원들을 독려하는 인센티브들	
☐ **expenditure** 지출, 소비	• The company reduced its expenditures. 그 회사는 지출을 줄였다. • eliminate unnecessary expenditure 불필요한 지출을 없애다	
☐ **location** 위치, 장소	• pinpoint a location 위치를 정확히 찾아내다 • open new plants in different locations 여러 장소에 새 공장들을 열다	
☐ **responsibility** 책임, 의무	• the department's responsibilities 그 부서의 책임 • assume additional responsibilities 추가적인 책임을 맡다	
☐ **flair** 천부적 재능, 솜씨	• She has a flair for languages. 그녀는 언어에 재능이 있다. • with real flair 정말 솜씨 있게	
☐ **site** 현장, 장소, 부지	• arrive at the construction site 건설 현장에 도착하다 • communicate with the site supervisor 현장 감독관과 연락하다	
☐ **entirety** 전체, 온전한 상태	• Fill out this form in its entirety. 이 서식을 전부 작성하세요. • maintain it in its entirety 그것을 온전한 상태로 유지하다	
☐ **experience** 경험, 경력	• No previous experience is required for this job. 이 업무에는 이전 경력이 필요하지 않습니다. • applicants with experience in the field 그 분야에 경험이 있는 지원자들	
☐ **productivity** 생산성, 생산력	• maximize employee productivity 직원들의 생산성을 극대화하다 • a dramatic increase in productivity 생산성의 급격한 증가	

Practice

정답 및 해설 p.62

A. 괄호에서 적절한 것을 고르세요.

1. Sarah Reed, who is a famous violinist, is recognized for her charm and (flair / form) for classical music.

2. Friaz Market is planning to offer discounts and other (incentives / impressions) on all grocery items to customers whose billing amounts exceed $50.

3. Many companies tend to offer bonuses, commissions and other forms of rewards to increase employee (productivity / tendency).

4. The Georgetown Weekly Newsletter illustrates recent growth in the global economy and lists the current job (vacancies / qualities).

B. 빈칸에 가장 적절한 것을 고르세요.

5. A salesperson must have the ------- to accept different buyer proposals.
   (A) flexibility
   (B) commission
   (C) destination
   (D) relativity

6. Real estate agent Neil Harrison offers retail ------- for lease in Chicago at reasonable prices.
   (A) locations
   (B) executives
   (C) meetings
   (D) expertise

7. Customers will be given refunds for any defective items only when they show some ------- of purchase, such as receipts.
   (A) print
   (B) change
   (C) goal
   (D) proof

8. All computer users have the ------- of backing up important files before system repairs are performed.
   (A) permission
   (B) responsibility
   (C) status
   (D) reference

어휘 1 famous 유명한 recognize 인정하다 charm 매력 2 grocery item 식료품 exceed 초과하다 3 tend to ~하는 경향이 있다 commission 수수료 reward 보상 4 illustrate 예를 들어 설명하다 recent 최근의 growth 성장 current 현재의 5 accept 받아들이다 proposal 제안 6 real estate agent 부동산 중개업자 retail 소매상의 lease 임대차 계약 reasonable 합리적인, 적당한 7 refund 환불 defective 결함 있는 receipt 영수증 8 repair 수리, 보수 perform 실행하다

Actual Test

1 Alsum Shoes Company provides footwear that is extremely ------- at reasonable prices.
(A) comfort
(B) comforts
(C) comfortably
(D) comfortable

2 Mobile broadband speeds are improving, but it is ------- that users will be receiving large amounts of data.
(A) doubt
(B) doubtful
(C) doubted
(D) doubtfully

3 Employees may improve their wages by working ------- shifts at overtime rates.
(A) addition
(B) additions
(C) additionally
(D) additional

4 In recent years, the ------- market has become less popular in the major cities of Indonesia.
(A) tradition
(B) traditionally
(C) traditionalism
(D) traditional

5 ------- salesperson should know how to prepare and present their products in a manner that will appeal to the clients and hold their interest.
(A) Every
(B) Whichever
(C) When
(D) Future

6 ------- businesses have recruited enthusiastic, creative and skilled graduates.
(A) Spare
(B) Least
(C) Short
(D) Small

7 If you are going to purchase new equipment, it is ------- to test it before making a final decision.
(A) advisable
(B) advisability
(C) advisory
(D) advising

8 Income will be ------- on the success of our new product and the state of the economy at the time.
(A) depend
(B) dependent
(C) dependable
(D) depends

Questions 9-12 refer to the following e-mail.

To: Fredric Martin (fredm@wemail.com)
From: Joshua Mangi (jmangi@healthylife.com)
Date: February 21
Subject: Healthy Life Monthly Magazine

Dear Mr. Martin,

I am glad to inform you that your article "Eating and Living" has been --- 9. --- for publication in our *Healthy Life Monthly Magazine*. I encourage you to contact our editor, David Lenard at davelen@healthylife.com within the next six days to discuss the --- 10. --- that need to be made to your article.
The article is slated to be published in our May issue; therefore, the revised version of the article must be submitted by April 10th. --- 11. ---. If the payment details and the schedule mentioned is --- 12. --- to you, please send me a confirmation by e-mail. We are looking forward to hearing from you.

Best Regards,
Joshua Mangi
Assistant Editor

9
(A) encouraged
(B) finalized
(C) accepted
(D) determined

10
(A) revisable
(B) reviser
(C) revises
(D) revisions

NEW
11
(A) You can pay either by cash or credit card.
(B) Next month's magazine will be delivered by mail.
(C) In terms of payment, you will receive a flat fee of $45 plus an additional $0.08 per word.
(D) You can find the payment details in the email.

12
(A) agreeably
(B) agreeable
(C) agreement
(D) agreed

Unit 09 부사

Part 5-6

부사는 문장에서 중심 역할을 하지 않고 부가적인 역할을 하는 말을 가리킵니다. 부사는 문장 속의 어떤 자리에서든 동사, 형용사 또는 다른 부사를 수식할 수 있습니다. 다만 부사는 형용사와 달리 명사는 수식하지 못합니다. 부사는 다른 품사나 문장 전체에 의미를 더해 주는 수식어이므로 한 문장 속에서 개수에 상관없이 사용할 수 있습니다. 부사의 위치 문제는 난이도가 낮아 쉽게 풀 수 있으나 요즘은 난이도가 약간 높은 짧은 부사 어휘가 많이 출제되고 있으므로 이에 대비해야 합니다.

부사의 형태

부사는 일반적으로 형용사에 -ly를 붙인 형태가 많습니다.

형용사	부사
rapid 빠른	rapidly 빨리
quick 빠른	quickly 빠르게
beautiful 아름다운	beautifully 아름답게
clear 분명한	clearly 분명하게
careful 신중한	carefully 신중하게
significant 상당한	significantly 상당하게
efficient 효율적인	efficiently 효율적으로

● 어미가 -ly로 끝나지 않는 부사도 많습니다.

| always 항상 | almost 거의 | just 단지 | still 여전히 | even 심지어 |
| sometimes 때때로 | already 이미 | besides 게다가 | also 또한 | then 그때 |

● 부사와 형용사 양쪽으로 모두 사용되는 단어들도 많습니다.

| early 일찍/이른 | near 가까이/가까운 | fast 빨리/빠른 | enough 충분히/충분한 |
| high 높게/높은 | far 멀리/먼 | daily 매일/매일의 | late 늦게/늦은 |

주의해야 하는 부사

형용사에 -ly가 붙어 부사가 되면 의미가 형용사와 완전히 달라지는 단어들이 있습니다. 토익에서는 보기에 두 단어가 함께 제시되므로 혼동하기 쉽습니다.

형용사	부사
high 높은	highly 매우, 상당히
late 늦은	lately 최근에
short 짧은	shortly 곧
close 가까운	closely 면밀히

a **short** story 짧은 이야기
late afternoon 오후 늦게

The meeting will be finished **shortly**. 회의는 곧 끝날 것이다.
It has snowed a lot **lately**. 최근에 눈이 많이 왔다.

부사의 위치

- 문장 맨 앞에서 문장 전체를 수식합니다.

  Regrettably, we are unable to meet the deadline. 유감스럽게도 우리는 마감 기한을 지킬 수 없습니다.

- 일반동사를 앞이나 뒤에서 수식합니다.

  My boss **always** comes late. 상사는 항상 늦게 온다.
  The machines are inspected **carefully**. 기계들은 신중하게 검사된다.

- be동사를 뒤에서 수식합니다.

  She is **currently** in the office. 그녀는 현재 사무실에 있다.

- 형용사를 앞에서 수식합니다.

  He made his report **completely** free of errors. 그는 보고서를 완전히 오류 없게 만들었다.

- 부사를 앞에서 수식합니다.

  Drivers are advised to drive **very** carefully on the icy road. 운전자들은 빙판길에서 매우 조심해 운전하도록 권고받는다.

- 형용사나 부사의 역할을 하는 전치사구(전치사+명사)를 앞에서 수식합니다.

  Today's low temperature is **mainly** because of a cold front. 오늘의 낮은 기온은 주로 한랭 전선 때문이다.

1 시험에 반드시 나오는 부사 자리

 부사의 위치

▶ **주어+동사+목적어+부사**

Sales people handle customers' complaints professionally. 영업사원들은 고객들의 불만을 프로답게 다룬다.
Scientists have failed to date the fossils accurately. 과학자들은 화석들의 연대를 정확히 측정하는 데 실패했다.

▶ **주어+부사+동사**

We sincerely regret any inconvenience. 불편을 드려 진심으로 유감입니다.
Tony finally realized how foolish he was. Tony는 마침내 자신이 얼마나 어리석은지 깨달았다.

▶ **부사+형용사**

This tool is extremely helpful. 이 도구는 무척 유용하다.
She is a highly sensitive woman. 그녀는 아주 예민한 여성이다.

▶ **자동사+부사**

I work collaboratively with a group of colleagues. 나는 동료들과 협력해 일한다.
Let's look for ways to work together productively. 생산적으로 함께 일할 방법을 찾아봅시다.

▶ **be동사, have+부사+p.p./-ing**

The market is continually changing due to unexpected events. 시장은 예상치 못한 사건들로 인해 계속 변하고 있다.
The final budgets can be formally accepted at the meeting. 최종 예산은 회의에서 정식으로 받아들여질 수 있다.
Analysts have repeatedly warned that stock prices will fall. 분석가들은 주가가 떨어질 것이라고 거듭 경고해왔다.

▶ **일반동사+more+부사 / be동사, 2형식 동사+more+형용사**

This system enables consumers to use energy more efficiently. 이 시스템은 소비자들이 에너지를 더 효율적으로 사용할 수 있게 해준다.
Raw materials have become more valuable. 원자재가 더 귀해지고 있다.

 수와 양을 수식하는 부사

approximately 대략	nearly 거의	almost 거의	about 대략
at least 적어도	up to 최대 ~까지	around 약	more than ~보다 많은, ~가 넘는

approximately thirty people 대략 30명   nearly 25 days 거의 25일

Practice

A. 괄호에서 적절한 것을 고르세요.

1. We need to develop alternative solutions to respond more (swiftly / swift) to the current market conditions.

2. The museum, located south from the train station, is (easy / easily) accessible by bus, car, or on foot.

3. The funds to renovate the public library were donated (overwhelmingly / overwhelming) by the educational foundation.

4. The sales team has accomplished the monthly goal by (innovational / innovatively) using its resources and talents.

B. 빈칸에 가장 적절한 것을 고르세요.

5. Over the past 3 years, shipping costs have increased ------- because fuel costs have risen.
   (A) considerably
   (B) considerable
   (C) considering
   (D) considered

6. Compared to last year, recycling in the Farmington District has increased by ------- 20 percent.
   (A) approximate
   (B) approximately
   (C) approximating
   (D) approximated

7. Pasadena has ------- negotiated a new long-term sales agreement with Regent Corporation.
   (A) success
   (B) successfully
   (C) successful
   (D) succeeded

8. Mr. Cooper has worked in the construction company for ------- 30 years.
   (A) neared
   (B) nearest
   (C) nearby
   (D) nearly

2 시험에 반드시 나오는 기출 부사와 비교급·최상급 강조 부사

주요 기출 부사

already	이미	I already met her. 그녀를 이미 만났다.
now	지금	He is working in Chicago now. 그는 지금 Chicago에서 일하고 있다.
just	방금, 막	I just met him here. 여기서 방금 그를 만났다.
still	아직, 여전히	She is still living in Seoul. 그녀는 여전히 서울에 살고 있다.
soon	곧	He will soon be back. 그는 곧 돌아올 것이다.
yet	아직	We have yet to win a game this year. 우리는 금년에 아직 한 경기도 이기지 못했다.
rather ★	꽤, 상당히, 다소	The computer is rather slow. 그 컴퓨터는 다소 느리다.
sometime	언젠가	I want to see her sometime. 언젠가 그녀를 보고 싶다.
ever	지금까지, 여태	I haven't ever been there. 나는 지금까지 그곳에 가 본 적이 없다.
early	일찍	The train arrived ten minutes early. 열차가 10분 일찍 도착했다.
thereby ★	그렇게 함으로써, 그것 때문에	Conflict of interests would thereby be avoided. 그렇게 함으로써 이해 충돌을 피하게 된다.
together	함께	They are spending time together. 그들은 함께 시간을 보내고 있다.
solely	혼자서, 오로지	He is solely responsible for it. 그가 혼자서 책임지고 있다.
rarely	드물게, 좀처럼 ~하지 않고	The Japanese rarely talk to strangers. 일본인들은 낯선 사람들에게 좀처럼 말하지 않는다.
altogether ★	전적으로	That's a different matter altogether. 그것은 전적으로 별개의 문제이다.

★고득점자도 많이 틀리는 부사들입니다.

비교급과 최상급을 강조하는 부사

▶ 비교급을 강조하는 부사: much, even, far, a lot, still

You are (much / so / very) better than me. 너는 나보다 훨씬 낫다.
　　　　　　비교급

▶ 최상급을 강조하는 부사: quite, by far, even, simply

He is (by far / much) the best artist. 그는 단연코 최고의 예술가입니다.
　　　　최상급

Practice

정답 및 해설 p.68

A. 괄호에서 적절한 것을 고르세요.

1. The Fixent Company has (rarely / just) completed its daily production of smartphones; soon they will be packaged and shipped for deliveries.

2. If you have (already / very) submitted your absence report, please disregard this e-mail.

3. Since Jenny works at the office until late afternoon, she (less / seldom) arrives home before dinner.

4. Mr. Madison will be back from his trip to Hong Kong (sometime / often) between late January and early February.

B. 빈칸에 가장 적절한 것을 고르세요.

5. Applications are ------- being accepted for the fifth Annual Midsummer Arts Fair.
   (A) much
   (B) now
   (C) further
   (D) more

6. Ms. Elliot will arrive ------- tomorrow to meet with the directors before attending the morning conference.
   (A) ever
   (B) seldom
   (C) early
   (D) yet

7. ------- after becoming a member of the society, Mary Owens was elected as the chairman.
   (A) How
   (B) Ever
   (C) Often
   (D) Soon

8. Sam ------- works at Buzz Wheel Motors, although he was demoted from the position of service manager two years ago.
   (A) nearly   (B) still
   (C) after   (D) much

어휘 ¹production 생산 package 포장하다 delivery 배송 ²submit 제출하다 absence 결석, 결근 disregard 무시하다 ³since ~이므로 arrive 도착하다 ⁴be back 돌아오다 between A and B A와 B 사이에 ⁵application 지원(서), 신청(서) accept 받아들이다 annual 연례의 midsummer 한여름 fair 박람회 ⁶attend 참석하다 conference 총회, 회의 ⁷society 학회 elect 선출하다 ⁸although 비록 ~이지만 demote 강등시키다

Unit 09 : 부사 105

3 반드시 알아야 하는 기출 명사 어휘 ❹

- [ ] **interest** 관심, 흥미
  - express great interest 커다란 관심을 표하다
  - He's never shown the slightest interest in politics. 그는 정치에 조금도 관심을 보이지 않았다.

- [ ] **gratitude** 감사, 고마움
  - Please relay my gratitude to her. 그녀에게 감사의 말을 전해주세요.
  - in token of our gratitude 우리의 감사의 표시로

- [ ] **majority** 대다수, 과반수
  - the majority of the survey respondents 설문조사 응답자들의 대다수
  - a majority of customers 대다수의 고객들

- [ ] **concept** 개념, 관념
  - grasp the basic concepts of economics 경제학의 기본 개념들을 파악하다
  - the concept of a public service 공공 서비스의 개념

- [ ] **approval** 승인
  - ask for approval 승인을 요청하다
  - obtain approval 승인을 얻다

- [ ] **sample** 견본, 표본
  - This product does not measure up to the sample. 이 제품은 견본과 같지 않다.
  - Send me a sample copy. 견본 한 부를 보내주세요.

- [ ] **adequacy** 타당성, 적당함
  - the adequacy of the contingency plans 비상 계획들의 적절성
  - adequacy assessment 타당성 평가

- [ ] **appearance** 겉모습, 출현
  - the original appearance of the building 빌딩의 원래 외형
  - She made a sudden appearance. 그녀가 갑자기 나타났다.

- [ ] **manner** 방식, 태도
  - act in a very stately manner 매우 당당한 태도로 행동하다
  - in a timely manner 시의적절한 방식으로

- [ ] **career** 직장 생활, 경력
  - He started his career as a reporter. 그는 기자로 직장 생활을 시작했다.
  - more opportunities for career growth 경력 향상을 위한 더 많은 기회

- [ ] **convention** 대회, 회의
  - the Republican Party Convention 공화당 전당 대회
  - teachers in convention 회의 중인 교사들

- [ ] **routine** 판에 박힌 일[절차], 일과
  - a daily routine 매일의 일과
  - go through the same old routine 오래된 똑같은 일상을 거치다

- [ ] **worth** 가치, 값어치
  - This book is of great worth. 이 책은 대단한 가치가 있다.
  - two thousand dollars' worth of cargo 2천 달러어치의 화물

- [ ] **reputation** 평판, 명성
  - earn a reputation for honesty 정직하다는 평판을 얻다
  - build up a reputation as a writer 작가로서 명성을 쌓다

- [ ] **registration** 등록
  - Advance registration is required. 사전 등록이 필수입니다.
  - vehicle registrations 차량 등록

Practice

정답 및 해설 p.69

A. 괄호에서 적절한 것을 고르세요.

1. It is impossible to tell the difference between fake luxury bags and the genuine ones from (absence / appearance).

2. There are some traditional trade theories that support the (concept / hesitation) of globalization.

3. If you would like to post an article in our magazine, please send us a (letter / sample) of your work for assessment.

4. The main discussion at the recent (convention / ceremony) was about gaining profitable opportunities in international trade.

B. 빈칸에 가장 적절한 것을 고르세요.

5. The newspaper shows a report stating that a ------- of the university graduates are aiming to apply for a multinational company.
    (A) majority
    (B) complaint
    (C) point
    (D) summary

6. Cartier Motors has agreed to buy the engineering company with 20 million dollars ------- of debt.
    (A) exception
    (B) worth
    (C) approval
    (D) account

7. Mr. Darrow, the CEO of Konex Enterprise has taken great ------- in the partnership plan with a Chinese company.
    (A) interest
    (B) benefit
    (C) attention
    (D) advantage

8. Butterpan has over 20 factories worldwide with a ------- for manufacturing kitchen tools and appliances.
    (A) reputation
    (B) caption
    (C) confirmation
    (D) recognition

어휘 1 tell the difference 차이를 구별하다 fake 가짜의, 위조의 luxury bag 명품 가방 genuine 진짜의, 진품인 2 theory 이론 globalization 세계화
3 post 게재하다 assessment 평가 4 profitable 수익성 있는 opportunity 기회 5 graduate 졸업생 aim to ~하는 것을 목표로 하다 apply for ~에 지원하다
6 debt 부채 7 partnership 제휴, 협력 8 factory 공장 tool 도구 appliance 가전제품

Actual Test

1. Erik Tyndale has been ------- reassigned to the office in Travor District until the DS3 project is completed.
   (A) temporary
   (B) temporariness
   (C) temporarily
   (D) most temporary

2. Infinite Home Express ensures that all care packages are always delivered -------.
   (A) safe
   (B) safer
   (C) safely
   (D) safest

3. Exchange rates are difficult to forecast because the market is ------- reacting to unexpected events or news.
   (A) continue
   (B) continual
   (C) continued
   (D) continually

4. ------- one in five individuals who attended the Global Outreach conference will be donors.
   (A) Approximately
   (B) Approximate
   (C) Approximation
   (D) Approximates

5. Karen Baker has ------- to receive a call from her manager concerning the changes in the project planning.
   (A) yet
   (B) finally
   (C) near
   (D) already

6. It is ------- necessary for small companies to create partnerships with much larger companies that have manufacturing and distribution capabilities.
   (A) every
   (B) often
   (C) when
   (D) after

7. A recent survey on health care shows that ------- half of the respondents only exercise for an hour or less per week.
   (A) less
   (B) even
   (C) early
   (D) almost

8. The new customized printing machine is faster, ------- reducing the time of delay.
   (A) throughout
   (B) between
   (C) thereby
   (D) such as

Questions 9-12 refer to the following notice.

Attention Occupants,

We aim to provide you a pleasant time at the public cottage. However, simultaneously, we also wish to be --- 9. --- of other residents residing in the neighboring buildings.
Recently, we received complaints about the --- 10. --- coming from our cottage area.
Therefore, we --- 11. --- ask that you would refrain from inconveniencing the neighbors by maintaining your conversation volumes at moderate levels while occupying the premises.
--- 12. ---. If you have any questions, feel free to contact management at 555-8249.

Yours sincerely,
Susan White, Owner
Greenville Residence

9   (A) considering
    (B) considerate
    (C) considerately
    (D) considered

10 (A) noise
    (B) light
    (C) litter
    (D) odors

11 (A) respects
    (B) respecting
    (C) respectable
    (D) respectfully

NEW
12 (A) Too much noise is bad for your health.
    (B) Thank you for your cooperation in advance.
    (C) Neighbors are always friendly and helpful.
    (D) Loud music prevents you from concentrating on the work.

Unit 10 전치사

Part 5-6

전치사는 명사나 대명사 앞에 와서 명사, 대명사와의 관계를 나타내는 품사입니다. 우리말의 조사처럼 '~에, ~에게, ~와, ~부터, ~로' 등의 의미를 나타내는 말이라고 생각하면 됩니다. 한 가지 차이점이 있다면 전치사는 명사 앞에 온다는 점입니다. 전치사는 문장에서 명사를 꾸미는 형용사 역할이나 동사를 꾸미는 부사 역할을 합니다. 접속사처럼 문장과 문장을 연결하는 것이 아니라 명사 또는 명사 상당 어구를 연결하는 역할을 합니다. 전치사는 종류에 따라 시간·기간·시점·참조·추가·이유 등 다양한 의미를 나타냅니다. 출제 비중 높은 중요한 유형입니다.

전치사의 종류

시간	at, in, on, for, during, after, by, until, within, over, before	**at** night 저녁에 **within** an hour 한 시간 안에 **during** the vacation 방학 동안에
장소	at, in, on	**at** the corporation 회사에서 **in** Tokyo 도쿄에서 **on** the roof 지붕 위에서
위치	over, along, across, beyond, beside	**over** the head 머리 위로 **beside** the baggage 여행용 가방 옆에
방향	to, toward, from, into	**to** the city hall 시청으로 **from** the people 사람들로부터
기타	with, except, for, about, as	**as** a sales manager 판매과장으로서 **except** you 당신만 제외하고

전치사 뒤 명사와 동명사의 구분

전치사 뒤는 명사나 대명사, 동명사가 옵니다. 이 둘의 구분은 이렇게 합니다.

▶ **전치사+(형용사/소유격)+명사/대명사**

of our procedures 저희 절차상의
     소유격   명사

▶ **전치사+동명사+명사**

for promoting company's image 회사 이미지를 홍보하기 위해
    동명사   명사

★ 전치사 뒤의 동명사는 뒤의 명사를 목적어로 취합니다.

전치사와 접속사의 구분

▶ 전치사 뒤에는 명사나 대명사, 동명사가 올 수 있습니다.

Because of space constraints on its bus, 주어+동사 ~ 그 버스의 공간에 제약이 있기 때문에. ~
전치사   명사

▶ 접속사 뒤에는 문장(주어+동사)이 올 수 있습니다.

Because the automatic sprinkler system was installed improperly, 주어+동사 ~
접속사   주어   동사
자동식 스프링클러 시스템이 제대로 설치되어 있지 않았기 때문에. ~

전치사구

전치사구는 '전치사+명사/대명사'를 말합니다. 문장에서 수식어 역할(형용사, 부사)을 하며 문장의 어디에라도 올 수 있습니다.

The people in the meeting room are our clients. 회의실에 있는 사람들은 저희 고객들입니다.
★ 전치사구가 앞의 명사 people을 수식하여 '회의실에 있는'이라는 뜻의 형용사 역할을 합니다.

Mr. Harris has worked for 30 years. Harris 씨는 30년째 근무해 왔습니다
★ 전치사구가 시간 부사의 역할을 합니다.

1 시험에 반드시 나오는 시간·장소 전치사

시간 전치사

at	시각, 시점	at 8 o'clock 8시에	at night 밤에
		at the end of the year 연말에	
on	요일, 날짜	on Monday 월요일에	on May 26 5월 26일에
in	월, 연도, 계절 오전/오후/저녁	in March 3월에	in 2014 2014년에
		in summer 여름에	
		in the morning/afternoon/evening 오전에/오후에/저녁에	
for	숫자 기간 앞에	for eight years 8년간	
during	특정 기간 앞에	during the vacation 방학 동안	
by	마감 기한이 있는 경우에	I will finish my homework by five o'clock. 나는 5시까지 숙제를 끝마칠 것이다.	
until	상태가 계속되다가 특정 시점에 종료될 때	The store is open until 9 p.m. 그 가게는 오후 9시까지 영업한다.	
after	~ 후에	She came back after a few hours. 그녀는 몇 시간 후에 돌아왔다.	
before	~ 전에	Wash your face before sleep. 자기 전에 얼굴을 씻어라.	
through throughout	~ 내내	I studied English through the night. 나는 밤새 영어 공부를 했다.	
over	~ 넘게	He stayed in L.A. for over a month. 그는 LA에서 한 달 넘게 머물렀다.	
within	~ 이내에	You must finish the work within two weeks. 당신은 2주일 내에 그 일을 마쳐야만 한다.	
since	~부터 줄곧, ~ 이후로	She has been off work since Friday. 그녀는 금요일부터 휴가 중이다.	

장소 전치사

at	정확한 장소나 위치 비교적 좁은 장소	at the station 기차역에	at work 직장에
		at the meeting 회의에서	at the corner 구석에
in	공간의 내부 비교적 넓은 장소	in the drawer 서랍 안에	in the office 사무실 안에
		in Canada 캐나다에	in Paris 파리에
on	표면 위	on the desk 책상 위에	on the floor 바닥 위에

Practice

정답 및 해설 p.74

A. 괄호에서 적절한 것을 고르세요.

1. Even though the lectures were being held (at / on) a Friday night, students were very diligent in attending them.

2. Please note that no refunds will be given for the purchased summer merchandise (after / toward) September 10.

3. The Dema Mobile Service Center opens (in / at) 10:00 a.m. five days a week.

4. Company policy clearly states that any worker caught using illegal software (through / in) the office will be denounced and dismissed from their position.

B. 빈칸에 가장 적절한 것을 고르세요.

5. Doctors always recommend patrons to follow a balanced diet to maintain the energy needed ------- the day.
   (A) throughout
   (B) considering
   (C) unless
   (D) least

6. For those traveling on flights departing ------- 7:00 a.m., please note that the terminal building does not open until 5:00 a.m.
   (A) below
   (B) with
   (C) before
   (D) inside

7. Companies predict that the MDM market will rapidly multiply in size ------- the next two years.
   (A) from
   (B) over
   (C) to
   (D) out

8. ------- the committee meeting, Ms. Murray proposed advertisement plans to increase the market sales of their products through publicity.
   (A) About
   (B) Against
   (C) At
   (D) Along

어휘 1 lecture 강의 diligent 부지런한 2 refund 환불 purchase 구입하다 merchandise 상품 3 mobile 휴대전화 4 illegal 불법적인 denounce 강하게 비난하다 dismiss 해고하다 5 patron 고객 balanced 균형 잡힌 diet 식단 6 flight 항공편 depart 출발하다 7 predict 예측하다 multiply 증가하다, 늘다 8 committee 위원회 advertisement 광고 publicity 홍보

2 시험에 반드시 나오는 위치·방향 전치사와 두세 단어 전치사

위치 · 방향 전치사

beyond ~ 너머	beyond the village 마을 너머	beyond control 통제할 수 없는
around ~ 주위에	around the park 공원 주위에	around the shop 가게 주위에
into ~의 속으로	into the water 물속으로	into the region 그 지역으로
within ~ 이내에	within walking distance 걸어서 갈 수 있는 거리 내에 within a mile 1마일 이내에	
toward ~로 향해	toward the river 강을 향해	toward a common goal 공동의 목표를 향해
over ~ 위로	over the world 전 세계에	over the sea 바다 위로
throughout 곳곳에	throughout the region 지역 곳곳에	throughout the country 나라 곳곳에
to ~로, ~에게	the way to the station 역으로 가는 길에	gave it to the director 감독관에게 제출했다
beside 옆에	beside the baggage carousel 수하물 컨베이어 옆에 beside the building 빌딩 옆에	
along ~을 따라	along the road 길을 따라	along the main route 주요 노선을 따라
across ~을 건너, 곳곳에	across Europe 유럽 곳곳에	across the street 길 건너편에
opposite ~ 반대편에	opposite the supermarket 슈퍼마켓 반대편에	
from ~에서	a memo from the accounting department 회계부서에서 온 메모	

두세 단어 전치사

prior to ~ 이전에	prior to submitting the application 신청서를 제출하기 전에
according to ~에 따르면	according to our recent survey 우리의 최근 조사에 따르면
instead of ~ 대신에	instead of the old one 예전 것 대신에
ahead of ~보다 앞서	ahead of the deadline 마감일자 보다 앞서
far from ~에서 먼	far from the city center 도심지에서 먼
in favor of ~을 찬성하여	in favor of the proposal 제안에 찬성하는
regardless of ~와 관계없이	regardless of age 나이에 상관없이
depending on ~에 따라	depending on experience 경력에 따라
aside from ~을 제외하고	aside from work 일을 제외하고

Practice

정답 및 해설 p.75

A. 괄호에서 적절한 것을 고르세요.

1. Known for its outstanding golf courses, Jennings Clubhouse is located (beside / within) 15 miles off the northern coast in St. Kingsbarn.

2. Many teachers promote outdoor educational programs, which enable students to learn (between / beyond) the school campus.

3. Engineers are progressing (toward / onto) new green fuels and energy storage devices.

4. Scheduled air tickets must be cancelled at least one hour (according to / prior to) departure.

B. 빈칸에 가장 적절한 것을 고르세요.

5. One particular study showed that a majority of students preferred face-to-face discussions ------- computer-mediated communication.

    (A) toward
    (B) over
    (C) during
    (D) along

6. Mr. Pacher, the sales manager, would often walk ------- the park continuously when he needed to calm himself and collect his thoughts.

    (A) around
    (B) of
    (C) plus
    (D) than

7. ------- attending the conference at New York next week, Wesley Jung has to manage the sales team at the office.

    (A) Beyond
    (B) Among
    (C) Due to
    (D) Instead of

8. Mr. Amerson reported that the final construction of the project was already two months ------- schedule.

    (A) ahead of
    (B) depending on
    (C) in exchange for
    (D) aside from

어휘 1 outstanding 뛰어난, 우수한 northern 북부의 coast 해안 2 promote 장려하다 enable 가능하게 하다 campus 교정 3 progress 전진하다 storage 저장 4 departure 출발 5 particular 특정한 majority 대다수 face-to-face 직접 대면하는 computer-mediated communication 컴퓨터 매개 의사소통 6 continuously 계속해서 collect 모으다, 가다듬다 7 conference 총회, 회의 8 construction 건설 schedule 일정

Unit 10 : 전치사 115

3 시험에 반드시 나오는 기타 전치사

 기타 전치사

regarding concerning ~에 관해	problems regarding your flight 당신의 항공편에 관련된 문제들
to ~하기 위해	to introduce its product 제품을 소개하기 위해
with ~와 함께	a meeting with clients 고객과 함께하는 회의
following ~의 뒤에 / ~에 이어	following the talk 연설 뒤에
except ~을 제외하고	except Friday 금요일을 제외하고는
for ~을 위해	for the dinner meeting 저녁 미팅을 위해
of ~의	the role of the new employee 신입 직원의 역할
without ~ 없이, ~이 없으면	without a valid driver's license 유효한 운전면허증 없이
on ~에	on management skills 경영 수완에
about ~에 관한	about exchange rates 환율에 관한
through ~을 통해	through a gate 문을 통해
between (둘) 사이에	between the candidates 두 명의 후보자 사이에
among (셋 이상) 가운데에	among producers 생산자들 가운데

Practice

정답 및 해설 p.76

A. 괄호에서 적절한 것을 고르세요.

1. The recall was announced (regarding / following) an FDA inspection for a manufacturing plant that found several deficiencies in meeting quality standards.

2. The Learner's Kit comes complete with everything that one need to have for successful camping in the mountains (unlike / except) for hiking boots.

3. Products available (on / for) purchase will be listed with an order form on the last page of the magazine.

4. If you missed the conference this morning, please speak with Martha Bell to obtain information (about / to) this week's event.

B. 빈칸에 가장 적절한 것을 고르세요.

5. Many of our member companies have repeatedly expressed concern over the potential consequences ------- further delay.
   (A) past
   (B) within
   (C) behind
   (D) of

6. During his visit to a southern boomtown, Mr. Evans declared that economic gains could be lost ------- reforms to the political system.
   (A) however
   (B) unless
   (C) against
   (D) without

7. Veceo Autos is ------- the 50 most innovative companies in the world with a history of 22 years.
   (A) toward
   (B) among
   (C) around
   (D) along

8. Professor Kim explained to students that the ability to write a good essay could only be gained ------- personal experience.
   (A) as
   (B) of
   (C) among
   (D) through

어휘 1 recall 회수 inspection 조사 plant 공장 deficiency 결함 standard 기준 2 kit 용구 한 세트 complete 전부 갖추어진 3 order form 주문서 4 obtain 얻다 information 정보 5 repeatedly 거듭해서 express 표현하다 potential 잠재적인 consequence 결과 6 boomtown 신흥 도시 declare 선언하다 reform 개혁 7 innovative 혁신적인 8 ability 능력

Unit 10 : 전치사 117

4 반드시 알아야 하는 기출 명사 어휘 ❺

- [ ] **rating**
  평가, 등급
  - receive the highest rating in customer satisfaction 고객 만족에서 최고 평가를 받다
  - Korea's credit rating 한국의 신용 등급

- [ ] **industry**
  산업, 업계
  - various manufacturing industries 다양한 제조 산업들
  - develop local industries 지역 산업을 발전시키다

- [ ] **option**
  선택할 수 있는 것, 옵션
  - change menu options seasonally 계절별로 선택할 수 있는 메뉴들을 바꾸다
  - The car comes with various options. 그 차는 다양한 옵션이 딸려 나온다.

- [ ] **quality**
  품질, 질
  - improve the quality of life 삶의 질을 향상시키다
  - ensure the quality of new goods 신제품의 품질을 보증하다

- [ ] **accuracy**
  정확(성)
  - This job requires a high degree of accuracy. 이 일은 고도의 정확성을 필요로 한다.
  - check the accuracy of the report 보고서의 정확성을 확인하다

- [ ] **decline**
  감소, 하락
  - in spite of the decline in profits 수익 감소에도 불구하고
  - the decline in stock prices 주가 하락

- [ ] **position**
  직위, 직책
  - apply for a position 구직 신청을 하다
  - secure the top position 1위 자리를 차지하다

- [ ] **mission**
  임무, 사명
  - He accomplished his mission. 그는 임무를 완수했다.
  - his mission in life 그의 평생의 사명

- [ ] **potential**
  가능성, 잠재력
  - have enormous potential for growth 엄청난 성장 가능성을 가지고 있다
  - have extraordinary potential for international sales 해외 영업에 비상한 잠재력을 가지고 있다

- [ ] **period**
  기간
  - for a limited period 한정된 기간 동안
  - within the warranty period 보증 기간 이내에

- [ ] **intention**
  의도, 의향
  - He hinted at his intention to retire. 그는 은퇴할 의사를 비쳤다.
  - with the intention of getting married 결혼할 작정으로

- [ ] **appliance**
  기기, 용품
  - the nation's largest maker of home appliances 국내 최대의 가전제품 제조업체
  - Turn off lights and appliances when they aren't being used. 전등과 전기기구는 사용하지 않을 때는 전원을 꺼주세요.

- [ ] **arrangement**
  준비, 마련, 주선
  - make arrangements for the trip 여행을 위한 준비를 하다
  - make arrangements for a meeting 만남을 주선하다

- [ ] **description**
  묘사, 기술, 설명
  - a detailed description of each character 각 인물에 대한 상세한 묘사
  - product descriptions 제품 설명서

- [ ] **award**
  상, 상품
  - He received an award for his acts of bravery. 그는 용감한 행동으로 상을 받았다.
  - cash awards 상금

Practice

A. 괄호에서 적절한 것을 고르세요.

1. The (status / mission) of Caffa Beans Company is to provide coffee lovers the fresh and exquisite taste of refined coffee beverages.

2. My secretary has made (authorities / arrangements) for me to meet with Mr. Pellicer regarding tax funding agreements.

3. A new Head Chef has been employed and he changes the menu (options / occasions) on a weekly basis.

4. Owing to the slight drizzle earlier this morning, commuters are doubting the (accuracy / enforcement) of the recent weather reports of a sunny week.

B. 빈칸에 가장 적절한 것을 고르세요.

5. The accountant of Hendri Beach Resort received an ------- for his contribution to the facility.
   (A) apology
   (B) interpretation
   (C) award
   (D) effort

6. Most schools have a 50-minute class ------- because students start to show signs of concentration loss.
   (A) location
   (B) idea
   (C) period
   (D) box

7. VS Productions has awarded its highest ------- in outstanding filmmaking to *Letters from Afar*.
   (A) priority
   (B) reliance
   (C) rating
   (D) personnel

8. The professor states that the ------- in the number of foreign exchange students is because of the failure of academic programs to provide financial support.
   (A) appraisal
   (B) decline
   (C) outpouring
   (D) overhead

Actual Test

1. All licensed drivers must register their operating vehicles in their names ------- 14 days of purchase.
   (A) around
   (B) beside
   (C) through
   (D) within

2. The general aviation exhibition scheduled for Farest Park in June has been postponed ------- next year.
   (A) often
   (B) during
   (C) until
   (D) soon

3. Glass walls have been used ------- the building to ensure that every workstation and meeting space receives natural light.
   (A) throughout
   (B) between
   (C) among
   (D) over

4. When you are finished with the exam, please proceed to the front and give your answer sheets ------- one of the assistant instructors before leaving the room.
   (A) in
   (B) to
   (C) of
   (D) at

5. The Axianta Company's business plan is focused ------- developing cost-effective, highly efficient and environmentally friendly solar energy products.
   (A) up
   (B) in
   (C) of
   (D) on

6. Not far ------- the city center is the Lotheim District, an area full of studio apartments with affordable rental prices.
   (A) on
   (B) with
   (C) about
   (D) from

7. ------- Mr. Grim's lack of experience, the directors had confidence in his judgment and potential.
   (A) Nonetheless
   (B) Insofar as
   (C) Simultaneously
   (D) Regardless of

8. Business analyst, Harlman Bothwick mentioned that relationships ------- farmers and processors are longstanding.
   (A) since
   (B) than
   (C) up
   (D) between

Questions 9-12 refer to the following information.

Ohani Homestay: Traveling from Mishi by train or bus

At Mishi station, board the train headed toward Saete station. --- 9. ---. Once at the station, walk approximately 700 meters north towards the large fountain. We are located directly --- 10. --- the entrance to the nature park.

From Mishi's central bus station, board any bus that is traveling toward Noime and ask the bus driver to let --- 11. --- get off at Shinsae bus station. Walk for approximately 1.3 kilometers west of the bus station and turn left at the corner of the public library.

For further information regarding --- 12. ---, please visit our website at www.ohanihomestay.com. Also, feel free to call us at (232) 5889-1645 with any questions you may have.

NEW
9   (A) Trains to Saete no longer runs now.
    (B) Trains leaving for Saete will arrive at one-hour intervals and take three hours to reach the destination.
    (C) Nature park is within walking distance.
    (D) The large fountain is one of the tourist's attractions.

10 (A) across from
    (B) up
    (C) between
    (D) along with

11 (A) your
    (B) yourselves
    (C) you
    (D) yours

12 (A) room rates
    (B) transportation
    (C) park fees
    (D) lodging

Unit 11 등위·상관접속사와 접속부사

Part 5-6

접속사는 말과 말을 연결해 주는 역할을 하는 문장 성분입니다. 등위접속사는 단어, 구, 문장 등을 동등하게 연결해 주는 기능을 합니다. 상관접속사는 두 단어 이상이 짝을 이루어 사용됩니다. 접속부사는 접속사와 유사한 기능을 하는 부사입니다.

 등위접속사

문장에서 단어, 구, 절을 동등하게 연결하는 접속사를 등위접속사라고 합니다.
등위접속사의 앞뒤로는 같은 문장 성분이 있어야 합니다.

The store sells meat and vegetables. 그 가게는 고기와 채소를 판다.
　　　　　　　　명사　　　명사
You have to take a vacation, or you will get sick. 휴가를 내셔야 해요, 아니면 병이 날 거예요.
　　　　　　　문장　　　　　　　　　문장

and	그리고
but	그러나
or	또는
so	그래서
for	~ 때문에

상관접속사

상관접속사는 두 개 이상의 단어가 짝을 이루어 사용되는 접속사입니다.

Both my mother and father will be there. 어머니와 아버지가 모두 그곳에 오실 것입니다.
Her house is neither big nor small. 그녀의 집은 크지도 않고 작지도 않다.

both A and B	A와 B 둘 다
either A or B	A나 B 둘 중의 하나
neither A nor B	A도 B도 아닌
not only A but also B	A뿐만 아니라 B도
not A but B	A가 아니라 B

접속부사

접속부사는 접속사와 유사하지만 부사이며, 한 문장 안에서 두 개의 문장을 연결할 때는 반드시 and 또는 세미콜론(;)을 사용합니다. 접속부사는 주로 Part 6에서 출제됩니다.

Part-time workers should be sure to sign in before starting each shift; otherwise, time worked may not be reflected in upcoming paychecks.
시간제 직원들은 교대 근무를 시작하기 전에 반드시 출근 서명을 해야 한다. 그렇지 않으면 일한 시간이 앞으로 받을 급여에 반영되지 않을 수도 있다.

★ therefore는 접속부사로 혼자서는 절을 연결할 수 없지만, 앞에 세미콜론(;)이 붙으면 문장을 연결할 수 있습니다.

1 시험에 반드시 나오는 등위접속사와 상관접속사

● 등위접속사

▶ 주요 등위접속사

and 그리고   or 또는, 아니면   so 그래서, ~하기 위해서   but 그러나   for ~ 때문에, 왜냐하면

▶ 등위접속사의 위치

등위접속사는 두 개의 단어, 구, 절을 중간에서 연결합니다.

Kelly is a highly intelligent girl, but she is rather lazy. Kelly는 아주 똑똑한 소녀이지만 다소 게으르다.
　　　　문장　　　　　　　　　　　　　　문장

It isn't the blue one but the red one. 그건 파란색이 아니라 빨간색이야.
　　　　구　　　　　　　　구

I told him to leave, for I was very tired. (O) 나는 피곤했기 때문에 그에게 떠나라고 말했다.
　　　문장　　　　　　　　문장

For I was very tired, I told him to leave. (X)

★ 등위접속사는 두 개의 절을 연결할 때 문장의 첫머리에는 쓰지 않으므로, Because로 고쳐야 합니다.

▶ 등위접속사의 앞뒤에는 같은 구조가 와야 합니다.

Everyone was singing and dancing. 모든 사람이 노래를 부르고 춤을 추었다.
I had nothing to eat or (to) drink all day. 나는 하루 종일 아무것도 먹거나 마시지 않았다.

★ to부정사를 연결할 때는 가급적 중복되는 to를 생략합니다.

● 상관접속사

▶ 주요 상관접속사

both A and B A와 B 둘 다　　　　　　　　either A or B A나 B 둘 중의 하나
neither A nor B A도 B도 아닌　　　　　　　not A but B A가 아니라 B
not only A but (also) B A뿐만 아니라 B도 역시　B as well as A A뿐만 아니라 B도

▶ 상관접속사의 출제 유형

You can contact us (either / ~~both~~) by phone or by letter. 당신은 전화나 편지로 저희에게 연락하실 수 있습니다.
You can contact us either by phone (or / ~~and~~) by letter.

Practice

정답 및 해설 p.82

A. 괄호에서 적절한 것을 고르세요.

1 The Majestic Tailor is known for making the best-quality suits (but / and) coats that can be worn for all types of occasions.

2 Mr. Khan's membership for Mondax Satellite Network TV may expire this month (or / so) the next.

3 (Either / Neither) the CFO nor the president will be attending the shareholder meeting.

4 Such cases have been reported not only nationwide (therefore / but) also worldwide.

B. 빈칸에 가장 적절한 것을 고르세요.

5 At Mobilith Customer Service, it usually takes approximately one ------- two days for a customer complaint to be fully resolved.

(A) so
(B) or
(C) yet
(D) but

6 All guests must present a valid identification for verification ------- surrender any electronic devices before entering the laboratory.

(A) and
(B) both
(C) so
(D) as

7 Payments for tax bills and insurance can be ------- made by mail or electronically withdrawn from your personal bank account.

(A) in case
(B) as well as
(C) not only
(D) either

8 Neobyte Electronics offers state-of-the-art desktop computers appropriate for ------- office work and home entertainment.

(A) few
(B) both
(C) many
(D) neither

어휘 1 suit 정장 occasion (특정한) 때, 경우 2 satellite 위성 expire 만료되다 3 CFO 최고재무책임자, 자금 관리 이사 president 사장 attend 참석하다 shareholder 주주 4 case 경우, 사례 report 보고하다 nationwide 전국적으로 worldwide 세계적인 5 approximately 대략, 약 complaint 불만, 항의 fully 완전히 resolve 해결하다 6 present 제시하다 valid 유효한, 타당한 identification 신분증 verification 확인, 입증 surrender 넘겨주다, 양도하다 electronic device 전자기기 laboratory 실험실 7 payment 납부, 결제 tax bill 세금 고지서 insurance 보험 electronically 온라인으로 withdraw 인출하다 account 계좌 8 state-of-the-art 최신식의 appropriate 적합한 home entertainment 가정용 오락 기구

Unit 11 : 등위·상관접속사와 접속부사   125

2 시험에 반드시 나오는 접속부사

필수 접속부사

however 그러나	afterward(s) 그 후에	as a result 그 결과로
therefore 그러므로	thus 따라서	for example/for instance 예를 들어
nonetheless 그럼에도 불구하고	in short 요약하면	instead 대신에
in contrast 반대로	if not 만약 ~ 아니라면	similarly 유사하게, 마찬가지로
accordingly 따라서, 그래서	otherwise 그렇지 않으면	on the contrary 반대로
also 또한	consequently 그 결과	on the other hand 반면에
And so 그래서	then 그리고 나서	in addition/besides 게다가
if so 만약 그렇다면	in fact 사실상	since then 그때 이후로
furthermore/moreover 더욱, 게다가		

접속부사의 위치

▶ 접속부사는 접속사가 아니라 부사이므로 and나 세미콜론(;), 마침표(.)가 없으면 절대 두 개의 문장을 연결할 수 없습니다.

주어+동사+~. However, 주어+동사+~
→ 마침표로 두 개의 문장으로 나눕니다.

주어+동사+~; therefore, 주어+동사+~
→ 세미콜론으로 두 개의 문장을 연결합니다.

주어+동사+~ and then, 주어+동사+~
→ and를 덧붙여서 두 개의 문장을 연결합니다.

Practice

A. 괄호에서 적절한 것을 고르세요.

1. Ms. Obrien will be attending the monthly staff meeting tomorrow at 10 A.M. (For example / Afterward), she will have lunch with the director at noon.

2. The news reported that a heavy snowstorm is heading towards the region. (Instead / As a result), public buildings have been shut down.

3. Analyst Vivian Fallapin stated that the total sales of TN Motors is likely to recover next year. (However / Therefore), in terms of market share, it will be impossible for the company to rebound to the 22 percent level that they were at before.

B. 빈칸에 가장 적절한 것을 고르세요.

4. Global bond markets posted their biggest monthly losses in May. -------, gains in employment and increases in housing and consumer confidence suggested the recovery of the economy.
   (A) Because of
   (B) In contrast
   (C) Moreover
   (D) Concerning

5. South Korea has over 50 beautiful tourist attractions. -------, it is an exciting destination for travelers.
   (A) Accordingly
   (B) Otherwise
   (C) Similarly
   (D) Nonetheless

6. Although solar panel electricity helps preserve the environment, the cost of installing solar panels is quite high. -------, the amount of solar power that they can generate significantly depends on the local climate.
   (A) On the contrary
   (B) Therefore
   (C) Furthermore
   (D) In spite of the fact

어휘 1 monthly 매달의, 월례의 director 이사, 임원 2 heavy 심한 snowstorm 눈보라 head towards ~로 향하다 region 지역 public building 공공건물 shut down 폐쇄하다, 휴업하다 3 state 말하다 be likely to ~할 것 같다 recover 회복하다 market share 시장 점유율 impossible 불가능한 rebound 반등하다 4 bond market 채권 시장 loss 손실 employment 고용 gain 증가 housing 주택 공급 consumer confidence 소비 의욕, 소비자 신뢰 suggest 암시하다 recovery 회복 economy 경제 5 tourist attraction 관광 명소 destination 목적지, 행선지 traveler 여행자 6 preserve 보존하다 environment 환경 install 설치하다 generate 발생시키다 significantly 상당히 depend on ~에 달려 있다 local 지역의 climate 기후

3 반드시 알아야 하는 기출 형용사 어휘 ❶

☐ **brief** 짧은, 간결한	• Could you make it brief? 짧게 말해 주시겠어요? • write a brief report 간결한 보고서를 쓰다
☐ **hopeful** 희망적인, 전도유망한	• She is very hopeful for the future. 그녀는 미래에 대해 매우 희망적이다. • These are hopeful signs for our economy. 이는 우리 경제에 희망적인 조짐이다.
☐ **scenic** 경치의, 경치 좋은	• The coastal route is more scenic. 연안 도로는 경치가 더 좋다. • The scenic river cruise will be offered. 경치 좋은 강 유람선 여행이 제공될 것이다.
☐ **available** 입수[이용]할 수 있는, 만날 수 있는	• The product is available at the market. 그 제품은 시중에서 구할 수 있다. • He is available any time. 그는 언제든 만날 수 있다.
☐ **exempt** 면제되는, ~이 없는	• be exempt from military service 병역을 면제받다 • be exempt from shipping charges 배송료가 면제되다
☐ **unable** ~할 수 없는	• They will be unable to attend the meeting. 그들은 회의에 참석하지 못할 것이다. • She was unable to see the difference. 그녀는 그 차이를 알 수 없었다.
☐ **healthful** 건강에 좋은	• healthful living habits 건강에 좋은 생활 습관 • maintain a healthful diet 건강에 좋은 식단을 유지하다
☐ **fortunate** 운이 좋은, 행운인	• I was fortunate in having a good wife. 나는 운이 좋아서 좋은 아내를 얻었다. • It was fortunate for us that the snow stopped. 우리에게 다행스럽게도 눈이 그쳤다.
☐ **leading** 선두의, 주요한, 일류의	• one of the leading suppliers 주요 공급 업체들 중의 하나 • become a leading manufacturer 선두 제조 업체가 되다
☐ **convenient** 편리한, 알맞은	• Which date is most convenient for you? 어느 날이 가장 편하신가요? • Chocolate is a convenient source of energy. 초콜릿은 편리한 에너지 공급원이다.
☐ **current** 현재의, 지금의	• follow the current regulations 현행 규정을 따르다 • figures for the current year 금년도 수치
☐ **previous** 앞의, 이전의	• because of a previous engagement 선약 때문에 • unlike the previous edition 이전 판과 다르게
☐ **empty** 빈, 비어 있는	• The dessert tray is empty. 디저트 쟁반이 비어 있다. • An empty bag will not stand upright. 빈 봉지는 곧바로 서지 않는다. (격언)
☐ **standard** 표준[기준]이 되는, 일반적인	• the standard weights and measures 표준 도량형 • standard rooms and deluxe rooms 일반실과 특실
☐ **proud** 자랑스러운, 자랑스러워하는	• I'm proud to be a member of this company. 이 회사의 일원인 것이 자랑스럽다. • I'm proud of my pretty daughter. 나는 예쁜 딸이 자랑스럽다.

Practice

A. 괄호에서 적절한 것을 고르세요.

1. The emergency hotline for urgent medical services must be (available / voluntary) to everyone at all times.

2. DSI Telecom is (general / proud) to present its latest smartphone model, which has an upgraded memory chip for enabling faster and easier use of applications.

3. Passengers were compelled to obtain the (current / occupied) schedules for the flights that were delayed due to unexpected weather conditions.

4. Yang Zhu was assigned to write a (brief / multiple) report on the autobiography of the famous golfer Luke Walmack.

B. 빈칸에 가장 적절한 것을 고르세요.

5. Parents with young children always try to serve only ------- meals at the dinner table.
   (A) grateful
   (B) healthful
   (C) rightful
   (D) wishful

6. The expedition team was ------- to have Mr. Pastel, an expert in jungle survival, when traveling through the Amazon.
   (A) obvious
   (B) fortunate
   (C) talented
   (D) encouraging

7. If the fruit tray is -------, it should be refilled with fresh fruits from the refrigerator.
   (A) empty
   (B) stuck
   (C) single
   (D) final

8. Although it is quicker to travel by plane, the train route is much more -------.
   (A) powerful
   (B) avoidable
   (C) accelerated
   (D) scenic

어휘 1 emergency 비상 사태, 비상용의 urgent 긴급한 medical service 의료 서비스 at all times 항상 2 present 내놓다, 소개하다 enable 가능하게 하다 3 be compelled to 할 수 없이 ~하다 obtain 얻다, 입수하다 delay 지연시키다 unexpected 예상치 않은, 뜻밖의 4 assign 배정하다 autobiography 자서전 5 serve (음식물을) 제공하다 meal 식사 6 expedition 원정, 탐험 expert 전문가 survival 생존 7 fruit 과일 tray 쟁반, 접시 refill 다시 채우다 fresh 신선한 refrigerator 냉장고

Actual Test

1 Mr. Valentine was promoted to Sales Director after his successful negotiations with Zeppino Inc. in Germany ------- Kiyoma Industries in Japan.

(A) nor
(B) but
(C) so
(D) and

2 The committee will congregate today to discuss how to improve the quality of their products ------- decide on the next month's budget plan.

(A) for
(B) but
(C) yet
(D) and

3 Conference participants who stay in the Hana hotel can go to the convention center ------- by bus or subway.

(A) in case
(B) as well as
(C) not only
(D) either

4 The production manager neither confirmed ------- denied that there were serious defects in the finished goods.

(A) yet
(B) and
(C) nor
(D) or

5 Whoever gets a two-third majority will be chosen. -------, the members will have another round of voting.

(A) If so
(B) Whereas
(C) Otherwise
(D) As long as

6 The position will have a strong focus on resolving issues such as responding to customer inquiries. -------, anyone applying should have experience of working in a call center environment or be proficient at complaint handling.

(A) Therefore
(B) Similarly
(C) For example
(D) Even though

7 CEO Ralph Kauffman has explained that the new BMI2 model is still in the early stages of its transition. -------, it has been only five months since the researchers began developing its operating system.

(A) Due to
(B) In fact
(C) On the other hand
(D) And so

8 When you are done carving your wooden sculpture, ensure that you add a finishing touch to it using lacquer spray. -------, store the sculpture indoors and wait for about a day for the coating to dry.

(A) What
(B) Through
(C) For example
(D) Then

Questions 9-12 refer to the following information.

Voice command function

As already stated before, the Blocktune MP4 player allows you to store --- 9. --- 50 gigabytes of media files.
One of Blocktune's most convenient functions is the traditional recording option. This function enables Blocktune to be used as a personal recorder, and it is integrated with a new technology that enables the execution of functions through voice commands.
--- 10. ---. Ensure that the person using the device is the one who will be speaking the commands. The MP4 player will not recognize more than one voice. Do not use voice commands in noisy places. --- 11. ---, when using voice commands, do not speak too quickly.
Please remember that the overuse of the voice command will drain the battery quickly. If your pronunciation while giving voice commands is not --- 12. ---, the feature will not function properly. For customer assistance with the voice command function, or any function, call 1-800-185-1864.

9
(A) without
(B) up to
(C) except
(D) as for

NEW
10
(A) A voice command device which is controlled by means of the human voice is available online.
(B) Some tips for using this feature are as follows.
(C) You are required to set the voice command function first.
(D) You need extra batteries to use the function.

11
(A) Whereas
(B) However
(C) Moreover
(D) Although

12
(A) melodic
(B) perceptive
(C) technical
(D) distinct

Part 5-6

Unit 12 to부정사

to부정사는 동사원형 앞에 to를 붙여 명사, 형용사, 부사로 사용하는 것입니다. to부정사는 문장 내에서의 위치에 따라 역할(부사, 형용사, 명사)이 달라지며 이것을 to부정사의 명사적 용법, 형용사적 용법, 부사적 용법이라고 부릅니다. 이렇게 역할이 하나로 고정되어 있는 것이 아니라서 부정사라고 부릅니다.

to부정사: to+동사원형

I am sorry to (hear / hearing) that. 그 말을 들으니 유감입니다.
It is time to (goes / go). 가야 할 시간입니다.
I want to (buy / bought) a new house. 새 집을 사고 싶어요.

to부정사는 동사가 아니다!

to부정사는 동사의 성질을 가지고 있기는 하지만 실제 동사는 아닙니다. 따라서 반드시 문장에 동사가 따로 있어야 합니다. 앞으로 다루게 될 동명사와 분사도 실제 동사가 아닙니다. 이 세 가지를 묶어서 준동사라고 합니다. 동사에 준하는 역할을 하지만 동사는 아니라는 것입니다.

The bank (to maintain / maintains) exceptional service. 그 은행은 우수한 서비스를 유지하고 있다.

All employees (are encouraged / to be encouraged) to review the parking policies.
모든 직원들이 주차 정책을 검토하도록 권장되고 있다.

Please (forward / to forward) all of my calls to Ms. Kelly. 나한테 오는 모든 전화는 Kelly 씨에게 돌려 주세요.

to부정사의 의미상의 주어

간혹 to부정사의 의미상 주어 형태인 'for+명사'도 출제됩니다.

It is necessary (for / ~~to~~ / ~~of~~ / ~~from~~) her to lose weight. 그 여자는 살을 뺄 필요가 있어요.
★ to lost weight의 주체는 her입니다.

It is hard (for / ~~what~~ / ~~that~~ / ~~if~~) me to get a job. 나는 일자리를 구하기가 어렵다.
★ to get a job의 주체는 me입니다.

to부정사의 태와 시제

- to부정사의 수동태는 'to be p.p.'입니다.
  I wanted the project to be finished by this afternoon. 나는 그 프로젝트가 오후에 끝나기를 원했다.
  ★ 프로젝트가 완료되는 것이므로 수동태를 사용해야 합니다.

- to부정사의 시제는 'to+동사원형'과 주절의 시제보다 한 시제 앞서는 'to+have p.p.' 형태로 나뉩니다.
  Mr. Ken seems to be rich. Ken 씨는 부자인 것 같다.
  Mr. Ken seems to have been rich. Ken 씨는 부자였던 것 같다.

1 시험에 반드시 나오는 to부정사의 역할

● 명사적 용법

문장에서 명사처럼 주어, 목적어, 보어 역할을 합니다. '~하기, ~하는 것'으로 해석합니다.

[주어]　　To save money seems completely impossible. 저축하는 것은 완전히 불가능한 것처럼 보인다.

[목적어]　The team has agreed to work extended hours. 그 팀은 근무 시간을 연장하는 것에 찬성했다.

[보어]　　Our mission is to support public art projects. 우리의 임무는 공공 예술 프로젝트를 지원하는 것이다.

● 형용사적 용법

명사를 뒤에서 수식하는 형용사 역할을 합니다. '~할, ~하는'으로 해석합니다.

He has a lot of money to spend. 그는 쓸 돈이 많다.
I know the way to go there. 나는 그곳으로 가는 길을 알고 있다.

● 부사적 용법

목적이나 원인을 나타냅니다. '~하기 위해, ~하게 되어'로 해석합니다.

[목적]　　My secretary went to the post office to buy stamps. 비서가 우표를 사려고 우체국에 갔다.
　　　　To make a reservation, call this number. 예약을 하려면 이 번호로 전화 주세요.

[원인]　　I'm sorry to hear about your accident. 당신의 사고 소식을 듣게 되어 유감입니다.

● 진주어와 진목적어 역할

주어나 목적어로 사용된 to부정사가 길 때, 그 자리에 it을 대신 넣고 to부정사는 문장 뒤로 보낼 수 있습니다. 이때 가주어, 가목적어 it은 해석하지 않습니다.

[진주어]　　It is important to exercise and maintain a healthful diet.
　　　　　　가주어　　　　　　　　　　　　　진주어
　　　　　운동을 하고 건강에 좋은 식단을 유지하는 것이 중요하다.

[진목적어]　To make it easier to select items, we offer free sample to customers.
　　　　　　　　 가목적어　　　　진목적어
　　　　　상품을 더 쉽게 고르시도록 하기 위해 저희는 고객들에게 무료 샘플을 제공합니다.

Practice

정답 및 해설 p.90

A. 괄호에서 적절한 것을 고르세요.

1. The main purpose of journalism is (provided / to provide) citizens with accurate and reliable information.

2. Elena Conrad hired a translator (assists / to assist) her in communicating with the Global Sales Manager in Japan.

3. The first and most important step in planning your retirement is (started / to start) saving.

4. (To celebrate / Celebration) its 20th anniversary, TC Soft Company will be holding a Summer Showcase Party for its employees and customers this week.

B. 빈칸에 가장 적절한 것을 고르세요.

5. ------- the reduction of food waste, government officials have decided to increase the prices of garbage bags that are used in homes and restaurants.
   (A) For the promotion
   (B) To promote
   (C) After promoted
   (D) Promotion

6. For reasons of security and privacy, it is necessary ------- a distinction between network connections.
   (A) made
   (B) make
   (C) to make
   (D) making

7. Mr. Kwan incorporated humor and material into his one-hour presentation to ------- his audience's attention and help them remember it.
   (A) keep
   (B) kept
   (C) keeps
   (D) keeping

8. ------- the process of economic and political integration, the assembly decided to convene a session.
   (A) To be expedited
   (B) To expedite
   (C) Will expedite
   (D) Expedite

어휘 1 purpose 목적 accurate 정확한 reliable 믿을 수 있는 2 hire 고용하다 translator 번역가 3 first and most important 우선 가장 중요한 step 단계 retirement 퇴직, 은퇴 saving 저축 4 anniversary 기념일 hold 개최하다 customer 고객 5 reduction 삭감, 감소 food waste 음식물 쓰레기 government 정부 official 공무원, 관리 increase 늘리다 garbage bag 쓰레기 봉투 6 reason 이유 security 보안, 안전 privacy 사생활 necessary 필요한 distinction 구별 connection 연결 7 incorporate 집어넣다 material 자료 audience 청중 attention 주의 remember 기억하다 8 process 과정, 진행 integration 통합 assembly 의회 convene 소집하다 session 회의

Unit 12 : to부정사 135

2 시험에 반드시 나오는 명사/동사+to부정사

명사+to부정사

to부정사의 수식을 받는 특정한 명사들이 있습니다. 다음 표현들은 반드시 알아 두어야 합니다.

way to ~하기 위한 방법	attempt to ~하려는 시도	ability to ~할 능력
time to ~해야 할 시간	duty to ~할 의무	willingness to ~하려는 의향
effort to ~하려는 노력	failure to ~하지 못함	plan to ~할 계획
need to ~할 필요	chance to ~할 기회	opportunity to ~할 기회

Parents have a duty to protect their children. 부모들은 자녀들을 보호할 의무가 있다.
You will have a chance to watch celebrities closely. 당신은 유명인들을 가까이서 볼 기회를 얻게 될 겁니다.

동사+to부정사

to부정사를 목적어로 취하는 특정한 동사들이 있습니다. 다음 표현들은 반드시 알아 두어야 합니다.

wish to ~하기를 희망하다	fail to ~하지 못하다	offer to ~하기를 제안하다
expect to ~하기를 기대하다	refuse to ~하기를 거절하다	attempt to ~하려고 시도하다
tend to ~하는 경향이 있다	intend to ~할 작정이다	promise to ~하기를 약속하다
decide to ~하기로 결정하다	aim to ~하는 것을 목표로 하다	hope to ~하기를 희망하다
desire to ~하기 원하다	afford to ~할 여유가 있다	manage to 가까스로 ~하다
ask to ~할 것을 부탁하다	want to ~하기 원하다	seem to ~인 것 같다
happen to 우연히 ~하다	learn to ~하기를 배우다	hesitate to ~하기를 망설이다

People tend to overuse credit cards. 사람들은 신용 카드를 남용하는 경향이 있다.
I cannot afford to buy a new cellular phone. 나는 새 휴대전화를 살 여유가 없다.

Practice

A. 괄호에서 적절한 것을 고르세요.

1. The ideal way (resolving / to resolve) disagreements between two negotiating parties is to place new proposals or items on the list of trade.

2. Netcraft.com reserves the right (limiting / to limit) the number of accounts that a user can make on the Netcraft Web site.

3. Once you contact our customer service department, the staff will attempt (remedy / to remedy) the issue by phone or e-mail as soon as possible.

4. Mr. Iverson took his medical examination two days ago, so he expects (have received / to receive) his results shortly.

B. 빈칸에 가장 적절한 것을 고르세요.

5. The school conducted a short campus orientation, which was an effort ------- the relatively small number of new students who enrolled in January.
   (A) to welcome
   (B) welcoming
   (C) welcome
   (D) welcomed

6. During the MCAT study program, students will get the opportunity ------- up to four AAMC practice tests.
   (A) take
   (B) takes
   (C) taking
   (D) to take

7. The names of shareholders who wish ------- the Annual General Meeting must be recorded in the share register no later than April 3.
   (A) attend
   (B) to attend
   (C) attended
   (D) attending

8. Many people who spend considerable hours at work fail ------- enough daily nutrition.
   (A) gets
   (B) got
   (C) getting
   (D) to get

3 시험에 반드시 나오는 형용사/p.p.+to부정사와 목적격 보어 to부정사

형용사/p.p.+to부정사

to부정사와 함께 쓰이는 특정한 형용사/p.p.가 있습니다. 다음 표현은 반드시 알아 두어야 합니다.

be able to ~할 수 있다	be likely to ~하게 될 것 같다	be eager to ~하기를 갈망하다
be eligible to ~할 자격이 있다	be supposed to ~하기로 되어 있다	be liable to ~하게 될 것 같다
be available to ~할 수 있다	be ready to ~할 준비가 되어 있다	be apt to ~하는 경향이 있다
be due to ~할 예정이다	be designed to ~하게 계획되어 있다	be sure to 반드시 ~하다

Ms. Smith was supposed to go back to Calgary. Smith 씨는 Calgary로 돌아가도록 되어 있었다.
He was eager to know what happened yesterday. 그는 어제 무슨 일이 있었는지 알기를 간절히 원했다.

동사+목적어+to부정사

주로 상대방의 행동을 촉구하는 동사의 경우에 목적격 보어로 to부정사를 취합니다. 다음 표현은 반드시 알아 두어야 합니다.

능동태 표현	수동태 표현
encourage+목적어+to ~에게 ~하기를 권장하다	be encouraged to
enable+목적어+to ~가 ~할 수 있게 하다	수동태 없음
advise+목적어+to ~에게 ~하도록 충고하다	be advised to
expect+목적어+to ~가 ~할 것을 기대하다	be expected to
permit/allow+목적어+to ~에게 ~하는 것을 허락하다	be permitted to / be allowed to
remind+목적어+to ~에게 ~할 것을 생각나게 하다	be reminded to
require+목적어+to ~에게 ~하기를 요구하다	be required to
force+목적어+to ~에게 ~하기를 강요하다	be forced to
ask+목적어+to ~에게 ~할 것을 부탁하다	be asked to
instruct+목적어+to ~에게 ~하도록 지시하다	be instructed to
would like+목적어+to ~에게 ~해 주기를 바라다	수동태 없음

All employees are asked to attend a meeting. 모든 직원들은 회의에 참석할 것을 요청받았다.
Money will enable you to do everything. 돈은 당신이 모든 것을 할 수 있게 해줄 것이다.

Practice

정답 및 해설 p.93

A. 괄호에서 적절한 것을 고르세요.

1 Foreign companies will not be able (to be bought / to buy) property in preservation zones.

2 Unfortunately, the flight to New York that is scheduled (depart / to depart) at 8:07 A.M. has been delayed until 9:33 A.M.

3 Mr. Winslow was encouraged to (participate / participating) in the next election.

4 Drivers with flat tires are advised (driving / to drive) to the nearest service station.

B. 빈칸에 가장 적절한 것을 고르세요.

5 Some students are eligible ------- financial aid from the government to enter certain colleges or career schools.
   (A) receives
   (B) to receive
   (C) receiving
   (D) received

6 Alforto Inc. would like ------- its staff members to contact the HR office.
   (A) remind
   (B) reminding
   (C) to remind
   (D) reminds

7 Visitors are permitted ------- in Canada for a maximum of six months.
   (A) staying
   (B) to stay
   (C) stayed
   (D) stay

8 Certain applications and software programs require the user ------- update their operating system to the latest version.
   (A) with
   (B) of
   (C) for
   (D) to

어휘 1 foreign 외국의 property 재산, 부동산 preservation 보존 zone 지구, 지역 2 unfortunately 운 나쁘게도 delay 지연시키다 3 encourage 권유하다 election 선거 4 flat (타이어에) 바람이 빠진 5 be eligible to ~할 자격이 있다 financial 재정적인 aid 도움 career school 직업 학교 6 staff member 직원 HR office 인사부 7 visitor 방문자 maximum 최대(한) 8 certain 어떤 operating system 운영 체제 latest 최신의

Unit 12 : to부정사 139

4 반드시 알아야 하는 기출 형용사 어휘 ❷

various
다양한, 여러 가지의
- various sizes of paper 다양한 크기의 종이
- students from various universities 여러 대학교에서 온 학생들

inaccessible
접근하기 어려운, 접근할 수 없는
- The facility is inaccessible to the public. 그 시설은 일반인이 출입할 수 없다.
- a remote area inaccessible by car 차로 접근하기 어려운 외딴 지역

practical
실제적인, 실용적인
- through practical experience of the work 실제적인 업무 경험을 통해
- The invention has been put to practical use. 그 발명품이 실용화되었다.

expensive
비싼
- offer a less expensive alternative 덜 비싼 대안을 제공하다
- Tickets were too expensive. 입장권이 너무 비쌌다.

incorrect
부정확한, 맞지 않는
- an incorrect calculation 틀린 계산
- Some incorrect information is being spread. 부정확한 정보가 퍼져 나가고 있다.

distinct
별개의, 뚜렷한
- two distinct groups 별개의 두 집단
- a distinct improvement 뚜렷한 개선

accurate
정확한
- gather accurate information 정확한 정보를 수집하다
- The figures were strictly accurate. 그 수치는 틀림없이 정확했다.

managerial
경영의, 관리의
- reduction in managerial positions 관리직 감축
- managerial experience 관리 경험

eligible
자격이 있는, 적당한
- All eligible applicants are fully funded. 자격 있는 모든 지원자들은 자금을 전액 지원받는다.
- be eligible for compensation 보상을 받을 자격이 있다

single
단 하나의, 유일한
- the single largest sales 단 한 번의 최대 세일
- He was the single survivor of the crash. 그는 그 충돌사고의 유일한 생존자였다.

upcoming
다가오는, 곧 있을
- the upcoming presidential election 다가오는 대선
- the upcoming Olympic Games 곧 있을 올림픽 대회

periodic
주기적인, 정기적인
- at periodic intervals 주기적인 간격으로
- periodic employee trainings 정기적인 직원 교육

dedicated
전념하는, 헌신적인
- She is dedicated to her work. 그녀는 자기 일에 전념하고 있다.
- dedicated sales representatives 헌신적인 영업 직원

reluctant
꺼리는, 마지못해 하는
- We are reluctant to purchase this model. 우리는 이 모델을 구입하기를 꺼린다.
- She gave him a reluctant smile. 그녀는 마지못해 그에게 미소를 지었다.

complimentary
무료의
- complimentary lunch coupons 무료 점심 쿠폰
- for a complimentary brochure 무료 안내책자를 받으시려면

Practice

정답 및 해설 p.94

A. 괄호에서 적절한 것을 고르세요.

1. The order form for products must be (average / accurate), so that our distributors know the quality of supplies that we need.

2. Those who have not missed a single training session during this month are (measured / eligible) to participate in the upcoming tournament.

3. Bestie Jeans Co. introduced everyday wear that is fashionable yet (practical / confined).

4. If your bill for payment is (unable / incorrect), please contact our Customer Service at 555-2332.

B. 빈칸에 가장 적절한 것을 고르세요.

5. The Feng Lai China Shop across from the station is selling ------- sizes of animal figurines which are believed to bring good fortune.
   (A) relative
   (B) following
   (C) various
   (D) developing

6. Official banners for the ------- National Sports Festival should be prepared as soon as possible.
   (A) patented
   (B) exchanged
   (C) welcoming
   (D) upcoming

7. Sunrise Travel Agency is pleased to offer customers ------- vouchers for a two-night stay, including breakfast at the Banloz Hotel.
   (A) receptive
   (B) complimentary
   (C) approximate
   (D) experimental

8. Studies show that most Internet users are ------- to share personal information on social Web sites.
   (A) subtle
   (B) distant
   (C) reluctant
   (D) conditional

어휘 1 order form 주문서 product 제품 distributor 배급 업체 quality 품질 supply 공급품, 비품 2 miss 놓치다, 빠지다 training session 훈련 시간 participate in ~에 참가하다 upcoming 다가오는 3 introduce 소개하다 everyday wear 일상복 4 payment 대금 5 figurine 작은 조각상 fortune 행운 6 official 공식적인 banner 기장, 현수막 prepare 준비하다 as soon as possible 가능한 빨리 7 be pleased to ~하게 되어 기쁘다 voucher 상품권 including 포함하여 8 share 공유하다 personal 개인적인

Actual Test

1. Modern medical workers have developed innovative surgical approaches ------- patients with ear, nose, and throat disorders.
   (A) is treating
   (B) treatment
   (C) to treat
   (D) treated

2. It is important ------- the contract carefully for policy inconsistencies or text mistakes before you sign it.
   (A) reading
   (B) to read
   (C) read
   (D) reads

3. Globalization makes it impossible ------- modern societies to collapse in isolation, like Easter Island and Greenland Norse did in the past.
   (A) from
   (B) if
   (C) of
   (D) for

4. Cultural competence refers to the ability ------- effectively with people of different cultures and socio-economic backgrounds.
   (A) to interact
   (B) interact
   (C) interacted
   (D) interacting

5. Professional body builders have suggested that calories tend------- burnt more effectively when exercising early in the morning than in the evening.
   (A) is
   (B) being
   (C) to be
   (D) will be

6. Nitre Corporation aims to ------- 50 additional employees after their new branch in Montreal is established next month.
   (A) hire
   (B) hiring
   (C) hired
   (D) be hired

7. Workers are ------- to inform the office manager if any replacement items are needed.
   (A) hired
   (B) charged
   (C) attempted
   (D) requested

8. The promoter reserves the ------- to alter, extend or delete the program without prior notice.
   (A) service
   (B) right
   (C) reflection
   (D) complication

Questions 9-12 refer to the following e-mail.

From: nbenstien@victorian.hcs.com
To: melvin.st@askys.net
Date: April 4
Subject: Hotel Reservation

Dear Dr. Stevens,

On behalf of Hotel Victorian, I would like to thank you for choosing us for your stay in Milan! I am writing to --- 9. --- your reservation at Hotel Victorian from April 26 to 30. We noticed that you are attending the Gruppo Atkins conference and have therefore given you the --- 10. --- rate. Kindly note that we will be charging £77 per night, which is £13 less than our regular price.
Lastly, you have asked for a single room during your booking, and we are happy to confirm that we will be able --- 11. --- your request.

You can find maps of the area and other useful information on our website: www.hotelvictorian.com. --- 12. ---. I hope you enjoy the conference.

Sincerely,
Nanna Benstein
Assistant Manager

9. (A) confirm
   (B) continue
   (C) cancel
   (D) correct

10. (A) standard
    (B) discounted
    (C) annual
    (D) maximum

11. (A) to accommodate
    (B) accommodating
    (C) having accommodated
    (D) be accommodated

NEW
12. (A) The hotel rate is the lowest in the city.
    (B) The conference will be rescheduled.
    (C) We look forward to working with you soon.
    (D) Please feel free to contact me should you have any further questions during your stay.

Unit 13 동명사

Part 5-6

동명사는 이름 그대로 동사에 -ing를 붙여 명사로 만든 것입니다. 동명사는 to부정사의 명사적 용법을 생각하면 이해하기 쉽습니다. to부정사의 명사적 용법과 마찬가지로 동명사도 명사 역할을 하기 때문입니다. 그러나 to부정사가 3가지 품사의 역할을 하는 반면에 동명사는 명사의 역할만을 합니다. 명사와 마찬가지로 문장에서 주어, 목적어, 보어 기능을 합니다.

동명사: 동사원형 + -ing

▶ 주어

Having a good friend is more than just time spent together. 좋은 친구를 가지는 것은 그냥 함께 시간을 보내는 것 이상이다.

▶ 동사의 목적어

I have finished installing software. 소프트웨어를 설치하는 것을 끝냈다.

▶ 전치사의 목적어

I'm tired of waiting for results. 결과를 기다리는 데 지쳤다.

▶ 보어

The most important thing is understanding the differences among cultures.
가장 중요한 것은 문화들의 차이를 이해하는 것이다.

동명사와 명사의 차이

동명사는 목적어를 취하지만 명사는 목적어를 취할 수 없습니다.

Before (~~introduction~~ / introducing) the product, I will show you the sample.
제품을 선보이기 전에 당신에게 샘플을 보여 드리겠습니다.

★ 문법적으로 전치사 Before 뒤에는 명사나 동명사가 모두 올 수 있지만, 뒤에 the product라는 목적어가 있으므로 동명사만 가능합니다.

After (explaining / ~~explanation~~) the procedure, we will begin accepting applications.
절차를 설명한 후에, 신청서를 받기 시작하겠습니다.

★ 문법적으로 전치사 After 뒤에는 명사나 동명사가 모두 올 수 있지만, 뒤에 the procedure라는 목적어가 있으므로 동명사만 가능합니다.

동명사의 의미상의 주어

동명사의 의미상 주어로 '소유격'을 사용합니다.

I'm sure of his passing the exam. 나는 그가 시험에 합격하리라 확신한다.
★ passing의 주체는 his입니다. 여기서 동명사 주어로 his를 묻는 문제가 출제됩니다.

동명사의 수동태와 시제

- 동명사의 수동태는 'being p.p.'입니다.

  I'm ashamed of being punished in front of my friends. 나는 친구들 앞에서 벌을 받는 것이 부끄럽다.
  ★ 자신이 벌을 받는 것이므로 수동태를 써야 합니다.

- 동명사가 주절의 시제보다 한 시제 앞서는 경우 완료형인 'having p.p.'를 씁니다.

  He is proud of having been a coach for the national team. 그는 국가 대표 팀 코치였던 것을 자랑스러워한다.
  ★ 자랑스러워하는 것은 현재, 코치가 된 것은 한 시제 앞선 과거이므로 완료형을 씁니다.

1 시험에 반드시 나오는 동명사의 역할

주어

문장의 주어로 사용되는 동명사는 단수 취급하므로 뒤에 단수 동사가 이어져야 합니다.

Exercising regularly is good for both body and mind. 규칙적으로 운동하는 것은 몸과 마음에 좋다.
Waiting in line makes me bored. 줄 서서 기다리는 것이 지루하게 만든다.

보어

진행 시제와 형태는 같지만 의미가 다릅니다.

His favorite hobby is watching a news program. 그가 가장 좋아하는 취미는 뉴스를 시청하는 것이다.
My dream is learning English in America. 나의 꿈은 미국에서 영어를 배우는 것이다.

동사의 목적어

Sam likes driving cars. Sam은 차를 운전하기를 좋아한다.
I have finished cleaning the living room. 거실을 청소하기를 끝냈다.

전치사+동명사+명사

in -ing ~하는 데 있어	by -ing ~함으로써	before -ing ~하기 전에
without -ing ~하지 않고	after -ing ~한 후에	at -ing ~하는 것에
of -ing ~하는 것의	on -ing ~하자마자	for -ing ~하기 때문에
from -ing ~하는 것으로부터	besides -ing ~하는 것 외에도	except -ing ~하는 것을 제외하고

He is good at speaking English. 그는 영어로 말하는 데 능숙하다.
You can memorize a word by repeating it several times. 당신은 몇 번 반복함으로써 한 단어를 암기할 수 있습니다.

★during -ing는 사용하지 않습니다.

~~During meeting~~

Practice

정답 및 해설 p.99

A. 괄호에서 적절한 것을 고르세요.

1. (Employing / Employment) more than 2,000 engineers at once is beyond the capacity of Mavrus Inc.

2. There is no way to hang an object on a wall without (leave / leaving) a mark.

3. Mr. Brant finally succeeded in (finds / finding) a job in the competitive job market.

4. Most advertisements are aimed at (encouraging / to encourage) customers to try a new product or switch from competitors.

B. 빈칸에 가장 적절한 것을 고르세요.

5. After ------- a degree in electrical engineering, Mr. Dawson decided to pursue a master's degree at Pinestone University.
   (A) acquiring
   (B) acquired
   (C) acquire
   (D) to acquire

6. Fendur Oil Company strictly protects confidential information for ------- its stability and competitiveness.
   (A) maintenance
   (B) maintains
   (C) maintaining
   (D) maintain

7. For security reasons, visitors are requested to refrain from ------- backpacks, luggage, or other parcels into the embassy premises.
   (A) bringing
   (B) to bring
   (C) bring
   (D) brought

8. The policy of DK Com clearly states that if its bills remain unpaid for three months, it has the right to cut Internet connections without ------- customers.
   (A) notifies
   (B) notified
   (C) notifying
   (D) notification

어휘 1 beyond the capacity of ~의 능력 밖인 2 hang 걸다, 매달다 object 물건 mark 표시 3 finally 마침내 succeed 성공하다 competitive 경쟁적인 4 advertisement 광고 aim 목표로 하다 switch 전환하다, 갈아타다 competitor 경쟁 업체 5 degree 학위 pursue 추구하다 master's degree 석사 학위 6 strictly 엄격하게 protect 보호하다 confidential 기밀의 stability 안정 competitiveness 경쟁력 7 security 보안 refrain from 삼가다 parcel 꾸러미, 소포 embassy 대사관 premises 구내 8 policy 정책 clearly 분명히 state 말하다 bill 청구서 unpaid 미납된 connection 연결, 접속

2 시험에 반드시 나오는 동명사를 목적어로 취하는 동사와 동명사 숙어

동사+동명사

동명사를 목적어로 취하는 특정한 동사들이 있습니다. 다음 동사들은 반드시 알아 두어야 합니다.

consider 고려하다	avoid/mind 피하다	suggest 제안하다
postpone 연기하다	discontinue/quit 중단하다	recommend 권하다
finish 끝내다	keep 계속하다	include 포함하다
begin 시작하다	deny 부인하다	enjoy 즐기다

Activities include playing football and singing in the choir. 활동들에는 축구하기와 합창단에서 노래하기가 포함된다.
Everyone began talking at once. 모든 사람들이 한꺼번에 말하기 시작했다.

동명사 숙어 표현

토익에 자주 출제되는 다음 동명사 숙어 표현들은 반드시 알아 두어야 합니다.

have difficulty -ing ~하는 데 어려움을 겪다	be capable of -ing ~할 수 있다
cannot help -ing ~하지 않을 수 없다	refrain from -ing ~하는 것을 삼가다
be worth -ing ~할 만한 가치가 있다	be busy -ing ~하느라 바쁘다
feel like -ing ~하고 싶다	spend 시간[돈] -ing ~하는 데 시간[돈]을 보내다[쓰다]
be committed[devoted] to -ing ~하는 데 전념하다	be opposed to -ing ~하는 데 반대하다
look forward to -ing ~하기를 고대하다	object to -ing ~하는 데 반대하다
be subject to -ing ~의 대상이 되다, ~될 수 있다	be used to -ing ~하는 데 익숙하다

It's worth making appointment before you go. 가기 전에 예약을 하는 게 좋다.
Children spend too much time watching television. 아이들은 텔레비전을 보는 데 너무 많은 시간을 보낸다.
Dr. Noah is committed to helping children. Noah 박사는 아이를 돕는 데 헌신하고 있다.
He objects to paying taxes. 그는 세금을 내기를 반대하고 있다.
We look forward to seeing you on May 11. 저희는 5월 11일에 뵙기를 바랍니다.

Practice

정답 및 해설 p.100

A. 괄호에서 적절한 것을 고르세요.

1. I suggest (assigned / assigning) one or two secretaries to facilitate a discussion each week.

2. When handling an issue that takes considerable time, people should try to avoid (using / to use) e-mails and instead communicate by phone.

3. Long-term consumers were shocked when Stivofilm announced that they would discontinue (make / making) film cameras.

4. Psychologist Erin Hopkins indicated that stress, depression, and caffeine are some of the reasons that people have difficulty (sleep / sleeping).

B. 빈칸에 가장 적절한 것을 고르세요.

5. Mr. Fisher mentioned that the Palmura Group committee is considering ------- the head office to Vancouver.
   (A) to relocate
   (B) relocation
   (C) has relocated
   (D) relocating

6. The board's main duties include ------- the company's strategy and budget and purchasing and selling major assets.
   (A) confirmation
   (B) confirms
   (C) confirming
   (D) confirmed

7. We are seeking instructors capable of ------- practical lessons.
   (A) teach
   (B) to teach
   (C) teaching
   (D) taught

8. Finance Minister, Mr. Simpson, said that the government was committed to ------- the rising inflation in the recent months.
   (A) moderate
   (B) moderating
   (C) moderation
   (D) moderately

어휘 1 suggest 제안하다 facilitate 수월하게 하다 discussion 토론 2 handle 다루다 considerable 상당한 avoid 피하다 3 long-term 장기간의 consumer 소비자 be shocked 충격을 받다 announce 발표하다 discontinue 중단하다 4 psychologist 심리학자 indicate 지적하다 depression 우울증 reason 이유 difficulty 어려움 5 mention 언급하다 committee 위원회 head office 본사 6 board 이사회 main 주된 duty 의무, 임무 include 포함하다 strategy 전략 budget 예산 asset 자산 7 seek 찾다 instructor 강사, 교사 practical 실용적인 8 Finance Minister 재무 장관 be committed to ~에 전념하다 recent 최근의

3 반드시 알아야 하는 기출 형용사 어휘 ❸

☐ **probable** 있을 법한, 가망성 있는	• It is highly probable that smoking causes lung cancer. 흡연이 폐암을 유발할 가능성이 매우 높다. • the probable outcome of the merger 그 합병으로 생길 수 있는 결과	
☐ **finest** 가장 훌륭한, 가장 뛰어난	• the world's finest automobile 세계에서 가장 훌륭한 자동차 • the finest watch in the world 세계에서 가장 좋은 손목시계	
☐ **accidental** 우연한, 우발적인	• an accidental death 변사, 사고사 • Our meeting was accidental. 우리의 만남은 우연이었다.	
☐ **sufficient** 충분한	• have sufficient time to work 일할 시간이 충분하다 • produce sufficient electricity 충분한 전기를 생산하다	
☐ **considerate** 사려 깊은, 배려하는	• He is always considerate toward his coworkers. 그는 직장 동료들을 항상 사려 깊게 대한다. • be considerate of the feelings of others 다른 사람들의 기분을 배려하다	
☐ **positive** 긍정적인, 자신 있는	• receive a positive reply 긍정적인 답변을 받다 • He is positive about his future. 그는 자기 미래에 대해 자신이 있다.	
☐ **drastic** 급격한, 과감한	• a drastic change in the economy 경기의 급변 • drastic cuts in spending 대폭적인 지출 삭감	
☐ **unprecedented** 전례 없는	• an unprecedented economic growth 전례 없는 경제 성장 • The event is unprecedented in the history. 그 사건은 역사상 유례가 없다.	
☐ **familiar** 잘 아는, 정통한	• analysts familiar with the housing market 주택 시장을 잘 아는 분석가들 • I'm not familiar with the area. 나는 그 지역을 잘 모른다.	
☐ **mutual** 상호간의, 서로의	• mutual understanding 상호 이해 • a mutual acquaintance 서로가 아는 사람	
☐ **frequent** 빈번한, 잦은	• conduct frequent sales meetings 영업 회의를 자주 하다 • a frequent visitor to the house 그 집에 자주 찾아오는 사람	
☐ **diverse** 다양한	• people from diverse backgrounds 다양한 배경을 지닌 사람들 • diverse energy sources 다양한 에너지원들	
☐ **common** 흔한, 공통의	• a common spelling mistake 흔한 철자 오류 • We have nothing in common. 우리는 공통점이 전혀 없다.	
☐ **moderate** 알맞은, 적당한	• a moderate rise in revenue 적당한 수입 증가 • conversation volume at moderate levels 적당한 수준의 대화 음량	
☐ **durable** 내구성 있는, 튼튼한	• Plastic is a very durable material. 플라스틱은 내구성이 좋은 물질이다. • The new wheeled suitcase is more durable. 바퀴 달린 새 옷가방이 더 튼튼하다.	

Practice

정답 및 해설 p.101

A. 괄호에서 적절한 것을 고르세요.

1. Also known as a peace activist, Malangatana is considered one of the (finest / closest) painters in Africa.

2. The headlines of Billberg Daily Newspaper reported only a (moderate / special) rise in inflation.

3. The technician informed the manager that (missing / frequent) paper jams caused the printer malfunction.

4. Hamdire University announced that they had collected (sufficient / contrived) funds for making further improvements, such as installing computers in the school library.

B. 빈칸에 가장 적절한 것을 고르세요.

5. Sales manager Frank Clinton's decision for promoting the product through advertisements led to an ------- increase in sales.
   (A) unprecedented
   (B) imminent
   (C) unsalvageable
   (D) extraneous

6. The recent seminar on Youth Entrepreneurship received a ------- response from many undergraduates studying economics and business.
   (A) chosen
   (B) practical
   (C) current
   (D) positive

7. Giraffe Waterpark Camp offers a ------- range of fun activities and events for families visiting during the summertime.
   (A) diverse
   (B) prolonged
   (C) several
   (D) valued

8. BIS Industry emphasized that employees need to be ------- with the new working hours.
   (A) recognizable
   (B) common
   (C) familiar
   (D) usual

어휘 1 activist 활동가, 운동가 consider 여기다, 간주하다 painter 화가 2 headline 헤드라인, 표제 기사 rise 상승 inflation 인플레이션 3 technician 기술자 jam 걸림, 엉킴 malfunction 오작동 4 announce 발표하다 collect 모으다 fund 자금 further 추가의 improvement 향상, 개선 5 decision 결정 promote 홍보하다 increase 증가 6 recent 최근의 response 반응 undergraduate 학부생 economics 경제학 7 range 범위 8 emphasize 강조하다

1. After ------- nine original works, Bethany Turner was hired to write a script for a film that would be directed by Douglas Zimmerman.
   (A) was selling
   (B) to have sold
   (C) had sold
   (D) having sold

2. Mr. Winston's presentation will focus on ------- the company's long-term strategic direction.
   (A) outline
   (B) outlined
   (C) outlining
   (D) outliner

3. Many business organizations have to keep ------- their customer service to stay ahead of their competitors.
   (A) improved
   (B) improving
   (C) improvement
   (D) improvable

4. Mr. Lewis decided to donate a part of the money to charity by ------- a check of $5,000.
   (A) issuing
   (B) issue
   (C) issued
   (D) to issue

5. Besides ------- no oil, steaming is considered a simple and nutritious method of cooking.
   (A) require
   (B) requirements
   (C) requires
   (D) requiring

6. At this time of year, everybody is busy ------- for the monsoons that could last for the next four to five months.
   (A) preparing
   (B) prepares
   (C) preparation
   (D) to prepare

7. Students should review their school's Program Planning Guide before they begin ------- courses.
   (A) select
   (B) selecting
   (C) selected
   (D) selection

8. The design firm NIXEA is well-known for ------- the most advanced working environment in the industry.
   (A) leading
   (B) leads
   (C) leader
   (D) leadership

Questions 9-12 refer to the following letter.

To: Department employees
From: Billy Ernest
Subject: Announcement
Date: April 19

Dear employees:

It is my deepest pleasure to announce that owing to his hard work and outstanding dedication, Jae-ho Kim is being promoted. From April 22, Mr. Kim will be --- 9. --- the Immigration Consulting Division.
Mr. Kim began as a public service worker in this division five years ago, and he has exhibited diligence in all his consulting assignments with many clients. In his new position as the Director of Immigration Consulting, besides --- 10. --- contracts with clients' lawyers, Mr. Kim will be responsible for training and managing all the Security Team members.
--- 11. ---.
I trust that all of you will make every effort to help him during his --- 12. --- to his new role. Thank you in advance for your help and support.

Best Regards,
Billy Ernest
Chief of Bureau, Immigration

9 (A) leaving
   (B) leading
   (C) joining
   (D) purchasing

10 (A) negotiate
   (B) negotiating
   (C) negotiator
   (D) negotiations

NEW
11 (A) This is only a temporary job Mr. Kim will take.
   (B) Please join me in congratulating Mr. Kim on his promotion.
   (C) It's been over a decade since he joined the sales team.
   (D) Mr. Kim's retirement party will be held this coming Friday.

12 (A) occupation
   (B) acquisition
   (C) transition
   (D) interruption

Part 5-6

Unit 14 분사

분사는 동사에서 온 형용사 형태로서 명사를 앞뒤에서 수식해 주는 역할을 합니다. 명사를 수식할 형용사가 없는 경우 동사를 형용사로 변형해 사용하는 것이 분사입니다. 현재분사(-ing)는 능동·진행의 의미를 나타내며 과거분사(-ed)는 수동·완료의 의미를 나타냅니다. 이렇게 주로 의미를 기준으로 현재분사와 과거분사를 선택할 수 있습니다. 그러나 토익에서는 해석만으로 풀기 어려운 문제가 많이 나오므로 분사의 특성들을 더 자세히 연구해 보아야 합니다.

분사의 위치와 역할

▶ 명사를 앞뒤에서 수식

I read an interesting novel. 재미있는 소설을 읽었다.
Please review the attached files. 첨부된 파일을 검토해 주세요.
The man taking a walk looks young. 산책을 하고 있는 그 남자는 젊어 보인다.

▶ be동사, 2형식 동사의 주격 보어

The children became excited. 그 아이들은 신이 났다.

▶ 5형식 동사의 목적격 보어

The teacher kept the students studying hard. 교사는 학생들이 계속 열심히 공부하게 했다.

현재분사와 과거분사의 구별

▶ 현재분사(-ing)는 능동의 의미를 나타냅니다.

현재분사는 '~하는'이란 뜻으로 능동과 현재의 의미가 있습니다.

The (~~cried~~ / crying) baby is my cousin. 울고 있는 저 아기는 내 사촌이다.
★ 울고 있는 대상은 아기로 능동의 의미인 현재분사가 정답.

The new system is compatible with (existing / ~~existed~~) equipment. 새 시스템은 기존의 장비와 호환이 된다.
★ 장비가 존재하고 있는 것으로 능동의 의미인 현재분사가 정답.

▶ 과거분사(-ed)는 수동의 의미를 나타냅니다.

과거분사는 '~받는, ~된'이란 뜻으로 수동과 과거의 의미가 있습니다.

They found some (hidden / ~~hiding~~) treasure. 그들은 숨겨진 보물을 찾았다.
★ 보물은 숨겨져 있던 것이므로 수동의 의미인 과거분사가 정답.

The book (~~writing~~ / written) by Jerry is informative. Jerry가 쓴 책은 매우 유익하다.
★ 책은 쓰여진 것이므로 수동의 의미인 과거분사가 정답.

 분사구문

분사구문은 '부사절 접속사+주어+동사'가 '(부사절 접속사)+-ing/-ed'로 축약된 것을 말합니다.

~~After we~~ finished our project, we started to test it. 프로젝트를 끝낸 후에 우리는 그것을 시험하기 시작했다.
    능동은 -ing로 바뀜
→ Finishing our project, we started to test it.

~~When I~~ am faced with a problem like this, I really don't know what to do. 이런 문제에 직면하면 정말 어떻게 할지를 모르겠다.
    수동은 -ed로 바뀜
→ Faced with a problem like this, I really don't know what to do.

1 시험에 반드시 나오는 현재분사와 과거분사

현재분사와 과거분사

▶ 현재분사: 동사원형+ -ing

분사와 수식을 받는 명사의 의미가 능동일 때 '~하는'으로 해석됩니다.

Consumers will benefit from the (rising / ~~risen~~) competition between two companies.
소비자들은 두 회사의 경쟁의 증가로 이익을 볼 것이다. ★ 경쟁이 증가하고 있는 것이 맞으므로 현재분사가 정답.

We have to complete any (remaining / ~~remained~~) paperwork. 우리는 남아 있는 모든 서류작업을 완료해야 한다.
★ 남아 있는 서류작업이 맞으므로 현재분사가 정답.

▶ 과거분사: 동사원형+ -ed

분사와 수식을 받는 명사의 의미가 수동일 때 '~된'으로 해석됩니다.

분사는 품사가 형용사로 명사를 수식하거나, 동사의 보어 자리에 쓰입니다.

Please mail the (~~completing~~ / completed) rental agreement. 완성된 임대 계약서를 우편으로 보내주세요.
★ 계약서가 완료되는 것이므로 과거분사가 정답.

There is an (~~updating~~ / updated) job listing. 업데이트된 구인 목록이 있다.
★ 구인 목록이 업데이트되는 것이므로 과거분사가 정답.

감정 타동사의 현재분사와 과거분사

▶ 감정 타동사의 종류

interest 흥미를 끌다	embarrass 당황하게 하다	annoy 짜증나게 하다	frustrate 실망시키다
bewilder 당황하게 하다	disappoint 실망시키다	excite 흥미진진하게 만들다	impress 깊은 인상을 주다
exhaust 피곤하게 하다	fascinate 흥미를 끌다	overwhelm 압도하다	alarm 깜짝 놀라게 하다
confuse 당황하게 하다	satisfy 만족시키다	surprise 놀라게 하다	worry 걱정을 끼치다
please 즐겁게 하다	delight 기쁘게 하다		

▶ 감정 타동사는 수식을 받는 명사가 감정을 느끼는 주체일 때는 과거분사(-ed), 감정을 일으키는 주체일 때는 현재분사 (-ing)를 사용합니다.

There is an (annoying / ~~annoyed~~) noise. 짜증나게 하는 소음이 있다.
★ noise가 감정을 일으키는 주체이므로 -ing가 정답.

Customers are (~~frustrating~~ / frustrated) because the door does not close completely.
문이 완전히 닫히지 않아서 고객들은 실망했다. ★ customers가 감정을 느끼는 주체이므로 -ed가 정답.

Wendy Tours is (~~pleasing~~ / pleased) to announce its new line of outdoor adventures.
Wendy Tours는 새로운 야외 모험 경로를 발표하게 되어 기쁩니다. ★ Wendy Tours가 감정을 느끼는 주체이므로 -ed가 정답.

Practice

정답 및 해설 p.107

A. 괄호에서 적절한 것을 고르세요.

1. Pilotte Investment, an (established / establishing) Tokyo-based company, bought $793 million stocks of Metack Corp., becoming the company's biggest shareholder.

2. The testing procedures (outlining / outlined) in this document are designed to ensure the safety of the newly developed tracking device.

3. Voltimo Company will distribute informational slips to anyone (interested / interesting) in registering for the workshop.

4. Critics have acknowledged that the Red Carpet Group's musical was an (overwhelmed / overwhelming) success.

B. 빈칸에 가장 적절한 것을 고르세요.

5. DALE Graduate Business School is offering an ------- deadline until July 14 for candidates who wish to apply for scholarships.
   (A) extend
   (B) extends
   (C) extensive
   (D) extended

6. Please complete, sign, and return the application form in the ------- pre-addressed return envelope by August 21.
   (A) enclosure
   (B) enclosed
   (C) enclosing
   (D) enclose

7. Government employees are ------- because despite increase in expenses, their salaries have not been increased.
   (A) disappointed
   (B) disappointing
   (C) disappointment
   (D) disappoints

8. The January issue of Literary Review carried a ------- interview with Philip Reeve.
   (A) fascinate
   (B) fascinated
   (C) fascinating
   (D) fascination

어휘 ¹ stock 주식 shareholder 주주 ² procedure 진행, 절차 ensure 보장하다 safety 안전성 tracking device 추적 장치 ³ distribute 배포하다 informational 정보를 제공하는 slip 종잇조각, 메모 용지 register 등록하다 ⁴ critic 비평가 acknowledge 인정하다 success 성공작 ⁵ graduate business school 경영대학원 candidate 지원자 apply for 신청하다 scholarship 장학금 ⁶ application form 신청서 pre-addressed 수신자 주소가 적힌 ⁷ expense 경비, 비용 salary 급여 ⁸ issue 호, 쇄 carry (기사를) 싣다

Unit 14 : 분사 157

2 시험에 반드시 나오는 필수 분사 표현

현재분사

leading company 선도하는 회사	upcoming events 다가오는 행사
increasing need 증가하는 요구	lasting impression 지속적인 인상
promising member 전도유망한 회원	opposing sides 반대편
preceding year 지난해	following year 다음 해
growing demand 증가하는 수요	remaining work 남아 있는 업무
surrounding cities 주변 도시들	outstanding design 뛰어난 디자인
challenging period 힘든 기간	deteriorating condition 악화되는 상태
mounting pressure 증가하는 압력	demanding supervisor 까다로운 상사
ongoing renovations 진행되고 있는 보수작업	entertaining advertisements 흥미로운 광고
culminating event 절정에 달한 행사	rising cost 상승하는 원가
existing equipment 현재 장비들	missing luggage 분실된 짐

과거분사

reserved seats 지정된 좌석	preferred means 선호되는 수단
talented authors 재능 있는 작가들	qualified person 자질 있는 사람
designated/limited areas 지정된/제한된 장소	detailed information 자세한 정보
skilled workers 숙련된 노동자	written statement 진술서
damaged condition 손상된 상태	retired technician 은퇴한 기술자
finished product 완제품	enclosed form 동봉된 양식
increased productivity 증가된 생산성	dedicated service 헌신적인 서비스
authorized dealers 허가받은 상인들	unlimited access 무제한 이용
informed customer 현명한 고객	assessed value 평가된 가치
complicated process 복잡한 과정	attached schedule 첨부된 일정
repeated requests 반복적인 요청들	motivated candidate 진취적인 후보
sophisticated architecture 정교한 건축물	revised edition 개정판

Practice

정답 및 해설 p.108

A. 괄호에서 적절한 것을 고르세요.

1 The board of directors will discuss the results after each group presents their (finished / finishing) product.

2 Mr. Frazier's ability to adapt quickly made him a (promised / promising) member of our community.

3 Food and drinks in the Kingsport Aquatic Center are only permitted in (designated / designating) areas.

4 Though Michael Newman is an amateur artist, his transcendent paintings leave a (lasted / lasting) impression on spectators.

B. 빈칸에 가장 적절한 것을 고르세요.

5 Employees are entitled to receive a ------- statement from their employer, listing the terms and conditions of the employment.
   (A) write
   (B) wrote
   (C) written
   (D) writing

6 Electric and plug-in hybrid auto sales have increased by approximately 60 percent over the ------- year.
   (A) preceding
   (B) preceded
   (C) precedes
   (D) precede

7 Mobile devices have been the ------- means of digital contact for consumers.
   (A) preferring
   (B) preferred
   (C) preference
   (D) preferably

8 Please follow the ------- schedule, which I will hand out at practice.
   (A) attach
   (B) attaches
   (C) attached
   (D) to attach

어휘 1 board of directors 이사회 result 결과 present 제출하다 2 adapt 적응하다 quickly 빠르게 3 permit 허용하다 area 구역, 장소 4 transcendent 탁월한, 초월적인 impression 인상, 감명 spectator 관람객 5 statement 성명서, 진술서 employer 고용주 terms and conditions (계약의) 조건 employment 일자리, 고용 6 approximately 대략 7 mobile device 무선 통신 기기 consumer 소비자 8 follow 따르다 hand out 나누어 주다 practice 실습

3 시험에 반드시 나오는 분사구문

분사구문을 만드는 방법

분사구문은 '부사절 접속사+문장'을 축약해 '(부사절 접속사)+-ing/p.p.' 형태로 만드는 것입니다.

▶ **의미상 주절의 주어가 동사의 행동을 '하는 경우'는 현재분사(능동)를 사용합니다.**

While I watched TV, I fell asleep. TV를 보면서 잠이 들었다.
→ Watching TV, I fell asleep.
★ 부사절 접속사 while을 생략합니다. 의미를 살리고 싶을 때는 생략하지 않을 수도 있습니다.
★ 부사절의 주어가 주절의 주어와 같으므로 생략합니다. 동사 watched가 능동태이므로 현재분사를 씁니다.

▶ **의미상 주절의 주어가 동사의 행동을 '당하는 경우'는 과거분사(수동)를 사용합니다.**

Because I was left alone, I cried. 혼자 남겨져서 나는 울었다.
→ (Being) Left alone, I cried.
★ 부사절 접속사 Because를 생략합니다. 의미를 살리고 싶을 때는 생략하지 않을 수도 있습니다.
★ 부사절의 주어가 주절의 주어와 같으므로 생략합니다. 동사 was left가 수동태이므로 과거분사를 사용합니다.

▶ **분사 자리 뒤에 목적어(명사)가 있는 경우는 현재분사, 수식어(부사, 전치사+명사)가 있는 경우는 과거분사를 사용합니다.**

(Elected / Electing) in 2013, ~
★ 뒤에 전치사+명사가 있으므로 과거분사가 정답입니다.

특정 접속사 뒤에 잘 어울리는 분사구문

when / while	+ -ing/ed
after / before	+ -ing/being p.p.
once / until unless / as than / though	+ p.p.

When contacting ~, 주어+동사   After expanding ~, 주어+동사
As noted ~, 주어+동사   Unless stated, 주어+동사

Practice

정답 및 해설 p.110

A. 괄호에서 적절한 것을 고르세요.

1. When (designed / designing) the interface of the application, remember to consider your target audience.

2. Please read all procedures thoroughly before (entering / entered) the laboratory.

3. (To be / Being) the store manager, Mr. Oneil is responsible for checking supplies that need to be restocked and keeping the facility clean at all times.

4. Weather satellites help us track hurricanes, (allowing / allows) meteorologists to warn people days in advance.

B. 빈칸에 가장 적절한 것을 고르세요.

5. As ------- in the rental contract, all residents will be given a maximum of five extra days before monthly payments are due.
   (A) noted
   (B) noting
   (C) note
   (D) notations

6. Improving service, efficiency, and productivity while ------- cost will be the company's goal this year.
   (A) reducing
   (B) reduced
   (C) reduce
   (D) to reduce

7. After ------- chosen in amateur auditions, prospective new vocalists of the musical ensemble will perform in small theaters next week.
   (A) is
   (B) been
   (C) were
   (D) being

8. ------- in the city of Bilbao, the museum features historical exhibitions organized by the Buenaventura Foundation.
   (A) Located
   (B) Locating
   (C) Locates
   (D) Locate

어휘 1 application 응용 프로그램 consider 고려하다 target audience 광고 대상자 2 procedure 절차, 순서 thoroughly 철저히 3 be responsible for ~에 책임이 있다 supply 공급품, 비품 restock 보충하다 facility 시설 4 weather satellite 기상 위성 track 추적하다, 쫓다 meteorologist 기상학자 warn 경고하다 in advance 미리 5 rental contract 임대 계약 resident 거주자 due 만기의, 지불 기일이 된 6 efficiency 효율성 productivity 생산성 goal 목표 7 prospective 유망한 8 feature 특징으로 하다 historical 역사적인 exhibition 전시회 organize 준비하다

4 반드시 알아야 하는 기출 형용사 어휘 ❹

☐ **plain**
분명한, 평이한, 평범한
- The book is written in plain language. 그 책은 평이한 말로 쓰여 있다.
- The facts were plain. 그 사실들은 분명했다.

☐ **possible**
가능한, 있을 수 있는
- Come as early as possible. 가능한 한 일찍 오세요.
- There are several possible explanations. 몇 가지 설명이 가능하다.

☐ **perishable**
상하기 쉬운
- the transport of perishable items 상하기 쉬운 물품의 운송
- Cakes are perishable. 케이크는 상하기 쉽다.

☐ **essential**
필수의, 본질적인
- an essential part of business travel 출장의 필수적인 부분
- an essential difference 본질적인 차이

☐ **careful**
주의하는, 세심한
- Fragile products require careful handling. 깨지기 쉬운 제품은 주의해 다루어야 한다.
- after careful consideration 세심한 고려 후에

☐ **sudden**
갑작스러운, 돌연한
- people who gained sudden wealth 벼락부자가 된 사람들
- There was a sudden drop in temperature. 기온이 갑자기 떨어졌다.

☐ **straightforward**
직선적인, 간단한, 솔직한
- The contract's language is very straightforward. 그 계약서의 내용은 매우 간단하다.
- his straightforward attitude 그의 솔직한 태도

☐ **agreeable**
기분 좋은, 선뜻 동의하는
- The weather is agreeable. 날씨가 쾌적하다.
- He was perfectly agreeable to the plan. 그 계획에 완전히 동의했다.

☐ **revised**
개정된, 수정된
- explain the revised policy 개정된 정책을 설명하다
- the revised travel itinerary 수정된 여행 일정

☐ **local**
지역의, 현지의
- a local newspaper article 지역 신문의 기사
- provide reliable service to local customers 지역 고객들에게 신뢰할 만한 서비스를 제공하다

☐ **exceptional**
예외적인, 우수한
- only in exceptional circumstances 예외적인 상황에서만
- offer exceptional performance 우수한 성능을 제공하다

☐ **impressive**
인상적인, 감동적인
- Her background was very impressive. 그녀의 경력은 아주 인상적이었다.
- an impressive scene 감동적인 장면

☐ **innovative**
혁신적인, 획기적인
- a prize for the most innovative TV commercials 획기적인 TV 광고에 주는 상
- innovative cost-cutting measures 혁신적인 원가 절감 조치

☐ **additional**
추가의, 부가적인
- additional flights 추가 항공편
- build an additional parking garage 추가로 주차장을 짓다

☐ **competitive**
경쟁하는, 경쟁력 있는
- in a highly competitive market 경쟁이 심한 시장에서
- offer competitive compensation 경쟁력 있는 보수를 제공하다

Practice

정답 및 해설 p.111

A. 괄호에서 적절한 것을 고르세요.

1. Weather reports claim that there will be rain of up to 20 inches (possible / allowable) in some areas.

2. TA Intel's new LED screen is so delicate that it requires (typical / careful) handling to avoid damage.

3. The new sales director instructed all representatives to find (innovative / billable) ways to address the needs of customers.

4. Customers expressed that the (revised / deleted) version of the manual for FW700z video camera was easier and simpler to follow.

B. 빈칸에 가장 적절한 것을 고르세요.

5. The demands seem very -------, so all deliveries can be completed without delay.
   (A) accomplished
   (B) straightforward
   (C) immediate
   (D) negligible

6. Mr. Freddy Murphy's guide on career assessment is a(n) ------- read for students preparing to enter university.
   (A) fortunate
   (B) talented
   (C) admired
   (D) essential

7. The company immediately hired Ms. Josie White for a position in the management team because her background was very -------.
   (A) qualified
   (B) knowledgeable
   (C) pleased
   (D) impressive

8. Many job applicants seek employment in Satif Company because it offers ------- salaries, commissions and overtime payments.
   (A) reflective
   (B) competitive
   (C) protective
   (D) excessive

어휘 1 claim 주장하다 2 delicate 섬세한, 민감한 handling 취급 avoid 피하다 3 instruct 지시하다 representative 담당 직원 address 집중해 다루다 4 express 표현하다, 나타내다 5 delivery 배송 delay 지연 6 career assessment 직업 평가 7 immediately 즉시, 곧바로 background 배경, 경력 8 job applicant 구직자 employment 일자리 commission 판매 수수료

Actual Test

1. Interviews with several financial advisers have revealed workers' ------- needs for a steady retirement income.
   (A) overwhelmingly
   (B) overwhelming
   (C) overwhelmed
   (D) overwhelm

2. Since the introduction of digital photography, cameras have become much more -------.
   (A) sophisticate
   (B) sophisticating
   (C) sophisticated
   (D) sophistication

3. The majority of Internet users are not comfortable with ------- advertisements and online data collection.
   (A) to target
   (B) is targeting
   (C) targeted
   (D) targets

4. ------- information and specifications are only available to customers with verified access clearance.
   (A) Detailing
   (B) Details
   (C) Detail
   (D) Detailed

5. Professor Brown will be sending an e-mail with the schedules for the ------- work for the month.
   (A) remainder
   (B) remaining
   (C) remained
   (D) remain

6. When ------- an important presentation, keep it brief but include substantial details.
   (A) make
   (B) makes
   (C) made
   (D) making

7. This year, the net loss of Texfill Bank was 10.5 billion euros, ------- that it is one of the largest financial losses in the last 10 years.
   (A) confirms
   (B) confirming
   (C) confirmed
   (D) confirmation

8. When ------- new manufacturing machinery, operators should first consider what is best in terms of personnel safety.
   (A) order
   (B) orders
   (C) ordering
   (D) ordered

Questions 9-12 refer to the following e-mail.

To: henry.gibson@sletter.net
From: walls.fed3@mtm.com
Subject: Letter of regret
Date: May 12

Dear Mr. Gibson,

We would like to thank you for your interest in becoming a --- 9. --- author to the Malaysia Tourist Newsletter . Although your work is highly regarded, our annual staffing budget was recently reduced. --- 10. ---. However, we urge you to continue your contributions and hope that you will submit your work again as an independent writer in the future.

Once again, please remember that we typically accept short --- 11. --- regarding tourist sites. We are looking forward --- 12. --- more of your work soon. Thank you.

Sincerely,
Wallsa Fedre, Malaysia Tourist Newsletter

9. (A) contribute
   (B) contributable
   (C) contributing
   (D) contributes

NEW
10. (A) While we are running out of budget, we are hiring some more staff.
    (B) Therefore, we will not be able to offer you a contract currently.
    (C) The budget meeting will be held this Monday.
    (D) Otherwise, we have no choice but to cut down expenses.

11. (A) exhibits
    (B) assistance
    (C) donation
    (D) articles

12. (A) read
    (B) reading
    (C) to read
    (D) to reading

Unit 15 명사절 접속사

Part 5-6

명사절은 '명사절 접속사+주어+동사' 구조로 명사의 성질을 그대로 갖고 있으면서 절의 형태를 띠고 있는 것이므로 문장에서 명사와 같은 역할을 합니다. 명사절은 절을 이끄는 접속사에 따라 that절, if/whether절, 의문사절로 구분할 수 있습니다. 난이도가 높은 유형이므로 정답을 맞히면 고득점에 유리합니다.

명사절의 역할

절은 접속사에 문장이 붙어 '접속사+주어+동사'로 이루어진 형태를 말하며 절이 명사와 동일한 역할을 할 경우에 **명사절**이라고 부릅니다. 명사절은 명사처럼 문장 안에서 주어, 목적어, 보어의 역할을 할 수 있습니다.

▶ **문장의 주어 역할**

That he is honest is true. 그가 정직한 것은 사실이다.

명사절 접속사 that이 문장의 주어 자리에 쓰일 때 뒤에 동사가 두 개 나온다는 점이 중요합니다.

주어(That+주어+동사1)+동사2+목적어/보어

▶ **문장의 목적어 역할**

동사의 목적어 자리

I think that he is honest. 나는 그가 정직하다고 생각한다.

전치사의 목적어 자리

They are still talking about whether he is honest. 그들은 아직도 그가 정직한지 여부에 대해 이야기하고 있다.

▶ **문장의 보어 역할**

The truth is that the sun rises from the east. 사실은 해가 동쪽에서 뜬다는 것이다.

명사절 접속사의 종류

대표적인 명사절 접속사는 that, if, whether, 의문사(의문대명사, 의문부사)입니다.
가장 많이 출제되고 있는 것은 that, whether, what, how, when, where 정도입니다.

that	~라는 것	+ 완전한 문장
if, whether	~인지 (아닌지)	+ 완전한 문장
의문대명사	who 누가 what 무엇을 which 어떤 것을	+ 불완전한 문장(주어나 목적어가 빠진 문장)
의문부사	when 언제 where 어디서 how 어떻게 why 왜	+ 완전한 문장

That he won the prize is surprising. 그가 상을 받은 것이 놀랍다.

I wonder if/whether she will come to the party. 나는 그녀가 파티에 올지 궁금하다.
★ 동사의 목적어로는 if 와 whether가 모두 가능하지만 if가 불가능한 경우도 있습니다.

Mary liked what I bought for him. Mary는 내가 그에게 사 준 것을 좋아했다.
★ bought의 목적어가 빠진 불완전한 문장입니다.

I don't know when he came. 그가 언제 왔는지 모르겠어요.

명사절을 이끄는 복합관계대명사

복합관계대명사는 명사절과 부사절을 모두 이끌 수 있지만, 토익에서는 명사절 접속사로 자주 출제됩니다.

whoever
whichever } + 불완전한 문장 (주어나 목적어가 빠진 문장)
whatever

1 시험에 반드시 나오는 that/what/whether/if

that vs. what

▶ **that 뒤에는 완전한 문장이 옵니다.**

We know (**that** / what) it is not perfect. 우리는 그것이 완벽하지 않다는 것을 알고 있다.
★ 뒤에 it(주어), 동사(is), 보어(perfect)의 완전한 문장이 왔으므로 that이 정답입니다.

James suggests (what / **that**) he will write a theme song. James는 주제가를 작곡하겠다고 제안했다.
★ 뒤에 주어(he), 동사(will write), 목적어(a theme song)의 완전한 문장이 왔으므로 that이 정답입니다.

▶ **what 뒤에는 주어나 목적어가 빠진 불완전한 문장이 옵니다.**

You decide (that / **what**) you need to do. 무엇을 원하는지 당신이 결정하세요.
★ 뒤에 do의 목적어가 없는 불완전한 문장이 왔으므로 what이 정답입니다.

They didn't know (**what** / that) kind of company they wanted. 그들은 자신이 어떤 종류의 회사를 원하는지를 몰랐다.
★ 뒤에 wanted의 목적어가 없는 불완전한 문장이 왔으므로 what이 정답입니다.

whether vs. if

▶ **whether 뒤에는 완전한 문장이 오고, '~인지 (아닌지)'로 해석합니다.**

I'm not sure (when / **whether**) I'm doing this right. 내가 제대로 하고 있는지 확실치 않아요.
★ when은 의미상 어색하며, whether '~인지 (아닌지)'가 더 알맞습니다.

▶ **whether to(명사절 접속사)/whether or not(부사절 접속사)**
명사절 접속사 뒤에는 문장도 오지만 to부정사 형태도 가능합니다.

You have to choose (which / **whether**) to buy it. 당신은 그것을 살지 결정해야 합니다.
★ which 뒤에는 to부정사가 올 수 없고, 명사절 접속사 which가 가능합니다.

I would like to ask (**whether** / unless) or not it is your experience. 나는 그것이 당신의 경험인지 아닌지 묻고 싶습니다.
★ whether가 or not과 함께 쓰이면 부사절 접속사가 됩니다. 뒤에 or not이 있으므로 whether만 가능합니다.

▶ **명사절 접속사 if는 주어 자리와 전치사 뒤에 쓸 수 없습니다.**

(**That** / If) the earth is round is true. 지구가 둥글다는 것은 사실이다.
★ 명사절 접속사 if는 주어 자리에 쓸 수 없습니다.

There is some debate about (if / **whether**) Mr. Choi will attend the conference. 최 씨가 회의에 참석할지에 대해 논쟁이 있다.
★ 명사절 접속사 if는 전치사 about 뒤에 쓸 수 없습니다.

Practice

정답 및 해설 p.117

A. 괄호에서 적절한 것을 고르세요.

1. Perexo Corporation announced (what / that) it will be establishing a new branch in Hong Kong within the next six months.

2. Mr. Holmes wishes to know (what / when) happened to his baggage that was supposed to arrive with him at the airport.

3. When the metal bracelet began to rust, many people began doubting (whether / whenever) it was made of genuine silver.

4. (That / What) Mr. Turner has supervised the service department for nearly twenty years shows his devotion and passion.

B. 빈칸에 가장 적절한 것을 고르세요.

5. It is vitally important ------- we consume the right amount of nutrients and vitamins daily to enable our body to function properly.
   (A) which
   (B) what
   (C) who
   (D) that

6. ------- impresses readers the most is the author's writing style, which reveals the writer's personality in the novel.
   (A) Which
   (B) What
   (C) Nothing
   (D) Neither

7. Mr. Sanders asked ------- Ms. Cooper was aware of the renovation of the finance department that was scheduled to begin next Monday.
   (A) whether
   (B) whenever
   (C) either
   (D) although

8. For his vacation to Europe, Mr. Price is trying to decide ------- to use a travel agency or to travel on his own.
   (A) whether
   (B) both
   (C) not only
   (D) so

어휘 1 announce 발표하다 establish 설립하다 branch 지사 2 wish 원하다 happen 발생하다 baggage 짐, 수하물 be supposed to ~하기로 되어 있다 3 bracelet 팔찌 rust 녹슬다 doubt 의심하다 genuine 진짜의 4 supervise 감독하다, 관리하다 devotion 헌신 passion 열정 5 vitally 매우, 중대하게 consume 섭취하다 nutrient 영양소 function 기능하다 properly 적절히, 알맞게 6 impress 감동시키다 author 저자 reveal 드러내다 personality 개성 novel 소설 7 be aware of 알고 있다 renovation 보수 공사 8 vacation 휴가 travel agency 여행사 on one's own 혼자, 스스로

Unit 15 : 명사절 접속사   169

2 시험에 반드시 나오는 의문사와 복합관계대명사

의문사

▶ **의문대명사 who, which, what** 뒤는 주어나 목적어가 빠진 불완전한 문장이 옵니다.

The problem is who will take care of children. 문제는 누가 아이들을 돌볼 것이냐이다.
★ who 뒤에 주어 없음

Please tell Mr. Whitner which you prefer. 당신이 선호하는 것을 Whitner 씨에게 말하세요.
★ prefer 뒤에 목적어 없음

▶ **의문부사 when, where, why, how** 뒤는 완전한 문장이 옵니다.

I asked when he is going to Chicago. 나는 언제 그가 Chicago로 가는지 물었다.
No one knew why the CEO resigned. 아무도 왜 CEO가 사임했는지 알지 못한다.
I wonder how you became interested in mathematics. 네가 어떻게 수학에 관심을 갖게 되었는지 궁금하다.

특이하게 how는 'how+형용사/부사+주어+동사'도 가능하고, 시험에 자주 출제됩니다.

Look at how beautiful you are. 네가 얼마나 예쁜지 봐.
She likes to show off how well she speaks English. 그녀는 자기가 영어를 잘한다는 것을 뽐내고 싶어 한다.

복합관계대명사

복합관계대명사 중 whoever, whatever, whichever는 명사절을 이끌 수 있습니다.
해석상 어울리는 것을 찾는 문제로 출제됩니다.

| whoever 누구든지 | whatever 무엇이든지 | whichever 어떤 것이든 |

Whoever wants the book may have it. 누구든지 그 책을 원한다면 가져도 좋다.
I'll buy whatever you want. 네가 원하는 건 뭐든지 사 줄게.
He will like whichever song you choose. 그는 네가 어떤 노래를 선택하든 좋아할 것이다.

복합관계대명사 앞에는 선행사가 올 수 없습니다.

I will follow ~~the rule~~ whatever it is. 나는 그게 무엇이든 따를 것이다.

Practice

정답 및 해설 p.118

A. 괄호에서 적절한 것을 고르세요.

1. Assessment tests are frequently administered to students to check (how / that) well their learning is progressing.

2. The manager asked (what / where) the power supply cord for the Metrax grinder was stored.

3. Many people have been asking (which / why) the company decided to employ younger applicants rather than the ones with experience.

4. During an interview with lottery contestants, many interviewees said that if they won, they planned to spend almost half of the prize money on (however / whatever) they wanted.

B. 빈칸에 가장 적절한 것을 고르세요.

5. The worn-out gloves and running shoes indicate ------- hard Joe trained at the gym to prepare for the upcoming contest.
   (A) why
   (B) where
   (C) when
   (D) how

6. For invoice payments, customers may choose to pay by mail or through online banking, ------- they prefer.
   (A) however
   (B) whichever
   (C) whenever
   (D) wherever

7. With the new portable music player, the NanoTune permits users to listen to music ------- and whenever they please.
   (A) whoever
   (B) wherever
   (C) whatever
   (D) whichever

8. ------- acquires Rickey Fleming's business will get a chance to get more than what they paid for.
   (A) Who
   (B) Whoever
   (C) Whom
   (D) Whose

어휘 1 assessment 평가 frequently 자주 administer 실시하다 learning 학습 progress 진전되다 2 power supply cord 전원 공급 코드 grinder 분쇄기 store 보관하다 3 decide 결정하다 employ 고용하다 applicant 지원자 experience 경험 4 lottery 복권, 추첨 contestant 출전자 interviewee 인터뷰 대상자 prize money 상금 5 worn-out 낡은 indicate 나타내다 contest 대회, 경기 6 invoice 송장 payment 지급, 결제 prefer 선호하다 7 portable 휴대용의 permit 허용하다, 가능하게 하다 8 acquire 취득하다, 인수하다 business 사업(체) pay for 지불하다

3 반드시 알아야 하는 기출 부사 어휘 ❶

- ☐ **easily**
  쉽게
  - They can easily access their account. 그들은 자기 계좌에 쉽게 접근할 수 있다.
  - Iron is easily corroded. 철은 쉽게 부식된다.

- ☐ **effortlessly**
  노력하지 않고, 힘들이지 않고
  - come apart effortlessly 쉽게 부서지다
  - She danced gracefully and effortlessly. 그녀는 우아하고 자연스럽게 춤을 추었다.

- ☐ **broadly**
  폭넓게, 대체로
  - The term is too broadly defined. 그 용어는 너무 폭넓게 정의된다.
  - They broadly agree on the need for investment.
    그들은 투자의 필요성에 대해 대체로 동의한다.

- ☐ **mutually**
  서로, 상호간에
  - set up a mutually agreeable time 서로 편한 시간을 정하다
  - a mutually beneficial relationship 상호 유익한 관계

- ☐ **ideally**
  이상적으로, 완벽하게
  - He is ideally suited for the position. 그는 그 직책에 아주 적격이다.
  - It is ideally located with all amenities.
    그곳은 모든 편의 시설이 갖추어진 이상적인 위치에 있다.

- ☐ **explicitly**
  명확하게, 노골적으로
  - It is explicitly against the regulations. 그것은 명백히 규정에 어긋난다.
  - the work dealing explicitly with homosexuality 동성애를 노골적으로 다루는 작품

- ☐ **anonymously**
  익명으로
  - The information was sent anonymously to the newspaper.
    그 정보는 익명으로 신문사에 보내졌다.
  - The donation was made anonymously. 그 기부는 익명으로 이루어졌다.

- ☐ **relatively**
  비교적, 상대적으로
  - in a relatively short period of time 비교적 짧은 기간 내에
  - The road is relatively free of traffic. 도로에는 비교적 차량이 없는 편이다.

- ☐ **punctually**
  정시에, 시간을 지켜
  - Employees should arrive punctually. 직원들은 정시에 도착해야 한다.
  - Products are shipped to patrons punctually. 제품들은 고객들에게 제때에 발송된다.

- ☐ **regularly**
  정기[규칙]적으로
  - He travels regularly for business. 그는 사업차 정기적으로 여행한다.
  - She works out regularly. 그녀는 규칙적으로 운동을 한다.

- ☐ **subsequently**
  그 후에, 이어서
  - The original copy was subsequently lost. 원본은 그 후에 잃어버렸다.
  - He resigned and subsequently was found not guilty.
    그는 사임했고 그 후에 무죄임이 밝혀졌다.

- ☐ **diligently**
  부지런히
  - They carry out their work diligently. 그들은 부지런히 업무를 수행한다.
  - all employees who work diligently 부지런히 일하는 모든 직원들

- ☐ **already**
  이미, 벌써
  - The plan has already been implemented. 그 계획은 이미 시행되고 있다.
  - She is already deeply involved. 그녀는 이미 깊이 관련되어 있다.

- ☐ **primarily**
  첫째로, 주로
  - Korea has depended primarily on exports. 한국은 주로 수출에 의존해왔다.
  - What does the second paragraph primarily discuss?
    둘째 단락은 주로 무엇을 논하고 있는가?

Practice

정답 및 해설 p.120

A. 괄호에서 적절한 것을 고르세요.

1. Kello Company has exported its products to several markets in Southeast Asia, (primarily / temporarily) to the Philippines.

2. According to journalist Helen Salt, 3D animation films are (early / broadly) popular with both adults and children.

3. Mr. Timothy Lee had worked in the company for over 7 years and was (subsequently / inappropriately) promoted to the position of an assistant manager.

4. Students who log in to the system (perceptively / anonymously), will not be credited for their participation.

B. 빈칸에 가장 적절한 것을 고르세요.

5. Flight passengers are expected to arrive ------- at the airport, because a late check-in may delay the flight schedule.
   (A) punctually
   (B) eventually
   (C) randomly
   (D) accordingly

6. Sheila was ------- recognized by her fancy sunglasses and colorful floral pants.
   (A) shortly
   (B) easily
   (C) daily
   (D) lately

7. The last few lines in the user manual ------- state that the service will not be provided without the appropriate warranty.
   (A) hardly
   (B) closely
   (C) indefinitely
   (D) explicitly

8. The Red Sands Hotel is ------- located within walking distance to the world-famous historical sites.
   (A) largely
   (B) ideally
   (C) evenly
   (D) chiefly

어휘 1 export 수출하다 product 제품 2 journalist 기자 popular 인기 있는 adult 성인 3 be promoted 승진하다 position 직책 4 credit 학점을 주다 participation 참여 5 delay 지연시키다 6 recognize 알아보다 fancy 화려한, 고급의 floral 꽃의, 꽃무늬의 7 appropriate 적절한 warranty 품질 보증서 8 within walking distance to ~까지 걸어갈 수 있는 거리 이내에

Actual Test

1. A recent poll indicates ------- many people in the United States hold a combination of conservative and liberal political views.
   (A) that
   (B) but
   (C) what
   (D) like

2. ------- is so remarkable about Natalie receiving the Music Award is that she only took up the profession three years ago.
   (A) What
   (B) That
   (C) Which
   (D) Why

3. The green number below the chart indicates ------- many seats are currently available in each theater.
   (A) only
   (B) there
   (C) most
   (D) how

4. The committee has not yet determined ------- to discard the proposal because of the shortfalls in resources.
   (A) regarding
   (B) either
   (C) nearby
   (D) whether

5. The advertising team hopes ------- the new products will help increase market awareness.
   (A) that
   (B) about
   (C) why
   (D) how

6. Since most of the talented players will not be able to participate due to their injuries, it is doubtful ------- the team will win the next game.
   (A) so that
   (B) whether
   (C) why
   (D) when

7. You can attach additional stamps ------- there is empty space.
   (A) wherever
   (B) whoever
   (C) whichever
   (D) whatever

8. ------- Mr. Alexander has said is his personal opinion, the board has nothing to do with it.
   (A) However
   (B) Whatever
   (C) Whichever
   (D) Whenever

Questions 9-12 refer to the following article.

Nowadays, a growing number of businesses are beginning to offer flexible schedules to both part- and full-time workers. Working from home is another alternative to the traditional schedule and is gaining popularity. --- 9. --- employees are working solely from home or working for some hours a week from home, this arrangement benefits both companies and workers. --- 10. ---.

Several studies have indicated that working from home increases employee --- 11. ---. It has statistically been shown that numerous sales agents achieved 25 percent more product sales while working from home.

Although working from home is certainly not suitable for everyone, an increasing number of businesses are --- 12. --- such options.

9. (A) Either
   (B) Likewise
   (C) Therefore
   (D) Whether

NEW
10. (A) Working together in a group can be a great experience or a terrible one.
    (B) Sales have decreased over the last 6 months.
    (C) Employees can save time and money wasted on commuting.
    (D) Flexible working hours make employees unhappy.

11. (A) analysis
    (B) management
    (C) productivity
    (D) purchases

12. (A) considerably
    (B) considering
    (C) considered
    (D) considerable

Unit 16 형용사절 접속사

Part 5-6

형용사절은 '형용사절 접속사+(주어+)동사' 구조로 형용사처럼 앞의 명사를 수식하는 역할을 합니다. 예를 들어 a desk which you sit at to read and write(당신이 읽고 쓰기 위해 앉는 책상)에서 명사 desk를 수식하는 which 이하 절이 형용사절입니다. 형용사절 접속사에는 관계대명사와 관계부사가 있습니다. 형용사절 접속사 유형은 난이도가 높지 않기 때문에 반드시 정답을 고르도록 해야 합니다.

관계대명사

두 문장에서 공통되는 명사 중 하나를 관계대명사로 바꾸어 한 문장으로 만들 수 있습니다. 관계대명사는 앞에 나온 명사를 대신하는 대명사 역할을 하는 동시에 두 개의 절을 연결하는 접속사 역할을 합니다. 관계대명사 앞의 명사를 선행사라고 하고 그 선행사가 사람, 사물인지에 따라 다른 관계대명사가 사용됩니다. 관계대명사가 문장에서 하는 역할에 따라 주격, 소유격, 목적격으로 구분합니다.

선행사	주격	소유격	목적격
사람	who	whose	whom
사물	which	whose	which
사람/사물	that	whose	that

I know a woman. + She lives next door to me. 나는 한 여자를 안다. + 그녀는 우리 옆집에 산다.
　　　　명사　　　　　주어

→ I know a woman who lives next door to me. 나는 우리 옆집에 사는 여자를 안다.
　　　　　　선행사　주격

This is the book. + My friend likes it. 이것은 그 책이다. + 내 친구가 그것을 좋아한다.
　　　　명사　　　　　　　　　목적어

→ This is the book which my friend likes. 이것이 내 친구가 좋아하는 책이다.
　　　　　　선행사　목적격

관계부사

관계부사는 두 문장에서 공통되는 부사를 대신하며 두 문장을 이어 주는 것입니다. 관계부사에는 when, where, how, why가 있으며 선행사가 시간일 때는 when, 장소일 때는 where, 방법일 때는 how, 이유일 때는 why를 사용합니다. 관계부사 how를 사용할 때는 선행사 the way를 반드시 생략해야 합니다.

when	I know a time(선행사) when you study English. 나는 네가 영어를 공부하는 시간을 알고 있다.
where	I know a place(선행사) where you study English. 나는 네가 영어를 공부하는 장소를 알고 있다.
how	I know (the way)(선행사) how you study English. 나는 네가 영어를 공부하는 방법을 알고 있다.
why	I know the reason(선행사) why you study English. 나는 네가 영어를 공부하는 이유를 알고 있다.

관계대명사와 관계부사의 차이

관계대명사 뒤에는 불완전한 문장이 오지만 관계부사 뒤에는 완전한 문장이 옵니다.

She is the only woman that doesn't tell a lie. 그녀는 거짓말을 하지 않는 유일한 여자다.
★ 관계대명사 that 뒤에 주어가 생략된 불완전한 문장이 옵니다.

This is the book which I bought. 이것이 내가 산 책이다.
★ 관계대명사 which 뒤에 bought의 목적어가 생략된 불완전한 문장이 옵니다.

I want to know the reason why she hates me. 그녀가 나를 싫어하는 이유를 알고 싶다.
★ 관계부사 why 뒤에 주어(she), 동사(hates)와 목적어(me)가 있는 완전한 문장이 옵니다.

1 시험에 반드시 나오는 관계대명사

관계대명사의 종류

▶ **주격 관계대명사: 뒤의 문장에 주어가 없습니다.**

The company hired an applicant who was highly qualified. 회사는 고도의 자격을 갖춘 지원자를 채용했다.
★ 선행사가 사람(applicant)이고 was의 주어가 없으므로 주격 관계대명사 who를 사용합니다.

I read the article that is controversial. 나는 논란이 되는 그 기사를 읽었다.
★ 선행사가 사물(article)이고 is의 주어가 없으므로 주격 관계대명사 that을 사용합니다.

▶ **목적격 관계대명사: 뒤의 문장에 목적어가 없습니다.**

I reviewed the report which Roy wrote. 나는 Roy가 쓴 보고서를 검토했다.
★ 선행사가 사물(report)이고 동사 wrote의 목적어가 없으므로 목적격 관계대명사 which를 사용합니다.

▶ **소유격 관계대명사: 뒤에 명사가 옵니다.**

I met an artist whose paintings will be on display in August.
나는 자신의 그림들이 8월에 전시될 한 미술가를 만났다.
★ 선행사가 사람(artist)이고 뒤에 명사 paintings가 있으므로 소유격 관계대명사 whose를 사용합니다.

관계대명사의 생략

▶ **주격 관계대명사+be동사는 생략 가능합니다.**

The washing machine ~~which was~~ ordered last week will be delivered tomorrow.
지난주에 주문한 세탁기가 내일 배송될 것이다.

Any staff member ~~who are~~ attending the seminar should contact Ms. Gomez.
세미나에 참석하는 모든 직원은 Gomez 씨에게 연락해야 합니다.

▶ **목적격 관계대명사는 생략 가능합니다.**

We have received the package ~~which~~ you sent to our factory.
우리는 당신이 우리 공장으로 보낸 소포를 받았습니다.
★ 동사 sent의 목적어이므로 생략할 수 있습니다.

I know the man ~~whom~~ you told me about yesterday.
나는 당신이 어제 내게 이야기한 그 남자를 압니다.
★ 동사 told의 직접목적어이므로 생략할 수 있습니다.

Practice

A. 괄호에서 적절한 것을 고르세요.

1. We will not produce products (that / what) consumers don't want.

2. Please contact our Technical Support department to deal with any problems (you / that) may encounter while using version 1.11.

3. The New Enterprise Incentive Scheme assists people (when / who) are interested in establishing and running small businesses.

4. BBC3 is a radio station (where / that) features readings of stories, interviews, and reviews on literature, music, culture.

B. 빈칸에 가장 적절한 것을 고르세요.

5. Semmens said, "Any employee ------- wishes to receive free legal assistance may call his organization at 800-555-3600."
   (A) which
   (B) when
   (C) what
   (D) who

6. An opening reception will be held on Friday from 8 p.m. to 10 p.m. for Todd Wolf ------- paintings will be displayed at the National Museum.
   (A) which
   (B) their
   (C) whose
   (D) that

7. Rogers is currently the only service provider in Canada ------- offers unlimited data services.
   (A) that
   (B) they
   (C) whose
   (D) these

8. The museum has a collection of over 200,000 items ------- illustrate the history of ancient Assyria.
   (A) that
   (B) still
   (C) so
   (D) how

어휘 / 1 produce 생산하다 product 제품 2 contact 연락하다 department 부서 deal with 다루다 encounter 직면하다 3 scheme 계획 assist 돕다 establish 세우다, 설립하다 4 feature 특징으로 하다 5 legal 법률의 assistance 도움 organization 단체, 조직 6 reception 축하 연회 display 전시하다 7 currently 현재 offer 제공하다 unlimited 무제한의 8 museum 박물관 illustrate 예시하다

2 시험에 반드시 나오는 관계사 출제 유형

관계대명사와 대명사의 선택

▶ **문장과 문장을 연결할 때는 관계대명사를 사용합니다.**

This award is given to an individual (who / ~~she~~) has made a significant contribution.
이 상은 지대한 공헌을 한 사람에게 수여된다.

★ 문장에 2가지 동사(is given, has made)가 있으므로 두 문장을 연결하는 관계사인 who가 정답입니다.

▶ **접속사가 이미 있으면 대명사를 사용합니다.**

When employees speak to customers, (~~who~~ / they) should always speak clearly.
직원들이 고객들에게 말할 때는 항상 명확히 말해야 한다.

★ 접속사 When이 이미 문장을 연결하는 기능을 하고 있으므로 대명사 they가 정답입니다.

수량 대명사+of+whom/which

▶ **선행사의 수량을 표현하고 싶을 때 '수량 대명사+of+whom/which' 형태를 사용합니다.**

선행사 + many, most, some, all+of+whom(사람 선행사)/which(사물 선행사)
      any, each, half, both

The party will honor employees, all of (whom / ~~which~~) have dedicated themselves for many years.
그 파티는 직원들을 예우할 것인데, 그들 모두는 여러 해 동안 헌신해왔다.

★ 선행사가 사람(employees)이므로 whom이 정답입니다.

관계부사

▶ **관계부사 = 전치사+관계대명사**

관계부사 뒤에는 주어와 목적어가 모두 있는 완전한 문장이 옵니다.

[시간] when = in/at/on/to+which   [장소] where = in/on/at+which
[방법] how = in+which   [이유] why = for+which

The village in which he lives is surrounded by a rain forest. 그가 사는 마을은 열대우림에 둘러싸여 있다.
= The village where he lives is surrounded by a rain forest.

▶ **관계부사 앞에는 전치사를 사용하지 않습니다.**

~~in where~~ → where
~~at how~~ → how

Practice

정답 및 해설 p.126

A. 괄호에서 적절한 것을 고르세요.

1. We look forward to continuing to provide you with the high-quality service to (which / where) you have become accustomed.

2. Mr. Wang, (who / he) has helped us with our research, is serving as a temporary employee.

3. The ship will have 1,250 staterooms, most of (that / which) will have balconies, with a capacity of 2,500 passengers and a crew of 1,000.

4. The hotel (where / when) the conference is being held is situated in the center of Manila.

B. 빈칸에 가장 적절한 것을 고르세요.

5. Garrett was appointed professor of English at the University of Virginia, ------- he continued to hold until his retirement.
   (A) in which
   (B) together with
   (C) not only
   (D) instead of

6. After accountants joined the company, ------- eliminated unnecessary expenditures from the budget.
   (A) which
   (B) where
   (C) how
   (D) they

7. Ken is a researcher in the field of physical education, ------- he has received multiple awards over the past five years.
   (A) in which
   (B) whereas
   (C) how
   (D) for which

8. The convention center ------- the presentations will be held is equipped with a projector.
   (A) where
   (B) why
   (C) how
   (D) when

어휘 / 1 look forward to -ing ~하기를 고대하다 accustom 익숙해지다 2 serve 근무하다 temporary employee 임시 직원 3 stateroom 특등실 passenger 승객 crew 승무원 4 be situated 위치하다 5 appoint 임명하다 retirement 은퇴 6 accountant 회계사 eliminate 제거하다 unnecessary 불필요한 expenditure 지출 budget 예산 7 researcher 연구자 physical education 체육 award 상 8 be equipped with ~이 갖추어져 있다

3 반드시 알아야 하는 기출 부사 어휘 ❷

- [ ] **periodically**
주기[정기]적으로
  - E-mail lists are updated periodically. 이메일 명단은 주기적으로 갱신된다.
  - Check the coffee maker periodically. 커피메이커를 정기적으로 점검하세요.

- [ ] **highly**
높이, 대단히, 고도로
  - I highly recommend reading the book. 그 책을 읽어 볼 것을 강력히 권합니다.
  - highly qualified candidates 고도의 자격을 갖춘 후보들

- [ ] **directly**
직접, 곧바로
  - be shipped directly from the warehouse 창고에서 곧바로 발송되다
  - Feel free to contact me directly. 부담 갖지 마시고 제게 직접 연락하세요.

- [ ] **accordingly**
그래서, 그에 따라
  - Adjust your speed accordingly. 그에 따라 속도를 조절하세요.
  - Accordingly, we were forced to increase our prices.
    그래서 저희는 가격을 올릴 수밖에 없었습니다.

- [ ] **previously**
이전에, 미리
  - previously wooded areas 이전에는 숲이 무성했던 지역들
  - as previously scheduled 미리 일정을 잡은 대로

- [ ] **finally**
마침내, 결국
  - The day is finally here! 마침내 그날이 왔다!
  - He has finally been nominated for the presidency.
    그는 결국 사장직에 지명되었다.

- [ ] **originally**
원래, 처음에는
  - stronger than originally anticipated 원래 예상했던 것보다 더 강력한
  - The device was originally designed for vehicles.
    그 장치는 처음에는 차량용으로 고안되었다.

- [ ] **momentarily**
잠시, 순간적으로
  - The plant was halted momentarily. 공장 가동이 잠시 중단되었다.
  - She lost her consciousness momentarily. 그녀는 순간적으로 정신을 잃었다.

- [ ] **only**
오직, ~만
  - They use only the freshest ingredients. 그들은 가장 신선한 재료만 사용합니다.
  - Orders should be placed only through the Internet.
    주문은 인터넷을 통해서만 해야 합니다.

- [ ] **especially**
특히, 유별나게
  - His skills would be especially helpful. 그의 능력이 특히 도움이 될 것이다.
  - It is especially freezing this morning. 오늘 아침에는 유난히 춥다.

- [ ] **particularly**
특히, 각별히
  - The magazine is particularly popular. 그 잡지가 특히 인기가 있다.
  - with particularly great interest 각별히 큰 흥미를 가지고

- [ ] **incorrectly**
부정확하게, 틀리게
  - The term is often used incorrectly. 그 용어는 부정확하게 사용될 때가 많다.
  - The sentence was translated incorrectly. 그 문장은 틀리게 번역되었다.

- [ ] **probably**
아마도, 대체로
  - Where does this conversation probably take place?
    이 대화가 이루어질 것 같은 장소는?
  - This is probably the best offer. 이것이 아마 최상의 제안일 것입니다.

- [ ] **provisionally**
임시로, 잠정적으로
  - be provisionally appointed to the committee 임시로 위원회에 임명되다
  - The agreement is to provisionally take effect on July 7.
    그 협약은 7월 7일에 잠정적으로 발효된다.

- [ ] **reasonably**
합리적으로, 상당히
  - have a reasonably balanced diet 합리적으로 균형 잡힌 식사를 하다
  - earn a reasonably good wage 상당히 괜찮은 급여를 받다

Practice

A. 괄호에서 적절한 것을 고르세요.

1. When Anna Tanchi felt ill, she left class, took a taxi home and went (directly / maybe) to bed.

2. After working for over 30 years in the field, Mr. Patrick Gilmore has (finally / promptly) decided to plan his retirement.

3. Pioneer Ace Corporation is well-known for its large number of (highly / merely) trained technicians.

4. Ever since the new model was released, the customer service department has been (radically / particularly) busy.

B. 빈칸에 가장 적절한 것을 고르세요.

5. The letter stated that the enclosed coupons would ------- provide seats for two people at the Palace Buffet.
   (A) finely
   (B) only
   (C) lively
   (D) sharply

6. Officials say that the recent report was false due to an ------- filed document.
   (A) importantly
   (B) equally
   (C) usually
   (D) incorrectly

7. Oscar Leone, our team manager, gave us crucial information, which was ------- shared at the staff meeting.
   (A) instead
   (B) previously
   (C) behind
   (D) accordingly

8. If you took Professor King's Public Speaking class for two semesters, then you have ------- heard all of his success stories.
   (A) nicely
   (B) never
   (C) probably
   (D) presently

어휘 1 ill 아픈 home 집에 2 plan 계획을 세우다 3 well-known 유명한 technician 기술자 4 release 출시하다 5 state 명시하다 enclose 동봉하다 6 official 공무원 false 틀린, 사실이 아닌 due to ~ 때문에 7 crucial 결정적인 share 공유하다 8 public speaking 대중 연설 semester 학기

Actual Test

1. The NMC is constructing a two-level underground parking garage at the stadium ------- will be able to accommodate 1,500 cars.
   (A) whenever
   (B) this
   (C) what
   (D) which

2. The Fulbright Programs are full scholarships in the USA for international students ------- want to pursue a master's or Ph.D. degree.
   (A) whoever
   (B) who
   (C) them
   (D) themselves

3. The agency is representing photographers ------- work appeared in magazines.
   (A) which
   (B) their
   (C) whose
   (D) that

4. We conducted a survey on a number of workers, most of ------- are employed and living in urban areas.
   (A) who
   (B) whom
   (C) whose
   (D) that

5. Fort Clarence Tower was the heart of the Fort and it is next to Borstal Road ------- Priester's Park was once located.
   (A) near
   (B) beside
   (C) where
   (D) until

6. The company has focused on the packaging in ------- its consumer goods are shipped.
   (A) which
   (B) that
   (C) what
   (D) when

7. San Antonio opened a new library ------- local residents can be educated.
   (A) when
   (B) which
   (C) what
   (D) where

8. Members, some of ------- are upset now, want to participate in the debate.
   (A) whom
   (B) that
   (C) whoever
   (D) whose

Questions 9-12 refer to the following advertisement.

A New Art Exhibition is Coming to Fanel Art Museum

Fanel Art Museum is proud to present "The Future We Will See," a new exhibition, --- 9. --- the work of 3D graphic artist Jake Woodrow and his team of experts.

3D, or three-dimensional, graphic art is becoming a popular theme, both in filmmaking and video games. Mr. Woodrow describes his new work as "the future which we are not far from." This new style of art is often called "new age" or "mechanical art," a term that refers to displaying certain objects --- 10. --- may be found in or imagined to be used in the futuristic world.

The exhibition is scheduled to be open to the general public from May 11th through June 21st. --- 11. ---, a special raffle event will be held for all viewers, which will entitle the winner to receive a free art package from the gift shop.

--- 12. ---.

---

9   (A) feature
    (B) featuring
    (C) featured
    (D) features

10 (A) what
    (B) each
    (C) how
    (D) that

11 (A) Specifically
    (B) Instead
    (C) In addition
    (D) as a result

NEW

12 (A) Getting a free gift is as exciting as getting cash.
    (B) The souvenir shop is conveniently located at the center of the city.
    (C) The gift shop regularly send our loyal customers free prize.
    (D) For more information, find us at www.fanelartmuseum.org.

Unit 17 부사절 접속사

Part 5-6

부사절은 '부사절 접속사+주어+동사' 구조로 문장에서 부사 역할을 합니다. 시간, 조건, 이유, 양보, 목적 등의 의미로 주절을 수식하는 절을 부사절이라고 합니다. 부사절은 주절을 수식해야 하므로 주절 없이 단독으로는 사용될 수 없다는 것이 특징입니다. 부사절을 이끄는 부사절 접속사는 가장 비중 높은 유형이지만 난이도는 별로 높지 않습니다.

부사절의 형태

부사절은 '부사절 접속사+주어+동사'로 이루어집니다. 부사절과 주절의 위치는 서로 바뀔 수 있지만 부사절이 앞에 나올 때는 주절 앞에 쉼표를 사용해야 합니다.

Since the ticket was so affordable, we could take the airplane to get to Jeju Island.
= We could take the airplane to get to Jeju Island since the ticket was so affordable.
항공권 가격이 아주 적당했기 때문에 우리는 비행기를 타고 제주도에 갈 수 있었다.

부사절 접속사의 종류

시간	when / as ~할 때 until ~할 때까지	while ~하는 동안 since ~한 이래로	after ~ 후에 once 일단 ~하면, ~하자마자	before ~ 전에
조건	if 만약 ~한다면 as long as ~하기만 한다면	unless 만약 ~하지 않으면	only if ~하는 경우에만 provided that ~한다면	
양보	although / even though / even if / though ~에도 불구하고 while / whereas ~한 반면에			
이유	because / since / now that / as ~ 때문에			
목적	so that ~하도록			

[시간] You need to check the price of the products before you place an order.
주문을 하시기 전에 제품의 가격을 확인하실 필요가 있습니다.

[조건] Unless the budget increases, the problem will continue.
만약 예산이 증가하지 않는다면 문제는 계속될 것이다.

[양보] Although the materials are expensive, they are popular.
그 재료들은 비싼데도 불구하고 인기가 있다.

[이유] I couldn't go to the party because I had to finish the homework.
숙제를 끝내야 했기 때문에 파티에 가지 못했다.

[목적]　Mr. Gibson runs every day so that he can stay healthy.
Gibson 씨는 건강을 유지하기 위해 매일 달린다.

부사절 접속사와 전치사의 구별

같은 의미의 부사절 접속사와 전치사를 구별하는 문제는 매회 반드시 출제됩니다. 부사절 접속사 다음에는 절(주어+동사)이 이어지고 전치사 다음에는 명사/대명사/동명사가 이어집니다.

(Because / ~~Because of~~) he wants to attend a seminar, Dr. Noah will not be in the office today.
Noah 박사는 세미나에 참석하기를 원하기 때문에 오늘은 사무실에 없을 것입니다.

★ 주어(he)+동사(wants)를 이끄는 부사절 접속사 Because가 정답입니다.

(~~Although~~ / Despite) the bad weather, the renovation was completed on schedule.
나쁜 날씨에도 불구하고 보수 공사는 일정대로 완료되었다.

★ 명사구(the bad weather)를 이끄는 전치사 Despite이 정답입니다.

1 시험에 반드시 나오는 부사절 접속사

시간 · 조건 · 양보

시간	when/as ~할 때 while ~하는 동안 after ~ 후에 before ~ 전에 until ~할 때까지 since ~한 이래로 once 일단 ~하면, ~하자마자 as soon as ~하자마자 by the time ~할 때쯤에
조건	if 만약 ~한다면 unless 만약 ~하지 않으면 only if ~하는 경우에만 as long as ~하기만 한다면 provided that ~한다면
양보	although/even though/even if/though ~에도 불구하고 while/whereas ~한 반면에

★ 시간 부사절 접속사 while은 while -ing 구문으로 '~하면서'라는 의미의 동시 동작을 나타낼 때 자주 사용합니다.

[시간] As soon as a train arrives at the platform, information will be posted on the monitor.
열차가 승강장에 도착하자마자 정보가 모니터에 표시될 것이다.

[조건] Any employee will receive an award provided that the sales meet the expectations.
매출이 예상치를 충족한다면 어떤 직원이라도 상을 받게 될 것이다.

[양보] This software is as reliable as the old one even though it is much cheaper.
이 소프트웨어는 가격이 훨씬 더 싼데도 불구하고 예전 것만큼 신뢰할 만하다.

이유 · 목적

이유	because/since/now that/as ~ 때문에
목적	so that ~하도록

[이유] Now that the construction is complete, traffic will no longer be delayed.
이제 공사가 완료되었기 때문에 교통이 더 이상 지체되지 않을 것이다.

[목적] Set up your computer so that all users share the same files.
모든 사용자들이 동일한 파일을 공유하도록 컴퓨터를 설정하세요.

Practice

정답 및 해설 p.133

A. 괄호에서 적절한 것을 고르세요.

1. Customers can ride any of the rides in this amusement park (unless / during) they are pregnant or have health issues.

2. (Although / Rather) many people use smartphones these days, some choose to continue using old-fashioned cell phones.

3. (Since / In case of) the department store is located in a densely populated urban area, it attracts many customers.

4. Ms. Schmeling's delivery request will be delayed (just / because) the delivery truck is out of operation.

B. 빈칸에 가장 적절한 것을 고르세요.

5. Parcells Technology, Inc. will enjoy an increase in sales revenue next month ------- its customers' needs continue to grow.
   (A) in place of
   (B) as a result
   (C) as well as
   (D) provided that

6. Although the class tomorrow may need to be postponed due to heavy snow, students need to complete their assignments ------- the class will be held.
   (A) if any
   (B) than if
   (C) as if
   (D) only if

7. Please submit the reason for your absence to Mr. Rochester ------- your attendance record is not affected.
   (A) ever since
   (B) due to
   (C) in spite of
   (D) so that

8. ------- Tom's flight was postponed because of an engine problem, he was late for his first client meeting.
   (A) Nearly
   (B) Since
   (C) As if
   (D) Even

어휘 1 customer 고객 amusement park 놀이 공원 pregnant 임신하고 있는 health issue 건강 문제 2 continue 계속하다 old-fashioned 구식의 3 department store 백화점 densely 밀집하여 urban 도시의 attract 끌어들이다, 유치하다 4 delivery 배송 request 요청 out of operation 고장 난 5 increase 증가 sales revenue 판매 수입 6 postpone 연기하다 complete 완료하다 assignment 과제 7 submit 제출하다 reason 이유, 사유 absence 결근 attendance 출근 affect 영향을 미치다 8 late 늦은 client 고객

Unit 17 : 부사절 접속사

2 시험에 반드시 나오는 부사절 접속사와 전치사

의미가 같은 부사절 접속사와 전치사의 구별

부사절 접속사 다음에는 절(주어+동사)이 이어지고 전치사 다음에는 명사/대명사/동명사가 이어집니다.

뜻	부사절 접속사	전치사
~때문에	because/since/as/now that	because of/owing to/owe to due to/on account of
~하는 동안	while	during + 특정 기간 for + 숫자 기간
~에도 불구하고	although/even though/even if	despite/in spite of
~을 제외하고	except that	except (for)/aside from/apart from
~한다면, ~하는 경우에	if/unless/provided that	in case of/in the event of

★ after, before, until은 똑같은 의미로 전치사로도 사용됩니다.

(Owing to / ~~Now that~~) the expansion of its branch, the company has hired two accountants.
그 회사는 지사 확장 때문에 회계사 두 명을 고용했다.

★ 뒤에 명사구(the expansion of its branch)가 있기 때문에 전치사 Owing to가 정답입니다.

(Although / ~~In spite of~~) there is no charge, attendees must sign up in advance.
요금은 없지만 참석자들은 사전에 등록해야만 한다.

★ 뒤에 주어(there)+동사(is)가 있기 때문에 접속사 Although가 정답입니다.

(~~Unless~~ / In case of) an emergency, please dial 911. 비상 시에는 911로 전화하십시오.

★ 뒤에 명사(an emergency)가 있기 때문에 전치사 In case of가 정답입니다.

보기에 등장하는 기타 전치사

regardless of ~와 관계없이　　as of ~ 현재로, ~부터　　besides ~ 이외에도　　in addition to ~뿐만 아니라
instead of ~ 대신에　　　　　as a result of ~의 결과로　on behalf of ~을 대신하여　as far as ~하는 한
in terms of ~ 면에서는　　　　unlike ~와 달리　　　　　barring ~을 제외하고

대표적인 부사절의 축약

Workers are not allowed to use smartphones (while / ~~during~~) on duty. 작업자들은 근무 중에 스마트폰을 사용해서는 안 된다.

★ while (they are) on duty에서 주어와 be동사가 생략된 형태입니다.
★ (while / ~~during~~) working → during -ing 형태는 사용하지 않습니다.

Practice

정답 및 해설 p.134

A. 괄호에서 적절한 것을 고르세요.

1. (In addition to / Because) the tennis court in front of the dormitory, there is a large gymnasium on the campus.

2. (While / In terms of) residents' benefits, Irvine council decided to construct a huge outdoor mall in an accessible area.

3. Steve Miller awarded the most outstanding employee a prize (on behalf of / even if) the company president.

4. (Despite / Although) the recent downturn in the economy, Jamba Juice Smoothie is expected to generate considerable profits this year.

B. 빈칸에 가장 적절한 것을 고르세요.

5. ------- unexpected changes in air current, the flight experienced some turbulence.
   (A) As far as
   (B) Even though
   (C) Owing to
   (D) While

6. A sales report for the last quarter indicated that the overall sales increased by 10% ------- the launch of a new product line.
   (A) only
   (B) until
   (C) after
   (D) rather

7. The average grade in Economics 101 was much higher than expected ------- the professor's extraordinarily remarkable lectures.
   (A) because of
   (B) finally
   (C) once
   (D) now that

8. Bobby could not hang out with his friends on the weekend ------- a heavy load of homework.
   (A) although
   (B) caused
   (C) due to
   (D) because

어휘 1 dormitory 기숙사 gymnasium 체육관 2 resident 주민 benefit 혜택, 유익 council (지방 자치체의) 의회 decide 결정하다 construct 건설하다 huge 거대한 accessible 접근하기 쉬운 3 award 수여하다 outstanding 뛰어난 president 사장 4 recent 최근의 downturn 침체 generate 발생시키다 considerable 상당한 profit 수익 5 unexpected 예상치 못한 air current 기류 turbulence 난기류 6 quarter 분기 indicate 나타내다 overall 전체의, 종합적인 launch 출시 7 average 평균의 grade 성적 extraordinarily 엄청나게 remarkable 주목할 만한 lecture 강의 8 hang out with ~와 어울리다 load 작업량

Unit 17 : 부사절 접속사

3 반드시 알아야 하는 기출 부사 어휘 ❸

☐ **separately**
따로따로, 별도로
- send the invoices separately 송장들을 따로따로 보내다
- throw away food waste separately 음식 쓰레기를 분리해 버리다

☐ **immediately**
즉시, 당장에
- The contract will take effect immediately. 그 계약은 즉시 효력이 발생할 것이다.
- be ready to use immediately 즉시 사용하도록 준비되다

☐ **formerly**
이전에, 예전에
- The building was formerly an elementary school. 그 건물은 예전에 초등학교였다.
- Myanmar was formerly known as Burma. 미얀마는 전에 버마로 알려져 있었다.

☐ **calmly**
조용히, 침착하게
- address complaints calmly 침착하게 항의를 다루다
- react calmly to the situation 그 상황에 침착하게 대응하다

☐ **severely**
심하게, 혹독하게, 엄하게
- The car was severely damaged. 그 차는 심하게 파손되었다.
- be punished severely 엄하게 처벌받다

☐ **widely**
널리, 광범위하게
- a newspaper that is distributed widely 널리 배포되는 신문
- Internet has been widely used for decades. 인터넷은 수십 년간 널리 사용되어 왔다.

☐ **significantly**
상당히, 크게
- This system is significantly more effective. 이 시스템은 상당히 더 효과적이다.
- increase the number of employees significantly 직원 수를 크게 늘리다

☐ **briefly**
간략하게, 잠시
- It can be briefly summarized as follows. 그것은 다음과 같이 간략하게 요약될 수 있다.
- They briefly exchanged greetings. 그들은 잠시 인사를 나누었다.

☐ **cautiously**
조심스럽게, 신중히
- handle the laboratory equipment cautiously 실험실 장비를 조심해 다루다
- be advised to drive very cautiously 매우 조심해 운전하도록 권고받다

☐ **slightly**
약간, 조금
- Oil prices rose slightly. 석유 가격이 약간 올랐다.
- He moved to a slightly larger company. 그는 조금 더 큰 회사로 옮겼다.

☐ **regularly**
정기적으로, 규칙적으로
- the next regularly scheduled meeting 다음 정례 회의
- The plants are spaced regularly. 식물들은 규칙적인 간격으로 떨어져 있다.

☐ **fortunately**
운 좋게, 다행히
- He fortunately arrived on time. 그는 운 좋게 정시에 도착했다.
- Fortunately, no one was hurt. 다행히 아무도 다치지 않았다.

☐ **securely**
안전하게, 튼튼하게
- Make sure the door is securely locked. 문이 단단히 잠겼는지 확인하세요.
- wrap the mirror securely 거울을 튼튼하게 포장하다

☐ **initially**
처음에
- initially pay all class fees 처음에 모든 수업료를 내다
- They initially resisted the changes of billing policy.
  그들은 처음에는 결제 정책 변경에 저항했다.

Practice

정답 및 해설 p.136

A. 괄호에서 적절한 것을 고르세요.

1. Though the basic programs are already installed upon purchase, other advanced application programs must be installed (loosely / separately).

2. Within the short time, archaeologist Terry Ardman will (briefly / strongly) explain the history behind the strange writings on the wall.

3. Breaking news reported that the storm (severely / crisply) damaged the homes of residents in the State of Texas.

4. The new Italian restaurant that opened today was (consecutively / formerly) a French bakery.

B. 빈칸에 가장 적절한 것을 고르세요.

5. The air filters should be changed ------- to keep the fans clean.
   (A) gently
   (B) perfectly
   (C) considerably
   (D) regularly

6. While traveling by airplane, your seatbelt should be ------- fastened at all times.
   (A) securely
   (B) partially
   (C) vastly
   (D) hastily

7. Steel prices rose -------, which was followed by an increase in the transaction volume.
   (A) repeatedly
   (B) slightly
   (C) rarely
   (D) blindly

8. Meteorologist Ian Simeons has studied how the climate has changed ------- over the years.
   (A) delightfully
   (B) endlessly
   (C) distantly
   (D) significantly

어휘 1 install 설치하다 purchase 구매 application program 응용 프로그램 2 archaeologist 고고학자 explain 설명하다 strange 이상한 3 breaking news 속보 damage 피해를 입히다 4 bakery 빵집 5 air filter 공기 필터 fan 환풍기 6 fasten 매다, 고정시키다 at all times 항상 7 transaction volume 거래량 8 meteorologist 기상학자 climate 기후

Actual Test

1 ------- the problem persists after the machine is repaired, call the maintenance office.
(A) So
(B) If
(C) Such
(D) Even

2 Mrs. Smith will visit the new restaurant in the town ------- it is operational.
(A) thanks to
(B) due to
(C) as soon as
(D) as well as

3 ------- Ryan was fired due to a huge misunderstanding, he had been considered one of the most remarkable employees in the company.
(A) Until
(B) Unless
(C) Before
(D) Despite

4 ------- Macro Star Inc. claimed bankruptcy on television, most of its investors immediately sold their stocks.
(A) So
(B) Already
(C) Along
(D) Once

5 Owing to financial issues, the construction will be temporarily paused ------- the end of the year.
(A) whether
(B) until
(C) when
(D) yet

6 Please update your changed address online ------- you can receive the monthly statement.
(A) such as
(B) so that
(C) because of
(D) but also

7 ------- the difficulties he has faced in managing the company, Mr. Gatersman remains the number one CEO nationwide.
(A) Neither
(B) As
(C) Despite
(D) Although

8 Mike chose to remain at the headquarters of his company ------- being sent to a branch abroad as a new executive officer.
(A) in order that
(B) even if
(C) instead of
(D) because

Questions 9-12 refer to the following notice.

The leading IOA Company is currently offering job vacancies for recent university graduates who are searching for a career in the business world. No previous --- 9. --- is required.

The company will continuously provide training to new employees. Those who wish to apply should not only be creative but also possess strong communication and leadership skills. --- 10. --- it is not necessary for candidates to have majored in economics or marketing, it is preferable.

--- 11. ---. To apply for one of our positions, you must first send your complete résumé with a photograph to info@leadingioa.com. Subsequently, you --- 12. --- an application form that will need to be completed and returned. The deadline for sending the completed form will be mentioned in the e-mail containing the application form.

9 (A) product
   (B) account
   (C) technology
   (D) experience

10 (A) Even though
   (B) Because
   (C) Despite
   (D) Whenever

NEW
11 (A) Please first fill out an application through our website before sending your resume.
   (B) Currently, you cannot apply for jobs through our website.
   (C) Economics is a compulsory subject in college.
   (D) Most of the seniors in the company majored in economics and marketing.

12 (A) were sent
   (B) will be sent
   (C) are being sent
   (D) will have been sent

Part 5-6

Unit 18 비교 구문

비교 구문은 둘 이상의 대상들을 비교할 때 형용사와 부사의 변화형을 사용해 비교 대상의 상태나 성질의 정도를 나타내는 것입니다. 비교 구문에는 원급, 비교급, 최상급의 세 유형이 있습니다. 비교 구문은 난이도가 낮은 유형이라 반드시 정답을 선택해야 합니다. 기본 유형이 꾸준히 출제되고 있으므로 이에 대비해야 합니다.

원급, 비교급, 최상급의 형태

	원급	비교급	최상급
1음절	old	older	oldest
	long	longer	longest
	short	shorter	shortest
-e로 끝나는 단어	large	larger	largest
자음+y	easy	easier	easiest
	busy	busier	busiest
	heavy	heavier	heaviest
단모음+자음	hot	hotter	hottest
	big	bigger	biggest
2음절 이상 일부 단어 3음절 이상 모든 단어	famous	more famous	most famous
	difficult	more difficult	most difficult
	interesting	more interesting	most interesting
	useful	more useful	most useful
불규칙 변화	good/well	better	best
	bad/ill	worse	worst
	many/much	more	most
	little	less	least

▶ **비교급을 수식하는 부사**: much/even/far/still/a lot/significantly/considerably

This river is even wider than the one on the back of the building. 이 강은 건물 뒤의 강보다 훨씬 더 넓다.

▶ **최상급을 수식하는 부사**: even/simply/by far/single/ever/possible

One of the single most commonly used tools in today's society is the computer.
현대 사회에서 가장 흔히 사용되는 도구들 중의 하나는 컴퓨터이다.

원급, 비교급, 최상급 문장

원급, 비교급, 최상급이 문장에서 어떻게 쓰이는지 문장을 통해 알아보겠습니다.

	The quality is important. 품질이 중요하다.
원급	The quality is as important as the quantity. 품질이 양만큼 중요하다.
비교급	The quality is more important than the quantity. 품질이 양보다 더 중요하다.
최상급	The quality is the most important of all things. 품질이 모든 것들 중에서 가장 중요하다.

The population is now growing faster in urban as rural areas. (X)
→ The population is now growing faster in urban than in rural areas. (O)
★ 비교급에는 than을 사용하고 원급에는 as를 사용합니다.

비교 대상

▶ 짝 맞추기

비교 대상의 앞뒤에는 같은 형식이 와야 합니다.

The population is now growing faster in urban than rural areas. (X)
→ The population is now growing faster in urban than in rural areas. (O)
인구가 이제 농촌 지역보다 도시 지역에서 더 빠르게 증가하고 있다.

★ 비교급 앞뒤에는 같은 형식이 와야 하므로 전치사 in이 빠지면 안 됩니다.

▶ 비교급의 미묘한 의미 차이

He likes dogs more than I. 그는 개를 내가 좋아하는 것보다 더 좋아한다.
★ 개를 좋아하는 정도를 비교합니다.

He likes dogs more than me. 그는 나보다 개를 더 좋아한다.
★ 좋아하는 대상을 비교합니다.

1 시험에 반드시 나오는 원급

as+형용사/부사+as

▶ as+형용사+as

Home education is as important as school education. 가정 교육은 학교 교육만큼 중요하다.
★ be동사 뒤에서 보어 역할을 하는 형용사입니다.

The system is not as reliable as the traditional method. 이 시스템은 전통 방식만큼 신뢰할 수 없다.
★ be동사 뒤에서 보어 역할을 하는 형용사입니다.

▶ as+부사+as

This fax machine works as efficiently as a new model. 이 팩스 기계는 새 모델만큼 효과적으로 작동한다.
★ 앞의 일반동사 works를 수식하는 부사입니다.

Ms. Rocha did not have the time to examine the report as carefully as she had planned.
Rocha 씨는 계획했던 만큼 꼼꼼히 보고서를 조사할 시간이 없었다.
★ 앞의 일반동사 examine을 수식하는 부사입니다.

원급 표현

▶ the same+(형용사)+명사+as: ~와 같은

The school offers education at the same cost as government schools. 그 학교는 공립 학교와 같은 비용으로 교육을 제공한다.

▶ as+many/much/few/little+명사+as: ~만큼이나 많은

Fund managers make as many mistakes as beginner investors. 펀드매니저들은 초보 투자자들만큼이나 많은 실수를 한다.

▶ as+형용사/부사+as possible: 가능한 한 ~한/하게

After landing, please vacate the runway as rapidly as possible. 착륙한 후에는 활주로를 가능한 한 빨리 비워 주세요.

Practice

정답 및 해설 p.141

A. 괄호에서 적절한 것을 고르세요.

1. To minimize the hazards associated with takeoffs, the airplane's weight must be transferred from the wheels to the wings as (rapid / rapidly) as possible.

2. Smartphone users consume twice (as much / so many) data as devices from three years ago.

3. Patients who wish to save time and avoid waiting should be as (specific / specification) as possible when filling out the registration form.

4. The FlipBucket online shopping Web site offers brand-new golf clubs at the same price (that / as) secondhand golf clubs at the retail store.

B. 빈칸에 가장 적절한 것을 고르세요.

5. Participants were disappointed when they learned that the camping site would be the ------- as the one they had visited last year.
   (A) same
   (B) equal
   (C) repeat
   (D) fewest

6. New drivers have twice ------- accidents as experienced drivers.
   (A) as many
   (B) much more
   (C) more than
   (D) too much

7. Real estate agents must create a clear sale plan to ensure that the sales process runs as ------- as possible.
   (A) smoothing
   (B) smoother
   (C) smoothest
   (D) smoothly

8. Owing to the popularity of the Power-X5 energy drink, the beverage can be easily found in local convenience stores as ------- as in supermarkets and pharmacies.
   (A) good
   (B) far
   (C) well
   (D) near

어휘 1 minimize 최소화하다 hazard 위험 associated with ~와 관련된 takeoff 이륙 weight 무게 transfer 옮기다, 이동시키다 2 consume 소비하다 device 장치, 기기 3 patient 환자 avoid 피하다 fill out 기입하다 registration form 등록 양식 4 secondhand 중고품의 retail store 소매점 5 participant 참가자 disappointed 실망한 learn 알다 6 accident 사고 experienced 경험 많은 7 real estate agent 부동산 중개업자 create 만들다 ensure 반드시 ~하게 하다 process 과정 8 owing to ~ 때문에 popularity 인기 beverage 음료 convenience store 편의점 pharmacy 약국

2 시험에 반드시 나오는 비교급과 최상급

 비교급

▶ 비교급의 형태

[형용사] 2음절 이하 형용사+-er+than / more+3음절 이상 형용사+than

[부사] more+부사+than

Buying a new computer would be cheaper than fixing broken parts.
새 컴퓨터를 사는 것이 고장 난 부품들을 고치는 것보다 더 쌀 것이다.

This year's final exam was more difficult than I thought it would be.
금년 기말고사는 내가 생각했던 것보다 더 어려웠다.

▶ 비교급의 관용표현

- the+비교급, the+비교급: ~할수록 더욱 ~하다

  The more advanced your equipment is, the better its performance is. 장비가 고급일수록 성능이 더 좋다.

- of the two ~, the+비교급: 둘 중에서 더 ~한

  Of the two students, Kelly is the better in chemistry. 두 학생 중에서 Kelly가 화학을 더 잘한다.

- no later than (=by): 늦어도 ~까지는

  Applicants must submit their documents no later than October 20. 지원자들은 늦어도 10월 20일까지는 서류를 제출해야만 한다.

- no longer: 더 이상 ~ 아니다

  A visit to the moon is no longer a dream. 달에 가는 것은 더 이상 꿈이 아니다.

 최상급

▶ 최상급의 형태

[형용사] the+2음절 이하 형용사+-est / the most+3음절 이상 형용사

[부사] (the) most+부사

Sunflower Grill is the largest restaurant in this city. Sunflower Grill은 이 도시에서 가장 큰 식당이다.
The S100 is the most highly advanced digital camera. S100은 최첨단 디지털 카메라이다.

Practice

정답 및 해설 p.142

A. 괄호에서 적절한 것을 고르세요.

1. Based on the statistical data recorded this year, Tokyo Metro is still the (faster / fastest) transit system in the world.

2. The new DMX25 camera's shutter speed is far (quickly / quicker) than the famous FT40 model.

3. Melinda Love interviewed two of the (more prominently / most prominent) senators on their newly proposed immigration reform policy.

4. The batteries of laptops designed by SwitchTag Electronics lasted considerably longer (than / to) those produced by rival companies.

B. 빈칸에 가장 적절한 것을 고르세요.

5. Drivers were advised to drive even ------- than usual this week because of icy roads and heavy fog.
   (A) most careful
   (B) more careful
   (C) more carefully
   (D) most carefully

6. The chefs at Keiko Sushi restaurant said that they use the ------- fish, fruits, and vegetables in all their seafood dishes.
   (A) freshness
   (B) fresher
   (C) freshly
   (D) freshest

7. Mr. Barnet is the ------- of the two candidates to engage in negotiations with other nations.
   (A) good
   (B) better
   (C) best
   (D) any good

8. A person can lose up to 40 percent of body heat from an unprotected head and ------- more from the neck, wrist, and ankles when surviving cold weather.
   (A) all
   (B) very
   (C) any
   (D) even

어휘 ¹ based on ~에 근거하여 statistical 통계의 transit 운송, 수송 ² far 훨씬, 더 famous 유명한 ³ senator 상원 의원 propose 발의하다 immigration 이민 reform 개혁 ⁴ laptop 노트북 last 지속되다 considerably 상당히 ⁵ even 더욱, 한층 icy road 빙판길 ⁶ chef 요리사 seafood 해산물 dish 요리 ⁷ candidate 후보 engage in ~에 관여하다, 종사하다 negotiation 협상 ⁸ body heat 체열 wrist 손목 ankle 발목 survive ~에서 생존하다, 견뎌 내다

3 반드시 알아야 하는 기출 부사 어휘 ④

☐ **carefully** 주의 깊게, 신중히	• **carefully** examine the problems 그 문제들을 주의 깊게 조사하다 • by **carefully** considering their special needs 그들의 특별한 욕구를 신중히 고려함으로써	
☐ **currently** 현재는, 지금은	• The Web site is **currently** unavailable. 그 웹사이트는 현재 이용할 수 없다. • We are **currently** processing orders. 우리는 지금 주문들을 처리하고 있다.	
☐ **evenly** 평평하게, 고르게	• spread paint **evenly** on walls 벽들에 페인트를 고르게 칠하다 • apply the cream **evenly** over the skin 크림을 피부에 골고루 바르다	
☐ **thoroughly** 완전히, 철저히	• We have finished the project **thoroughly**. 우리는 그 프로젝트를 완전히 끝냈다. • Wash apples **thoroughly** before eating. 사과를 먹기 전에 철저히 씻어라.	
☐ **quickly** 빨리, 신속히	• as **quickly** as possible 가능한 한 빨리 • He **quickly** learned the ropes. 그는 재빨리 요령을 터득했다.	
☐ **smoothly** 부드럽게, 순조롭게	• The interview went very **smoothly**. 면접은 아주 순조롭게 진행되었다. • Traffic is flowing **smoothly**. 교통 흐름이 원활하다.	
☐ **fairly** 상당히, 꽤	• This type is **fairly** common. 이런 유형은 무척 흔하다. • a **fairly** difficult book 아주 어려운 책	
☐ **skillfully** 솜씨 있게, 교묘하게	• The house was **skillfully** constructed. 그 집은 솜씨 좋게 지어졌다. • **skillfully** evade the law 법망을 교묘히 빠져나가다	
☐ **instantly** 즉시, 당장	• His face is memorable, **instantly** recognizable. 그의 얼굴은 기억하기 쉽고 즉시 알아볼 수 있다. • **instantly** turn into a madhouse 순식간에 아수라장으로 변하다	
☐ **repeatedly** 되풀이해, 거듭해	• **repeatedly** deny the allegations 혐의를 거듭 부인하다 • **repeatedly** underline that point 그 점을 거듭 강조하다	
☐ **sparingly** 절약하여, 조금만	• Use water **sparingly**. 물을 아껴 쓰세요. • Use lengthy footnotes **sparingly**. 긴 각주는 조금만 사용하세요.	
☐ **strictly** 엄격히, 엄밀히	• The regulations will be **strictly** enforced. 그 규정은 엄격하게 시행될 것이다. • Smoking is **strictly** forbidden. 흡연이 엄격하게 금지된다.	
☐ **tightly** 단단히, 꽉, 엄중히	• He hugged his daughter **tightly**. 그는 딸을 꼭 껴안았다. • a substance which is **tightly** regulated 엄중히 규제되는 물질	
☐ **unexpectedly** 뜻밖에, 예상외로	• The restaurant has been **unexpectedly** busy. 그 식당이 뜻밖에 분주하다. • due to **unexpectedly** high shipping costs 예상외의 높은 발송비로 인해	
☐ **urgently** 긴급히	• They **urgently** need security guards. 그들은 경호원이 긴급히 필요하다. • We are **urgently** seeking full-time instructors. 긴급히 정규직 강사를 구합니다.	

Practice

정답 및 해설 p.143

A. 괄호에서 적절한 것을 고르세요.

1. A conference was held (totally / urgently) this morning to announce a temporary halt in the production processes at all factories.

2. Ensure that the cap is screwed on (warmly / tightly), so that no detergent can enter the container during the wash cycle.

3. Ms. Loren Amelia examined the weekly reports (thoroughly / interestingly) and filled in the assessment papers.

4. The company's new Web site was (skillfully / recklessly) designed by Mr. Cory Hans, our computer specialist.

B. 빈칸에 가장 적절한 것을 고르세요.

5. The final changes need to be submitted ------- so that the complete book may be published as per schedule.
   (A) terribly
   (B) kindly
   (C) nearly
   (D) quickly

6. The negotiation talks proceeded ------- and both parties were satisfied in the end.
   (A) extremely
   (B) personally
   (C) smoothly
   (D) constantly

7. Scientists are ------- researching new sources of energy, such as hydroelectricity, to protect the ecosystem.
   (A) miserably
   (B) currently
   (C) silently
   (D) furiously

8. Students were advised to listen to the instructor ------- and ask any questions that they wanted answered.
   (A) anxiously
   (B) carefully
   (C) elegantly
   (D) wonderfully

어휘 **1** announce 발표하다 temporary 일시적인 halt 중단 **2** ensure 반드시 ~하게 하다 cap 뚜껑 screw 죄다, 비틀어 돌리다 detergent 세제 container 용기 **3** fill in 기입하다 assessment paper 평가서 **4** specialist 전문가 **5** submit 제출하다 complete 완전한 publish 출판하다 **6** negotiation 협상 proceed 진행되다 party 당사자 satisfied 만족한 **7** source 원천 hydroelectricity 수력 전기 protect 보호하다 ecosystem 생태계 **8** instructor 강사

Actual Test

1 If the floors, carpets, and walls become wet, it's imperative to dry them out as ------- as possible to prevent mold growth.

(A) quick
(B) quicker
(C) quickest
(D) quickly

2 Please provide us ------- information as possible so that we can best assist you with your needs.

(A) so far
(B) so long
(C) as much
(D) as long as

3 A research study has found that babies as young ------- six months of age can read each other's moods in certain situations.

(A) as
(B) than
(C) of
(D) at

4 You should handle the books in the public library as ------- as you do your own property.

(A) carefully
(B) careful
(C) to care
(D) more careful

5 Allen Ramirez said that his ------- accomplishment at Tibejin University was constructing the student service center.

(A) gratify
(B) more gratified
(C) most gratifying
(D) gratifyingly

6 After a series of rigorous meetings and negotiations, the committee finally agreed upon purchasing the product with the ------- design.

(A) more efficiencies
(B) more efficiently
(C) most efficiently
(D) most efficient

7 The construction projects planned this season in Nebraska's largest city are starting ------- than expected because of the prolonged winter.

(A) late
(B) lately
(C) later
(D) latest

8 Due to the drastic changes in technology, film is ------- the dominant cinematic medium in the digital world.

(A) another
(B) no longer
(C) anymore
(D) not enough

204

Questions 9-12 refer to the following e-mail.

To: Bluewind Office Staff <staffnotice@bluewind.com>
From: Ella Friscal, Assistant Director <ellafriscal@bluewind.com>
Re: VIKI messenger system
Date: April 13
Attachment: viki_messenger.txt

As you all know, our IT communications team has finished developing a new one-touch messenger program, which will be --- 9. --- our current e-mail system on May 20. I have attached a document that explains how the new program has to be installed and introduces the different features of the program. All staff members are required to review this document to ensure that the transition goes as --- 10. --- as possible.
Besides conducting hands-on training for the people who have opted for it, we are offering an in-person information session on Thursday, the 5th of May. However, this session is --- 11. --- to 50 participants only, so if you feel that it is necessary for you to attend this session, do not miss this opportunity.
--- 12. ---.

9 (A) pricing
   (B) replacing
   (C) connecting
   (D) analyzing

10 (A) smoothing
   (B) smoother
   (C) smoothest
   (D) smoothly

11 (A) limit
   (B) limited
   (C) limitation
   (D) limitations

NEW
12 (A) Contact Cindy, our secretary, for any questions and reservations.
   (B) To make a keynote speech, don't forget to contact me.
   (C) Once you've finished filling the application out, please submit it.
   (D) We have large venues to accommodate over a hundred people.

Unit 19 가정법과 도치

Part 5-6

가정법은 실제 일어나지 않은 상황을 일어난 것처럼 가정하는 문장을 말합니다. 현재의 사실을 다르게 가정하는 것을 가정법 과거, 과거의 사실을 다르게 가정하는 것을 가정법 과거완료라고 합니다. 도치는 강조하고 싶은 문장 요소를 문장 맨 앞으로 보내고 주어와 동사의 순서를 바꾸는 것을 말합니다. 문법적으로는 어려운 부분이지만 출제되는 문제 유형은 단순한 편입니다. 실제 토익 시험에 출제되는 가정법과 도치 유형은 주요 개념들만 숙지하면 어렵지 않게 해결할 수 있습니다.

가정법의 종류

▶ **가정법 과거: 현재 사실의 반대를 가정합니다.**

If I had money, I would treat you. 내게 돈이 있다면 네게 한턱낼 수 있을 것이다.
If he were rich, he would buy that building. 그가 부자라면 그 건물을 살 것이다.
If I were you, I would visit his home. 내가 너라면 그의 집을 방문할 것이다.

★ be동사의 경우 주어의 수와 인칭에 관계없이 항상 were를 사용한다는 것에 유의해야 합니다.

▶ **가정법 과거완료: 과거 사실의 반대를 가정합니다.**

If she had not been sick, she could have done it within the deadline.
그녀가 아프지 않았다면 마감 기한 내에 그것을 끝낼 수 있었을 것이다.

If I had enough money, I would have bought a car. 내게 충분한 돈이 있었다면 차를 샀을 것이다.

▶ **가정법 미래: 미래의 희박한 가능성을 나타냅니다.**

If it should rain, I will stay home. 내일 비가 온다면 나는 집에 있을 것이다.
If you should find any defects, you can call me. 혹시 결함을 발견하신다면 제게 전화하시면 됩니다.

★ please+동사원형과 can/may/should+동사원형도 미래 의미로 사용됩니다.

도치

강조하고 싶은 말을 앞으로 보낼 때 주어와 동사의 순서가 바뀌게 됩니다.

▶ **일반동사의 도치**

He rarely called her at night. → Rarely did he call her at night. 그가 그녀에게 밤에 전화하는 일은 거의 없었다.
★ 동사 do(does, did)를 주어 앞으로 보내고 원래 동사를 원형으로 바꾸어 줍니다.

▶ **be/have/조동사의 도치**

I had never dreamed I would work under her.
→ Never had I dreamed I would work under her. 내가 그녀 밑에서 일하게 될 줄은 꿈에도 생각하지 못했다.
★ be/have/조동사가 주어 앞으로 나갑니다.

1 시험에 반드시 나오는 가정법 형태

가정법 과거

▶ ~하다면 ~할 것이다 (현재 사실의 반대)

If+주어+과거 시제, 주어+would/could/might+동사원형

If the car had an automatic transmission, I would buy it. 그 차에 자동변속기가 있다면 그것을 살 것이다.

가정법 과거완료

▶ ~했다면 ~했을 것이다 (과거 사실의 반대)

If+주어+과거완료 (had p.p.), 주어+would/could/might+have p.p.

If he had remained in the race, Mr. Chen would have won the election.
Chen 씨가 선거 경쟁에 남아 있었더라면 선거에서 이길 수 있었을 것이다.

가정법 미래

▶ 혹시 ~하면 ~할 것이다/하세요. (실현 가능성이 낮은 미래)

If+주어+should+동사원형, 주어+미래 시제/동사원형 (명령문)

If you should have any concerns, please feel free to contact me. 혹시 걱정되는 게 있으시면 부담 갖지 마시고 제게 연락하세요.

- if 조건절: ~하다면 ~할 것이다/하세요. (실현 가능성이 있는 미래)

    If+주어+현재 동사, 주어+현재/미래 시제

    If the report is true, I will employ him. 그 보고서가 사실이라면 그를 고용할 것이다.

혼합 가정법

▶ ~했다면 지금 ~할 것이다

If+주어+과거완료 (had p.p.), 주어+would/could/might+동사원형+(by) now

If you had listened to my advice, there would be no problem now.
네가 내 충고에 귀를 기울였다면 지금 아무런 문제가 없을 것이다.

Practice

정답 및 해설 p.148

A. 괄호에서 적절한 것을 고르세요.

1. If your visa application is submitted, you (are sent / will be sent) a package with your passport and visa soon.

2. If anyone (will wish / wishes) to enter the Shin Technology Inc. building, he or she will be requested to show an ID card to a security officer.

3. If the product had been advertised, we (would have achieved / achieved) our monthly sales goal.

4. If our company had received more financial support, the factory renovation (had been beginning / could have begun) much earlier.

B. 빈칸에 가장 적절한 것을 고르세요.

5. If the fresh ingredients ------- on time, the restaurant could sell much more of its dessert now.
   (A) had been arriving
   (B) would arrive
   (C) had arrived
   (D) will arrive

6. If the mall was built in a larger area with more shops, it ------- more employees.
   (A) could have hired
   (B) could hire
   (C) will hire
   (D) hired

7. If I had been promoted last quarter, I ------- earning much more than I am now.
   (A) have been
   (B) could have been
   (C) will be
   (D) had been

8. Cindy wouldn't have missed the seminar if she ------- the flight last night.
   (A) had been caught
   (B) had caught
   (C) caught
   (D) catch

어휘 / 1 application 신청(서) submit 제출하다 passport 여권 2 security officer 경비원 3 advertise 광고하다 goal 목표 4 support 지원 factory 공장 5 ingredient 재료, 성분 dessert 디저트 6 area 지역, 구역 employee 직원 7 be promoted 승진하다 quarter 분기 8 miss 놓치다

2 시험에 반드시 나오는 도치 유형

가정법의 도치

가정법 문장에서 if가 생략되면서 동사가 주어 앞으로 나옵니다.

If+주어+had p.p. → Had+주어+p.p. / If+주어+should+동사원형 → Should+주어+동사원형
Had I been there, I could have helped you. 내가 거기 있었다면 너를 도울 수 있었을 것이다.
Should you need further information, contact me. 혹시 더 많은 정보가 필요하시면 제게 연락하세요.

그 외의 도치

▶ **부정어가 문장 앞에 올 때**

hardly/seldom/scarcely/rarely+동사+주어: 거의/좀처럼 ~하지 않다
never+동사+주어: 결코 ~하지 않다   not only+동사+주어: ~할 뿐만 아니라
Never did I imagine that you would become a professor. 나는 네가 교수가 되리라고는 전혀 상상하지 못했다.

▶ **so, nor, neither가 문장 앞에 올 때**

긍정문, so+동사+주어: ~하고 ~하기도 한다 / 부정문, nor[neither]+동사+주어: ~하지 않고 ~하지도 않는다
The people thought it was a type of medication, and **so did others**.
그 사람들도 그것이 약의 일종이라고 생각했고 다른 사람들도 그렇게 생각했다.

He didn't call me, **nor did he answer** the phone. 그는 내게 전화하지도 않았고 전화를 받지도 않았다.
There is no railroad system in Tanzania, **nor is there** a subway system. 탄자니아에는 철도도 없고 지하철도 없다.

▶ **be동사의 보어가 문장 앞에 올 때**

Attached+be동사+주어: ~에 첨부된 / Enclosed+be동사+주어: ~에 동봉된
Attached is a tentative schedule of the event. 첨부된 것은 임시 행사 일정입니다.

▶ **only+부사/부사구/부사절이 문장 앞에 올 때**

Only+부사/부사구/부사절+동사+주어: ~에야 비로소
Only recently have we decided to move. 최근에서야 우리는 이사하기로 결정했다.

▶ **as가 문장 앞에 올 때**

as+동사+주어: 마찬가지로, ~처럼
We continue to do research on it **as are many other companies**.
우리는 다른 여러 회사와 마찬가지로 그것에 관해 연구를 계속하고 있습니다.

Practice

정답 및 해설 p.149

A. 괄호에서 적절한 것을 고르세요.

1 (Not only / Even if) did the samples arrive two weeks late but they were also severely damaged.

2 Had we (been found / found) out that the CEO was involved in embezzlement, we would have fired him.

3 (Solely / Rarely) has the weather in London been much better than it was last summer.

4 (Seldom / Also) have the sales volumes of Best Trekkers Inc. been higher than they are currently.

B. 빈칸에 가장 적절한 것을 고르세요.

5 ------- you have any concerns about our service, please find our receptionist in the lobby.
   (A) Should
   (B) Could
   (C) Can
   (D) May

6 ------- is a letter that Galen recently wrote to his father.
   (A) Enclosure
   (B) Enclosed
   (C) Encloses
   (D) Enclose

7 Mark Lieberman proposed a solution for the company's current downturn and ------- did his coworker, Nina Haruka.
   (A) or
   (B) so
   (C) either
   (D) and

8 Mr. Brown graduated the university with honors this summer, ------- did Ms. Bailey.
   (A) as
   (B) although
   (C) more
   (D) very

어휘 1 severely 심하게 damage 손상시키다 2 embezzlement 횡령 fire 해고하다 3 weather 날씨 4 volume 양 currently 현재는, 지금은 5 concern 관심사, 용무 receptionist 접수 직원 6 recently 최근에 7 propose 제안하다 solution 해결책 current 현재의 downturn 하락, 침체 8 graduate 졸업하다 with honors 우등으로

3 고득점을 위한 고난이도 어휘

- [ ] **lapse**
  실수, 과실
  - even a minor lapse in product quality 제품 품질의 사소한 실수조차도
  - a remarkable lapse of judgment 중대한 판단 착오

- [ ] **disruption**
  붕괴, 중단, 장애
  - recent disruption in Internet service 최근의 인터넷 서비스 중단
  - avoid disruption to production 생산 차질을 피하다

- [ ] **inquisitive**
  캐묻기 좋아하는, 호기심 많은
  - They are so inquisitive about his research. 그들은 그의 조사에 대해 무척 궁금해한다.
  - Children are naturally inquisitive. 아이들은 본래 캐묻기 좋아한다.

- [ ] **methodically**
  체계적으로, 조직적으로
  - methodically arrange the papers 서류를 체계적으로 정리하다
  - methodically search the drawers 서랍들을 찬찬히 뒤지다

- [ ] **premises**
  건물, 구내
  - take a tour of the premises 구내를 둘러보다
  - Smoking is not allowed on the premises. 구내에서는 흡연이 허용되지 않습니다.

- [ ] **impeccable**
  흠잡을 데 없는
  - the owner's impeccable taste 주인의 흠잡을 데 없는 취향
  - provide passengers with impeccable service 승객들에게 완벽한 서비스를 제공하다

- [ ] **ample**
  충분한, 풍부한
  - ample parking space 충분한 주차 공간
  - He has ample experience. 그는 경험이 풍부하다.

- [ ] **improbable**
  일어날 것 같지 않은, 사실 같지 않은
  - It seems improbable that the recession will continue. 불황이 계속될 것 같지는 않다.
  - an improbable story 사실 같지 않은 이야기

- [ ] **deliberate**
  의도[계획]적인, 신중한
  - deliberate efforts to appeal to readers 독자의 흥미를 끌려는 계획적인 노력
  - a deliberate political decision 신중한 정치적 결정

- [ ] **maneuverable**
  조종[조작]하기 쉬운
  - develop a more maneuverable ship 기동성이 더 좋은 배를 개발하다
  - The cars are not very maneuverable in the narrow streets. 그 차들은 좁은 거리에서 운전하기가 쉽지 않다.

- [ ] **courteous**
  예의 바른, 공손한
  - Please be courteous. 예의 바르게 행동해 주시기 바랍니다.
  - in a very polite and courteous manner 아주 예의 바르고 공손한 태도로

- [ ] **attentively**
  주의 깊게, 조심스럽게
  - listen attentively to her words 그녀의 말을 경청하다
  - handle customer suggestions more attentively 고객 의견들을 더 주의 깊게 다루다

- [ ] **conceive**
  구상하다, 마음에 품다
  - She conceived a warm affection for her son. 그녀는 아들에게 따뜻한 애정을 품었다.
  - He conceived the idea of building a hotel. 그는 호텔을 지을 아이디어를 구상했다.

- [ ] **exclusively**
  배타적으로, 독점적으로, 전적으로
  - those exclusively responsible for that work 그 일을 전담하는 사람들
  - She works as a model exclusively for that agency. 그녀는 그 에이전시의 전속 모델로 활동하고 있다.

- [ ] **waive**
  (권리를) 포기하다,
  (규정을) 적용하지 않다
  - waive tuition for students from low-income families 저소득 가정 학생들에게 수업료를 면제해 주다
  - The museum waives admission fee on Sundays. 그 박물관은 일요일에는 입장료를 받지 않는다.

Practice

정답 및 해설 p.151

A. 괄호에서 적절한 것을 고르세요.

1. Queens.com uses a better cardboard box with (ample / temporary) packing material for your item.

2. Even a minor (lapse / inclination) can cause the rejection of the enrollment.

3. We look for people who are so (confidential / inquisitive) about the world that they're willing to try anything.

4. Bridge rehabilitation work will be completed by tomorrow to minimize the traffic (outbreak / disruption).

B. 빈칸에 가장 적절한 것을 고르세요.

5. The goal of this meeting is to teach counselor how to listen to workers' problems more -------.
   (A) structurally
   (B) immediately
   (C) unexpectedly
   (D) attentively

6. Anyone who likes the same songs as me has ------- taste in music.
   (A) fragile
   (B) impeccable
   (C) surpassed
   (D) worthwhile

7. This special offer is available ------- to the members who purchase a used vehicle from Enterprise Car Sales.
   (A) exceptionally
   (B) impossibly
   (C) exclusively
   (D) unclearly

8. Under the law, the government will ------- the current 15.4 percent tax on such gains for three years.
   (A) reject
   (B) delete
   (C) waive
   (D) obtain

어휘 1 cardboard box 종이 상자 packing material 포장 재료 2 minor 중요하지 않은 rejection 거부, 거절 enrollment 등록 3 look for 찾다 be willing to 기꺼이 ~하다 4 rehabilitation 재건 minimize 최소화하다 5 counsellor 상담가 problem 문제 6 taste 취향, 안목 7 available 이용할 수 있는 purchase 구입하다 used vehicle 중고 차량 8 tax 세금 gains 소득

Unit 19 : 가정법과 도치

Actual Test

1. If you ------- a new patient at this hospital, please fill out the personal information form.
   (A) were
   (B) will
   (C) be
   (D) are

2. If the chief executive officer ------- the supervisor's inability to manage the factory line, some action could have been taken.
   (A) has known
   (B) had known
   (C) knew
   (D) have known

3. If the items you borrowed are not turned in by tomorrow, your membership ------- terminated.
   (A) would be
   (B) will be
   (C) be
   (D) was

4. If Mr. Kawasaki had not brought the document with him, his boss ------- to the office.
   (A) being return
   (B) will return
   (C) would have returned
   (D) have returned

5. ------- to this e-mail are the instructions that should be followed at work.
   (A) Attaching
   (B) Attached
   (C) Attach
   (D) Attachment

6. ------- has Mr. Brown been seen in his office since he was elected as vice president of the local committee.
   (A) Hard
   (B) Hardly
   (C) Hardness
   (D) Harden

7. Hospal Inn does not refund the deposit, ------- does it guarantee vacancy of unreserved rooms.
   (A) nor
   (B) but
   (C) or
   (D) and

8. Only recently have organizations ------- that their success is directly linked to the quality of their leaders.
   (A) to recognize
   (B) recognized
   (C) recognition
   (D) recognizing

Questions 9-12 refer to the following letter.

S.A.F.E. Security Corporation
4112 Westwood Street
Stamford on T3L4A7

Dear Mrs. and Mr. Chester:

Thank you for visiting us regarding your home security installments. Upon your request, your monthly payments for our services of $350 will be automatically withdrawn on the 27th of every month from your checking account. --- 9. --- your security alarm device encounter any problems, we will be able to observe these from our monitoring channels.
In case you wish to cancel this service, you need to file an --- 10. --- request. You can visit us at our office, send a mail to the address mentioned above, or fax us at 711-555-1131.
For further questions, please contact our Customer Service Center at 711-555-1132. We will be available to assist you over the phone every day from 9 a.m. to 10 p.m.
--- 11. ---, if you wish to contact us through e-mail, please send an e-mail to service@safesecurity.com. --- 12. ---.

9 (A) Did
   (B) Had
   (C) Should
   (D) Could

10 (A) equivalent
   (B) official
   (C) intended
   (D) outstanding

11 (A) Favorably
   (B) Originally
   (C) Accordingly
   (D) Alternatively

NEW
12 (A) In order to change your email address, please contact me directly.
   (B) All public phones in this building are temporarily out of order.
   (C) We will respond to your email within 24 hours.
   (D) Your feedback is very important to us.

Unit 01 ● 주제와 목적	Unit 11 ● 기사
Unit 02 ● 구체적 정보	Unit 12 ● 송장과 양식
Unit 03 ● NOT/TRUE	Unit 13 ● 초대장
Unit 04 ● 추론	Unit 14 ● 편지·이메일 연계 지문
Unit 05 ● 동의어	Unit 15 ● 광고 연계 지문
Unit 06 ● 편지와 이메일	Unit 16 ● 알림 연계 지문
Unit 07 ● 광고	Unit 17 ● 기사 연계 지문
Unit 08 ● 공지	Unit 18 ● 기타 연계 지문
Unit 09 ● 회람	Unit 19 ● 고득점을 위한 독해 연습
Unit 10 ● 안내문	

Part 7

Unit 01 주제와 목적

Part 7

Part 7에서 20% 정도의 높은 비중을 차지하는 문제 유형이 글의 주제와 목적을 찾는 문제입니다. 이 유형은 대개 각 지문의 첫 번째 문항으로 출제됩니다. 지문의 전체적인 문맥을 파악하고 풀어야 하는 문제 유형이므로 평소 속독의 방법으로 문장을 빠르게 훑어보는 연습을 해두는 것이 좋습니다.

문제유형

▶ **주제를 묻는 유형**

What is the main topic of this memo? 이 회람의 주제는?
What is this article about? 이 기사의 내용은?
What does the notice mainly discuss? 공지에서 주로 논의하는 것은?

▶ **목적을 묻는 유형**

What is the purpose of the letter? 편지의 목적은?
Why was this e-mail written? 이 이메일이 쓰여진 이유는?
What made John write this memo? John이 이 메모를 쓰게 된 이유는?

풀이전략

▶ **주제문은 대부분 지문의 앞부분에 있습니다.**

정보 전달 중심의 실용문들은 대부분 주제를 앞에서 밝히고 세부 내용을 뒤에서 설명하는 구조로 되어 있습니다. 따라서 지문의 첫 두 문장을 읽다 보면 주제를 찾을 수 있는 경우가 많습니다. 그러나 지문의 중간이나 뒤에 주제문이 나오거나 전체 내용을 읽고 주제를 파악하는 문제도 나옵니다. 따라서 첫머리에 주제문이 나오지 않을 때는 글을 계속 읽어 다른 문제들부터 풀어 가며 주제문을 찾아야 합니다.

▶ **주제나 제목 부분을 읽어 문제를 푸는 시간을 절약해야 합니다.**

이메일이나 회람에서는 주제를 밝히는 Subject와 Re: 부분에서 정답의 단서가 제시되기도 합니다. Re:는 Regarding의 약자입니다. 기사문에서는 제목만 읽어도 정답이 나오는 경우가 있습니다.

▶ **다음과 같은 지문 속의 특정 어구 주변에 주제문의 단서가 있습니다.**

Thank you for ~에 대해 감사드립니다
would like to ~하고 싶다
will ~할 것이다
be pleased to ~하게 되어 기쁘다
It is a pleasure to ~하게 되어 기쁘다
therefore 그러므로
regarding ~에 관하여
however 그러나

Sample Test 문제풀이전략을 적용해 기출 유형 예제를 풀어 보세요.

To: Parents of Rifler School District
From: Thomas Bagington
Subject: Closings and Delays
Date: October 3

Dear Parents:

Numerous questions have been raised about the school's policy on closings and delays. As a school district, we realize that the parents must also be kept informed about such issues; therefore, we are sending this e-mail. Schools will only be closed when inclement weather makes it too difficult for buses and other means of transportation to operate safely throughout a school day. Delays and the like will be issued only when it is difficult or dangerous for students to reach school at normal hours due to problems or events.

Events of a school closing or delay will be called in to local radio stations and television networks. I encourage all parents to listen and tune in to more than one method of announcement.

Sincerely,
Thomas Bagington
Superintendent of Schools

Q. What is the purpose of this e-mail?
(A) To hire bus drivers
(B) To announce the closing of a school
(C) To ask parents to volunteer
(D) To notify parents of the school policy

어휘 school district 학군 delay 연기, 지연 policy 정책 realize 실현하다, 깨닫다 keep informed 계속 정보를 통보받다 inclement (날씨가) 험악한, 궂은 means 방법, 수단 transportation 교통수단 operate 작동하다 and the like 기타 비슷한 종류의 것 issue 발표하다 normal 정상적인 call in 전화로 알려주다 encourage 권장하다 method 방법, 방식 volunteer 자원하다 notify 알리다, 통지하다 superintendent 감독관

문제분석

To: Parents of Rifler School District 수신: Rifler 학군 학부모님들께
From: Thomas Bagington 발신: Thomas Bagington
Subject: Closings and Delays 제목: 휴교와 등교 지연
Date: October 3 날짜: 10월 3일

Dear Parents: 학부모님들께

Numerous questions have been raised about the school's policy on closings and delays. As a school district, we realize that parents must also be kept informed about such issues; therefore, we are sending this e-mail. Schools will only be closed when inclement weather makes it difficult for buses and other means of transportation to operate safely throughout a school day. Delays and the like will be issued only when it is difficult or dangerous for students to reach school at normal hours due to problems or events.

휴교와 등교 지연에 관한 학교 방침에 관해 수많은 문의가 있어왔습니다. 학군으로서 저희는 부모님들께서도 이러한 사안들에 대해 항상 알고 계셔야 한다고 생각하여, 이렇게 메일을 보내게 되었습니다. 수업일 하루 종일 악천후로 인해 버스와 다른 교통수단이 안전하게 운행하기가 매우 어려워질 경우에만 휴교할 것입니다. 등교 지연 등의 조치는 문제나 사건으로 인해 학생들이 정상 등교 시간에 학교에 도착하기 어렵거나 위험할 때에만 발표될 것입니다.

Events of a school closing or delay will be called in to local radio stations and television networks. I encourage all parents to listen and tune in to more than one method of announcement.

휴교나 등교 지연 사항은 지역 라디오 방송국과 TV 네트워크로 통보될 것입니다. 모든 부모님들께 한 가지 이상의 공지 방식에 귀를 기울이고 경청해주시기를 권해드립니다.

Sincerely,
Thomas Bagington
Superintendent of Schools 교육감

> 2. 제목을 보면 문제가 되는 내용이 나올 것임을 짐작할 수 있습니다.
>
> 3. 첫 문장과 둘째 문장에서 이메일의 목적을 쉽게 찾을 수 있습니다. 접속사 therefore의 앞뒤에 정답의 단서가 있습니다.

Q. What is the purpose of this e-mail? 이 이메일의 목적은?

(A) To hire bus drivers 버스 기사를 채용하기 위해
(B) To announce the closing of a school 휴교를 발표하기 위해
(C) To ask parents to volunteer 부모들에게 자원봉사를 요청하기 위해
(D) To notify parents of the school policy 학교 방침을 부모들에게 알리기 위해

> 1. 글을 쓴 목적을 묻고 있습니다.
>
> 4. 지문의 be kept informed를 notify로 바꾸어 쓴 (D)가 정답입니다.

해설 지문의 앞부분 we realize that the parents must also be kept informed about such issues; therefore, we are sending this e-mail에서 이 글이 학교 방침에 관해 부모에게 설명하는 글임을 알 수 있다. 따라서 정답은 (D)이다.

Practice

정답 및 해설 p.158

Question 1 refers to the following letter.

> Dear Mrs. Annia,
>
> On behalf of the members of the Storytelling Kids Club, I would like to thank you for creating a wonderful environment for the children at our institute during the past 10 months. Your leadership and devotion as a supervisor has inspired everyone.

1. What is the purpose of this letter?
   (A) To show appreciation of Mrs. Annia's services
   (B) To hire a new supervisor

Question 2 refers to the following memo.

> Dear Colleagues,
>
> Please join us from 5:00 P.M. to 7:00 P.M. on August 27 at the Barkley Conference Room, which is located on the second floor of the Jordan Building, to celebrate Sean Lonergon's return to the company. As you all probably know by now, after spending six months at the hospital, Sean has now fully recovered and will be resuming his duties as assistant director at Calbest Connections next week.

2. What is the main topic of this memo?
   (A) A welcoming party
   (B) An outdoor event

어휘 **1** on behalf of ~을 대표해 environment 환경 institute 기관, 건물 devotion 전념, 헌신 supervisor 감독, 부서장 appreciation 감사, 인정 inspire 자극하다, 영감을 주다 **2** join ~와 함께하다 be located 위치하다 celebrate 축하하다 return 귀환, 복귀 recover 되찾다, 회복하다 duty 근무, 업무 assistant director 차장

Questions 1-2 refer to the following letter.

Dear Mr. Francis,

We are sending you this letter regarding an incorrect payment made. Your telephone bill for January 15-February 15 was $177.87 and we received a payment against this on February 22 from your credit card company. However, the current balance for your bill still shows an unpaid amount of $29.31. This is owing to a previous bill amount that is still outstanding. Please make the payment for this as soon as possible.

Payment can be made by either check or credit card. In case you wish to pay by credit card, the payment can be made online by simply visiting our Web site and logging in. Subsequently, please click on "My Bills" and then make the payment.

If you believe that you have received this letter by mistake, please contact the Billing Department at 1800-845-1836.

Thank you.

Sincerely,

The Accounts Department

United Telecom

1   Why was this letter written?
    (A) To confirm an order
    (B) To change a delivery address
    (C) To pay for a bill
    (D) To draw a customer's attention

2   What is the company requesting Mr. Francis to do?
    (A) Subscribe to a service
    (B) Send payment to the company
    (C) Check the Web site
    (D) Contact a phone number

Unit 02 구체적 정보

Part 7

구체적 정보를 묻는 유형은 Part 7 전체 유형의 60% 정도를 차지할 만큼 비중이 높기 때문에 이 유형을 완전히 공략해야 고득점이 가능합니다. 세부 사항을 묻는 유형은 문제를 먼저 읽고 특정 핵심어를 중심으로 지문을 살펴보면 정답 찾는 시간을 절약할 수 있습니다. 그러나 아래쪽에 짧은 글을 덧붙여 지문과 연계시키거나 특정 정보에서 추론해야 하는 문제가 나오기도 하므로 전체 내용 파악을 소홀히 할 수는 없습니다.

문제유형

When does contest voting end? 콘테스트 투표는 언제 끝나는가?
When did the promotional program start? 홍보 프로그램은 언제 시작되었는가?
What are employees asked to do? 직원들이 하도록 요청받는 것은?
What will the hotels offer? 호텔이 제공하게 될 것은?
Who is Angela Franco? Angela Franco는 누구인가?
Who completed the survey? 설문조사를 완료한 사람은?
Where is Ms. Ellise from? Ellise 씨는 어디에서 왔는가?
Where should employees put their lab coat? 직원들은 실험실복을 두어야 하는 곳은?
Why are residents of ACE TOWER upset? ACE 타워의 주민들이 화가 난 이유는?
Why should people enroll by January? 사람들이 1월까지 등록해야 하는 이유는?
Which has the highest test performance rating? 가장 높은 시험 성적을 기록한 것은?
Which products are most customers interested in? 대부분의 고객들이 관심을 가진 제품은?
How can Mr. Hoyt order the product? Hoyt 씨가 제품을 주문할 수 있는 방법은?
How many employees will be hired? 고용될 예정인 직원의 수는?

풀이전략

▶ 문제에서 언급하고 있는 숫자나 이름, 요일, 대문자 등은 중요한 단서가 됩니다.
문제에 있는 고유명사나 숫자에 표시를 한 다음 지문을 읽으면서 해당 부분을 찾으면 쉽게 문제가 풀립니다.

▶ 요구나 요청의 내용에 관한 질문의 단서는 대부분 지문의 끝에 나옵니다.

▶ Although, Because, If, Since, However, Despite, Nevertheless 등의 접속사나 접속부사의 앞뒤에 정답의 단서가 있습니다.

Sample Test 문제풀이전략을 적용해 기출 유형 예제를 풀어 보세요.

FAX

Recipient: Blake Artoshire
Sender: Arthur Huntings
Subject: Field trip form

Message:
As per your request, I am sending you a copy of the form for the field trip to the city zoo. The due date for returning the completed form is today; however, I will extend this deadline until the end of this week. Please ensure that this form is signed by your parents at the designated place at the bottom of the form. This signature is required so that I know that they have granted you permission to go on the field trip. Once it is signed, you could either e-mail it to me, or, preferably, hand it over to me during class.

Sincerely,
Arthur Huntings

Q. What should Blake do after the form is completed?

(A) Give it to the teacher
(B) Prepare for the trip
(C) Ask his parents for permission
(D) Extend the due date

어휘 as per ~에 따라, ~대로 request 요청 field trip 현장 학습, 현지 조사 여행 due date 마감일 extend 연장하다 ensure 반드시 ~하다 designated 지정된 bottom 아래쪽 grant 동의하다 permission 허락, 허가 preferably 되도록이면

문제분석

FAX 팩스

Recipient: Blake Artoshire 수신: Blake Artoshire
Sender: Arthur Huntings 발신: Arthur Huntings
Subject: Field trip form 제목: 현장 학습 양식

Message: 메시지
As per your request, I am sending you a copy of the form for the field trip to the city zoo. The due date for returning the completed form is today; however, I will extend this deadline until the end of this week. Please ensure that this form is signed by your parents at the designated place at the bottom of the form. This signature is required so that I know that they have granted you permission to go on the field trip. Once it is signed, you could either e-mail it to me, or, preferably, hand it over to me during class.

학생이 요청한 대로 시립 동물원 현장 학습 신청 양식 한 부를 보냅니다. 작성한 양식의 반송 마감일은 오늘까지이지만 이 기한을 이번 주말까지 연장하겠어요. 이 양식은 아래쪽 지정된 위치에 부모님의 서명을 꼭 받도록 해요. 이 서명은 부모님이 현장 학습에 참가하는 것을 허락했음을 내가 알기 위해 필요해요. 일단 서명을 받게 되면 내게 이메일로 보내거나 되도록이면 수업 때 제출하세요.

Sincerely,
Arthur Huntings

---

2. 구체적 정보를 찾는 유형에서 요청이나 요구에 관련된 문제의 단서는 대부분 지문의 끝부분에 있습니다.

1. 요청이나 요구에 관련된 문제임을 알 수 있습니다.

3. 지문의 hand it over to me를 Give it to the teacher로 바꾸어 쓴 (A)가 정답입니다.

Q. What should Blake do after the form is completed? 양식을 작성한 후에 Blake가 해야 하는 것은?
   (A) Give it to the teacher 선생님께 드릴 것
   (B) Prepare for the trip 여행을 준비할 것
   (C) Ask his parents for permission 부모님께 허락을 구할 것
   (D) Extend the due date 마감일을 연장할 것

해설 마지막 문장 Once it is signed, you could either e-mail it to me, or, preferably, hand it over to me during class.에서 서명함으로써 양식 작성을 완료한 후에는 자신에게 이메일로 보내거나 수업 시간에 제출해 달라고 요구하고 있다. 따라서 (A)가 정답이다.

Practice

정답 및 해설 p.160

Question 1 refers to the following notice.

NOTICE TO ALL EMPLOYEES

As you are already aware, T-Voice Company will begin installing the new communication system into the personal computers stationed in every office at 10 A.M. on Monday, October 15. All computers will remain offline during this time. Furthermore, a meeting regarding safe system management will be held during the following week.

1. What will happen on October 15th?
   (A) A meeting for safe system management will be held.
   (B) Office computers will be unavailable online.

Question 2 refers to the following advertisement.

Job Vacancy

Jewls Company, one of the top architectural design companies located in Hong Kong, is recruiting new employees to work on future project plans with their partners in Australia. These new employees will be tasked with checking legal documents, communicating with company representatives, and frequently attending business conferences in Singapore.

2. Where is the job located?
   (A) Australia
   (B) Hong Kong

어휘 **1** install 설치하다 station 배치하다 furthermore 게다가, 더 나아가 **2** architectural 건축의 recruit 모집하다 employee 직원 legal 법률적인 document 서류, 문서 representative 대표, 담당자 frequently 자주

Questions 1-2 refer to the text message chain.

Siennna Middleton — Jan. 23 8:31 A.M.
Good morning. Kevin. I'm scheduled to preside over the weekly meeting at 9 A.M. but I'm afraid I'm going to be late.

Jennifer Monroe — Jan. 23 8:32 A.M.
What's the problem?

Siennna Middleton — Jan. 23 8:32 A.M.
I got stuck in a traffic jam. I think there was a traffic accident. We'd better postpone the meeting until tomorrow.

Jennifer Monroe — Jan. 23 8:33 A.M.
Hmm… Most of our team members are already here and we need to urgently talk about the contract with Jason Inc. Why don't we ask Mr. Lee in Sales to lead the meeting instead?

Siennna Middleton — Jan. 23 8:34 A.M.
That's a great idea. He is the right person to replace me. Thank you.

---

1 What does Ms. Monroe indicate she will do?
(A) Ask someone to chair the meeting
(B) Arrive late for the meeting
(C) Reschedule the meeting
(D) Go to the airport

NEW
2 At 8:34 A.M. what does Ms. Middleton most likely mean when she writes, "That's a great idea"?
(A) She likes Ms. Monroe's solution.
(B) She is excited to see the contractor.
(C) Brainstorming will generate a lot of great ideas.
(D) She is satisfied with Jennifer's transfer.

Part 7

Unit 03 NOT/TRUE

지문의 내용과 일치하거나 일치하지 않는 것을 고르는 NOT/TRUE 유형은 Part 7에서 10~15%의 비중을 차지하고 있습니다. 최근 Part 7의 난이도가 높아지면서 이 유형의 난이도도 점점 높아지고 있습니다. 지문과 보기를 일일이 대조하는 데 시간이 많이 걸릴 수 있으므로 평소에 속독 훈련을 통해 대비해야 합니다.

문제유형

▶ **NOT 유형**

What is NOT true about the Suprema Clock? Suprema Clock에 대해 사실이 아닌 것은?
What is NOT mentioned as an open position? 공석에 대해 언급되지 않는 것은?
What is NOT included in the benefit packages? 복지 혜택에 포함되지 않는 것은?
What is NOT stated in the article? 기사에 진술되지 않는 것은?

▶ **TRUE 유형**

What is true about the Emerton Tire? Emerton 타이어에 대해 사실인 것은?
What is stated about the database? 데이터베이스에 대해 진술된 것은?
What is mentioned about Thursdays? 목요일에 대해 언급된 것은?
What is indicated about the event on March 30? 3월 30일의 행사에 관해 지적된 것은?

풀이전략

▶ **다른 유형의 문제부터 해결하며 지문 내용을 파악한다.**

지문마다 거의 1문항씩 출제되는 NOT/TRUE 유형 문제를 풀려면 지문 전체를 훑어보아야 하므로 시간이 많이 걸리고 정답을 찾아야 한다는 강박감 때문에 다른 문제를 푸는 데도 지장을 받게 됩니다. 따라서 다른 유형의 문제부터 해결하면서 지문의 전체 내용을 파악하고 나서 시간이 허락할 때 풀도록 해야 합니다.

▶ **보기를 먼저 읽고 핵심어를 중심으로 정답을 찾는다.**

문제를 풀 때에는 보기를 먼저 읽은 후 다른 문제를 풀면서 살펴본 내용들을 바탕으로 지문을 빠르게 읽어 나가며 핵심어를 중심으로 정답을 찾아야 합니다. 질문의 about과 in 다음의 명사가 핵심어입니다. 보기들을 하나씩 지문의 핵심어 부분들과 대조해야 합니다. 소거법을 이용해 NOT 유형에서는 지문 내용과 일치하는 보기를 제거하고, TRUE 유형에서는 일치하지 않는 보기를 제거하면 됩니다.

▶ **문제에 NOT이 있는지 확인한다.**

경험 많은 수험자도 NOT 유형 문제에서 NOT을 보지 못하고 오답을 고르는 경우가 많습니다.

Sample Test   문제풀이전략을 적용해 기출 유형 예제를 풀어 보세요.

Frank's Movie Review: *Return to the Cape*

Through the dense lush of movies, a certain movie happened to catch my eye. It was neither the story nor the cast that interested me, but the director behind the film. The title of Richard Olsvek's new movie is called *Return to the Cape* and it tells the rather overdone story of a man returning to his home at a farm after an unsuccessful career working in the bustle of a city.

It sounds timeworn at first due to the large number of movies that have the same subject, but the way the director was able to capture and successfully portray the inner workings of the protagonist was simply movie-making at its best. It certainly was a great way for Olsvek to return to the cinema after a 10-year pause. The movie opened in select theatres across the country on April 12 and thus far, it has received remarkable reviews from critics. Owing to its success, the movie is scheduled to open in more theatres on May 2. To see if your local theatre is showing *Return to the Cape*, check the "Theatre: Now Playing" section of our blog.

Q. What is mentioned about Olsvek?
(A) He owns a movie theatre.
(B) He is a former actor.
(C) He reviewed *Return to the Cape*.
(D) He has returned from a break.

어휘 / review 비평, 비평하다 dense 빽빽한 lush 무성한, 우거진 cast 배역, 출연진 rather 다소 overdone 과도한, 과장된 career 직장 생활 bustle 분주함 timeworn 케케묵은, 진부한 subject 주제 capture 포착하다 portray 묘사하다 protagonist 주인공 simply 그야말로, 단순히 at one's best 최고 상태인 pause 중단, 휴지기 remarkable 주목할 만한 critic 평론가

문제분석

Frank's Movie Review: *Return to the Cape* Frank의 영화 비평: Return to the Cape

Through the dense lush of movies, a certain movie happened to catch my eye. It was neither the story nor the cast that interested me, but the director behind the film. The title of **Richard Olsvek's new movie** is called *Return to the Cape* and it tells the rather overdone story of a man returning to his home at a farm after an unsuccessful career working in the bustle of a city.

엄청나게 많은 영화들 틈에서 한 특정한 영화가 우연히 내 시선을 끌었다. 나의 흥미를 끈 것은 이야기도 출연진도 아니었고 그 영화 뒤의 감독이었다. Richard Olsvek의 새 영화 제목은 'Return to the Cape'라고 하며 이 영화는 분주한 도시에서 신통치 않은 직장생활을 한 후 농장에 있는 자기 집으로 돌아가는 한 남자에 대한 다소 과장된 이야기를 들려준다.

It sounds timeworn at first due to the large number of movies that have the same subject, but the way the director was able to capture and successfully portray the inner workings of the protagonist was simply movie-making at its best. It certainly was a great way for **Olsvek to return to the cinema after a 10-year pause**. The movie opened in select theatres across the country on April 12 and thus far, it has received remarkable reviews from critics. Owing to its success, the movie is scheduled to open in more theatres on May 2. To see if your local theatre is showing *Return to the Cape*, check the "Theatre: Now Playing" section of our blog.

같은 주제를 가진 영화가 많은 까닭에 처음에는 진부하게 느껴지지만 감독이 주인공의 내면 작용을 포착해 성공적으로 묘사할 수 있었던 방식은 그야말로 영화 제작의 백미였다. 이는 Olsvek이 10년 공백 후에 영화계로 복귀하는 훌륭한 방법이었음이 확실하다. 이 영화는 4월 12일에 전국의 선별된 극장들에서 개봉했으며 지금까지 비평가들로부터 주목할 만한 평가를 받고 있다. 이 영화는 흥행 성공에 힘입어 5월 2일에 더 많은 극장들에서 개봉될 예정이다. 여러분의 지역 극장에서 'Return to the Cape'를 상영하는지 확인하려면 우리 블로그의 '현재 상영관' 항목을 확인할 것.

Q. What is mentioned **about Olsvek**? Olsvek에 대해 언급된 것은?
(A) He owns a movie theatre. 영화관을 소유하고 있다.
(B) He is a former actor. 전직 배우이다.
(C) He reviewed *Return to the Cape*. 'Return to the Cape'를 비평했다.
(D) **He has returned from a break.** 공백기를 마치고 돌아왔다.

1. 문제에서 about 다음의 Olsvek이라는 이름이 핵심어이므로 지문에서 Olsvek이 나오는 문장을 신속히 찾아야 합니다.

2. Olsvek이 영화감독이나 배우임을 짐작할 수 있습니다. 따라서 우선 보기 중의 (A)와 (C)를 오답으로 제거할 수 있습니다.

3. 이 문장에서 (D)가 정답이 되는 근거를 찾을 수 있습니다.

4. 지문의 pause를 break로 바꾸어 쓴 (D)가 정답입니다.

해설 둘째 단락의 It certainly was a great way for Olsvek to return to the cinema after a 10-year pause.에서 Olsvek이 활동을 중단한 지 10년 만에 영화계에 복귀했음을 알 수 있습니다.

Practice

정답 및 해설 p.162

Question 1 refers to the following announcement.

> Caring 4 Earth, a non-profit organization, is declaring April 7 as the official community day; this has been approved by the mayor of San Rodriguez. During the last few years, our organization has offered services for the ecological restoration of urban areas and promoted educational seminars emphasizing the importance of water preservation and recycling at several high schools. On this official community day, we invite everyone to join us once again in saving the environment by planting trees, cleaning public streets, and exercising a conservative lifestyle.

1. What is NOT mentioned about Caring 4 Earth?
   (A) It is inviting people to plant trees on April 7.
   (B) It has promoted seminars for reducing the wastage of food.

Question 2 refers to the following advertisement.

> Summer is here and so is the Hansel Summer Camp! This year, the camp will be held at the Orion Hill campsite from July 11 to July 28. Like every year, the camp will be organizing various activities. Hiking trails, swimming, survival games, barbecues, campfires, and other outdoor recreational activities are waiting for you! The number of registrations is limited, so register quickly so that you don't miss out on the fun.

2. What is NOT mentioned as an activity in the summer camp?
   (A) Survival games and campfire
   (B) Mountain biking and rock climbing

어휘 1 non-profit 비영리의 organization 단체, 조직 declare 선포하다 official 공식적인 approve 승인하다 mayor 시장 ecological 생태계의 restoration 복원 urban 도시의 area 지역 promote 주최하다 emphasize 강조하다 importance 중요성 preservation 보존 recycle 재활용하다 conservative 검소한 2 campsite 캠프장 organize 조직하다, 준비하다 various 다양한 outdoor 야외의 registration 등록 register 등록하다 miss out on 놓치다

Questions 1-2 refer to the following article.

January 20

There has been a considerable increase in the number of companies joining the technology competition. Limitoo Incorporated is no exception, as it has publicly announced the unveiling of a new type of computer processor.

The official unveiling of Limitoo Incorporated's new product is currently scheduled for March 15, during their next conference at their hometown of Dallas. The company is also expected to announce their new long-term plans during this conference. The announcement of their new product has surprised many people worldwide; however, they are expecting a good product due to Limitoo's long-standing reputation in the computer software business.

Besides us, many other news portals and television networks will also be attending this conference. To follow our story as we provide coverage of the event, please subscribe to our live feed through our Web site.

1. What can be inferred about Limitoo Incorporated?
   (A) They recently decided to launch computer processors.
   (B) They only manufacture computer hardware components.
   (C) They are only known in the United States.
   (D) They will hold an event on January 20.

2. What is NOT mentioned about the product?
   (A) It is Limitoo's first product.
   (B) Many people are looking forward to its unveiling.
   (C) It will be announced in Dallas.
   (D) It is a part of a new field of technology.

Unit 04 추론

질문에 inferred, indicated, suggested, implied, most likely, probably 등의 단어들이 나오면 추론 유형 문제입니다. 이 유형에서는 보기에 적혀 있는 단어와 똑같은 단어나 동의어가 지문 속에 없습니다. 따라서 질문에서 핵심어와 똑같은 단어가 나오는 문장을 찾아서 그 문장을 근거로 추론하여 정답을 찾아야 합니다. 추론 유형은 Part 7에서 5~10% 정도의 비중을 차지하지만 세부 사항과 관련된 추론 유형은 가장 난이도가 높은 유형 중의 하나이므로 충분히 대비해야 합니다.

문제유형

▶ **지문 전체를 파악해야 하는 유형**

For whom is the announcement intended? 이 공지는 누구를 대상으로 하는가?
Where will this ad most likely be posted? 이 광고는 어디에 실릴 가능성이 가장 높은가?
What most likely is Marshall Enterprises? Marshall Enterprises는 무엇일 가능성이 가장 높은가?

▶ **세부 사항을 찾아야 하는 유형**

What is implied about the travel guide? 여행 안내서에 대해 암시된 것은?
What is suggested about Mr. Knox? Knox 씨에 대해 언급된 것은?
What can be inferred about Sonito's sales last year? Sonito의 작년 매출에 대해 추론할 수 있는 것은?
What will probably happen if the store is successful? 매장이 성공한다면 어떤 일이 벌어지겠는가?

풀이전략

▶ **지문의 첫 문항이 추론 유형일 때는 대개 지문의 초반이나 첫 단락에 정답이 제시됩니다.**

▶ **지문 전체를 파악해야 하는 추론 문제는 나중에 풉니다.**

Where would this information most likely appear?라고 물었다면, 이 질문은 전반적인 내용을 묻고 있으므로 다른 문제를 먼저 풀면서 힌트를 얻고 나서 나중에 푸는 것이 유리합니다.

▶ **세부 사항에 관련된 추론 문제는 지문에서 질문의 핵심어 관련 부분만 찾아 읽습니다.**

질문에 핵심어가 있으면 그 내용만을 지문에서 찾으면 됩니다. 예를 들어 세부 내용을 묻는 What is suggested about the books Mr. Thompson has written?이라는 질문에서 핵심어는 about 다음의 명사들입니다. 지문에서 핵심어와 관련된 부분을 찾은 다음 그 앞뒤에서 정답의 단서를 찾으면 됩니다.

▶ **지문에서 보기의 핵심어와 같은 글자가 아니라 의미를 찾는다.**

보기를 다 읽고 문제를 풀어야 하는 경우에는 보기의 핵심어 몇 개만 기억하고 지문을 읽어야 합니다. 지문 속의 문장과 보기의 문장이 완전히 일치하지 않으므로 글자가 아니라 의미가 같은 부분을 찾아야 합니다.

Sample Test 문제풀이전략을 적용해 기출 유형 예제를 풀어 보세요.

Online
Thank You
Giveaway!

We are currently conducting a giveaway in appreciation of our regular customers. The giveaway will last for a total of four weeks, with a prize being given away at the end of each week, that is, a total of four prizes and a total of four chances to win! Please read the information provided below for additional details on the fabulous prizes that you could win!

Week 1: $1,000 gift card for our store
Week 2: Brand-new smartphone
Week 3: Brand-new 15.6-inch laptop
Week 4: Brand-new 30-inch HDTV

Please enter the contest each week to be eligible for a chance to win. Winners will be chosen at random and their names will be announced by e-mail at the end of each week.

This offer is limited to residents of the Continental U.S.

For more details and information, visit us at www.electronicsup.com/giveaway.

Q. What kind of products does the company most probably sell?

(A) Electronic products
(B) Computer parts
(C) Gift cards
(D) Cellular phones

어휘 giveaway 경품, 증정품 in appreciation of ~에 감사하여 regular customer 단골 고객 win 우승하다, 차지하다 additional 추가의 detail 세부 사항 fabulous 굉장한 eligible 자격이 있는 at random 무작위로 announce 발표하다 offer 제안 limit 제한하다 resident 주민 Continental U.S. 미국 본토 (알래스카 주와 하와이 주를 제외한 미국의 48주)

문제분석

Online Thank You Giveaway! 온라인 감사 경품 행사!

We are currently conducting a giveaway in appreciation of our regular customers. The giveaway will last for a total of four weeks, with a prize being given away at the end of each week, that is, a total of four prizes and a total of four chances to win! Please read the information provided below for additional details on the fabulous prizes that you could win!

저희는 현재 단골 고객 여러분께 감사의 표시로 경품 행사를 하고 있습니다. 본 경품 행사는 총 4주 동안 진행될 예정이며 매주말마다 상품을 증정할 것입니다. 다시 말해 총 4개의 상품과 총 4번의 당첨 기회가 있습니다! 당신이 당첨될 수도 있는 굉장한 상품들에 대한 추가 세부 사항을 알고 싶으시면 아래 제공된 정보를 읽어주시기 바랍니다.

Week 1: $1,000 gift card for our store 첫째 주: 본 매장용 1,000달러 상품권
Week 2: Brand-new smartphone 둘째 주: 최신 스마트폰
Week 3: Brand-new 15.6-inch laptop 셋째 주: 최신 15.6인치 노트북 컴퓨터
Week 4: Brand-new 30-inch HDTV 넷째 주: 최신 30인치 고화질 TV

> 2. 경품 품목을 알려 주고 있습니다.

Please enter the contest each week to be eligible for a chance to win. Winners will be chosen at random and their names will be announced by e-mail at the end of each week.

당첨 기회를 얻을 자격이 되시려면 매주 콘테스트에 참여해 주세요. 당첨자는 무작위로 선정되며 당첨자 명단은 주말마다 이메일로 발표될 예정입니다.

This offer is limited to residents of the Continental U.S.
이번 행사는 미국 본토 주민에 한합니다.

For more details and information, visit us at www.electronicsup.com/giveaway.
더 많은 세부 사항과 정보를 얻기 원하시면 www.electronicsup.com/giveaway를 방문해 주세요.

> 3. 전자제품 매장임을 알 수 있습니다.

Q. What kind of products does the company most probably sell?
이 회사에서 판매할 가능성이 가장 높을 것 같은 제품 종류는?

(A) Electronic products 전자제품
(B) Computer parts 컴퓨터 부품
(C) Gift cards 상품권
(D) Cellular phones 휴대폰

> 1. most probably가 있으므로 추론 문제임을 알 수 있습니다. 전체 내용을 파악해야만 풀 수 있는 추론 유형입니다.

> 4. 본문의 스마트폰, 노트북 컴퓨터, TV가 경품이고, 웹사이트 주소에서 (A)가 정답임을 추론할 수 있습니다.

해설 상품 설명에 대한 내용을 보면, 둘째 주에는 스마트폰, 셋째 주에는 노트북 컴퓨터, 넷째 주에는 TV를 증정하고 있으므로 전자제품 회사라는 것을 추론할 수 있다. 따라서 (A)가 정답이다.

Question 1 refers to the following notice.

FINE MAPLE CAFÉ COUPON

This limited coupon will entitle customers to a 25% discount on the lunch menu and a 10% discount on hot beverages. This coupon cannot be used with other discount coupons and customers must present this coupon at the time of placing the order to claim the discount. There are no discounts on cold beverages and desserts. Coupon discounts cannot be combined with membership discounts. The offer on the discount coupon expires on May 4. For additional information, please visit our Web site at www.finemaple.com.

1. What is indicated about Fine Maple Café?
   (A) It offers a membership discount.
   (B) It gives 10% discount on all drinks.

Question 2 refers to the following message.

Hi, Russell.

I just received your message. I remember that we had scheduled a meeting for Monday to discuss the company's budget management; however, unfortunately, I will have to reschedule this meeting. A representative manager of our partner company in Hamburg will be arriving on Monday for the final contract negotiation. He will then be accompanying me to Tokyo on Tuesday for our product introduction at the Machinery Expo conference. Can we reschedule our meeting for Thursday? I will be back in Seoul by then. In case Thursday does not suit you, please inform my assistant of your availability during the next week.

2. Where does Russell most likely work?
   (A) In Hamburg
   (B) In Seoul

어휘 **1** entitle 자격을 주다 beverage 음료수 present 제시하다 claim 요구하다 combine 결합하다 expire 만료되다 **2** budget 예산 unfortunately 불행하게도 reschedule 일정을 다시 잡다 representative 대표 negotiation 협상 accompany 동행하다, 수행하다 introduction 소개 suit ~에 맞다, 적합하다 inform 알리다 availability 이용 가능함, 만날 수 있음

Actual Test

정답 및 해설 p.165

Questions 1-2 refer to the text message chain.

Owen Justin 8:31 A.M.
Hi, Grace. Can you help me? My computer isn't working.

Grace Lee 8:31 A.M.
Sure. What's the problem?

Owen Justin 8:32 A.M.
I'm not sure. I can't access the Internet.

Grace Lee 8:33 A.M.
Have you checked the network cable?

Owen Justin 8:33 A.M.
Yes. I think it's connected. I have an important email to send in half an hour.

Grace Lee 8:34 A.M.
I think you should check the basics on your computer. please first reset the router on your desk. Let me get there and help you. I'll be there in about 10 minutes.

Owen Justin 8:34 A.M.
Thank you so much.

NEW

1 At 8:33 A.M. what does Mr. Justin most likely mean when he writes, "I have an important email to send in half an hour"?

(A) He must use the Internet right now.
(B) His email inbox is full.
(C) He still have time to revise his email.
(0) He knows several technicians to repair his computer.

2 What will Ms. Lee most likely do next?

(A) Ask help from technical support team
(B) Purchase a new computer
(C) Go help Mr. Justin
(D) Send an email

Part 7

Unit 05 동의어

동의어 유형은 지문 속의 한 단어와 가장 유사한 의미의 단어를 고르는 것입니다. 이 유형은 Part 7에서 차지하는 비중이 5% 정도이지만 매년 난이도가 높아지고 있는 추세입니다. 단순히 일차적으로 유사한 의미의 어휘가 아니라 지문에서의 특정한 의미와 유사한 어휘를 골라야 합니다.

문제유형

▶ 질문 유형

The word "ordered" in line 4, is closest in meaning to
4행에 나온 단어 'ordered'와 의미상 가장 가까운 것은?

▶ 자주 출제되는 동의어

uniform = consistent (오답: outfitted / accustomed / fashionable)
current = valid (오답: present / moving / formal)
fields = responds to (오답: disciplines / raises / involves with)
carries = keeps in stock (오답: moves between locations / holds a majority of / gives support to)
extended = offered (오답: described / increased / guaranteed)
impact = effect (오답: strike / measure / outlook)
turn out = produce (오답: switch off / become / tear down)
shape = condition (오답: pattern / figure / plan)
issued = distributed (오답: resulted / reported / published)
under = less than (오답: beneath / through / down from)

풀이전략

▶ 질문을 읽고 신속히 단어의 위치를 확인해야 합니다.

The word "ordered" in line 4, is closest in meaning to라고 묻는 질문이 나오면 신속히 지문을 살펴보아 넷째 줄에 있는 ordered라는 단어를 찾아 표시해야 합니다.

▶ 문맥 안에서의 단어 의미를 파악해야 합니다.

'ordered'를 보통 '주문했다'라는 뜻으로만 알고 있지만 지문에서 정말 그 의미로 쓰였는지 아니면 또 다른 의미로 쓰였는지 앞뒤 문장을 보면서 파악해야 합니다. 앞뒤 문장만으로 의미가 파악되지 않으면 다른 문제를 먼저 풀면서 전체 문맥을 파악해야 합니다. 정답을 찾기 어려울 때는 소거법을 이용해 정답과 거리가 먼 보기들부터 제거해 나가야 합니다.

Sample Test

문제풀이전략을 적용해 기출 유형 예제를 풀어 보세요.

To: Keith Winters
From: Fortis Mackenzie
Date: Monday, February 11
Subject: Temporary Consent

Dear Mr. Winters:

I am writing to let you know about your recent job performance. I have been informed that you have transferred to the public relations department. It is surprising to hear how well you are taking on new responsibilities and performing tasks that may be unfamiliar to you. I admire your enthusiasm and attitude in the face of such challenges, which others would normally not accept.

However, I have been receiving reports from your supervisor about your progress. It has been nearly one month since your transfer and unfortunately, not much efficiency has been observed in your area. More importantly, I hear that your health is under distress. Lack of physical strength will only lead to losing focus. Therefore, I am permitting you to accept official leave from work until further notice. Please correspond with Mr. Gheed in this regard and I hope that you will return to work fully recovered.

Sincerely,

Fortis Mackenzie

Q. In the e-mail, the word "leave" in line 10 is closest in meaning to

(A) permission
(B) departure
(C) removal
(D) absence

어휘 / recent 최근의 job performance 업무 수행 inform 알리다 transfer 옮기다, 이동 public relations department 홍보부 responsibility 책임 task 과제, 직무 unfamiliar 낯선, 생소한 admire 감탄하다, 칭찬하다 enthusiasm 열정 attitude 태도 normally 통상적으로 supervisor 부서장 progress 경과 observe 관찰하다 physical strength 체력 lead to ~으로 이어지다 official 공식적인 until further notice 추후 연락이 있을 때까지 correspond with ~와 연락하다 in this regard 이 점에 관해서 recover 회복하다

문제분석

To: Keith Winters 수신: Keith Winters
From: Fortis Mackenzie 발신: Fortis Mackenzie
Date: Monday, February 11 날짜: 2월 11일 월요일
Subject: Temporary Consent 제목: 임시 동의

Dear Mr. Winters: Winters 씨께

I am writing to let you know about your recent job performance. I have been informed that you have transferred to the public relations department. It is surprising to hear how well you are taking on new responsibilities and performing tasks that may be unfamiliar to you. I admire your enthusiasm and attitude in the face of such challenges, which others would normally not accept.

당신의 최근 업무 수행에 대해 알려드리고자 이 편지를 보냅니다. 당신이 홍보부로 자리를 옮겼다고 들었습니다. 당신이 아주 훌륭하게 새 책임들을 맡아 낯설지도 모르는 과제들을 수행하고 있다는 말을 들으니 놀랍습니다. 다른 사람들은 대개 받아들이려고 하지 않을 그러한 도전들을 대하는 당신의 열정과 태도를 높이 평가합니다.

However, I have been receiving reports from your supervisor about your progress. It has been nearly one month since your transfer and unfortunately, not much efficiency has been observed in your area. More importantly, I hear that your health is under distress. Lack of physical strength will only lead to losing focus. Therefore, I am permitting you to accept **official leave from work** until further notice. Please correspond with Mr. Gheed in this regard and I hope that you will return to work fully recovered.

그러나 나는 당신의 부서장으로부터 당신의 업무 경과에 대한 보고를 받고 있습니다. 부서 이동 후 거의 한 달이 되어 가는데, 안타깝게도 당신의 영역에서 많은 효율성이 관찰되지 않고 있습니다. 더 중요한 것은 당신의 건강이 좋지 않다는 소식을 듣고 있다는 것입니다. 체력 부족은 집중력을 잃게 할 뿐입니다. 그러므로 나는 당신이 추후 공지가 있을 때까지 공식 휴가를 받는 것을 허락합니다. 이 점에 관해 Gheed 씨와 연락하십시오. 그리고 당신이 완전히 회복되어 돌아오게 되기를 바랍니다.

Sincerely,

Fortis Mackenzie

> 2. 질문하는 단어를 찾았으면 문장의 앞뒤를 보면서 단어의 의미를 파악합니다. '공식적인 leave'에서 leave는 '휴가 기간'을 의미합니다.

> 1. 지문의 10행에서 단어를 빨리 찾습니다.

Q. In the e-mail, the word "leave" in line 10 is closest in meaning to
이메일에서 10행에 나온 단어 'leave'와 의미상 가장 가까운 것은?

(A) permission 허가
(B) departure 출발
(C) removal 제거
(D) absence 부재

> 3. '휴가'라는 의미와 가장 유사한 단어는 (D)입니다. leave of absence는 '휴가'라는 의미입니다.

해설 leave는 '휴가', 즉 자리를 비움을 말하기 때문에 '부재'라는 의미의 (D)가 정답이다.

Practice

정답 및 해설 p.166

Question 1 refers to the following article.

> **NABI Entertainment Opens International Expo**
>
> Tokyo, November 18: Last week, November 13 was a landmark occasion for NABI Entertainment and their worldwide fans, who are especially interested in their popular animated work, *Eternal Carnival*. The response to the first exposition was surprising, with over 120,000 visitors in 4 days.

1. The word "landmark" in line 1, is closest in meaning to
   (A) typical
   (B) important

Question 2 refers to the following article.

> In a press conference that was held this Monday, February 3, Richard Eames, the Chief Executive of Ace Corporation and the largest investor in BTC Co. Ltd., mentioned that he plans to retire. Though he will be stepping down from his position, he intends to continue working as Head Advisor to help his successor, Fredrick Eames, who is also his son. Fredrick has already served in the corporation for over 10 years.

2. The word "served" in line 4 is the closest in meaning to
   (A) assisted
   (B) worked

어휘 1 occasion (특별한) 때, 행사 especially 특히 worldwide 전 세계의 animated work 애니메이션 작품 response 반응 exposition 박람회
2 press conference 기자회견 investor 투자자 mention 언급하다 retire 은퇴하다 step down 물러나다, 사퇴하다 intend to ~할 작정이다 successor 후계자 corporation 기업, 주식회사

Questions 1-3 refer to the following letter.

October 11

Dear Mr. Mercier:

It is my pleasure as the chief sales supervisor at Dandy Hardware Co. to welcome you to our stores in Dayton City. We have just received your complaint about the lack of customer service in our department. I apologize for the inconvenience that you experienced during your previous visit and as compensation, I am willing to offer a 20% discount on your next purchase. I like to remind our clients that our products are world renowned for their quality and durability, and are accompanied with a yearlong warranty. Furthermore, I encourage you to join our new premium membership. Since June 17 this year, we have been offering 10% discounts to members who purchase products worth more than $200 per transaction. Moreover, please look at our limited special sale items in the enclosed brochure. If you wish to make a purchase, please place an order before October 17.

Thank you,

Vicky Lee
Assistant Manager
Sales Department

1. Why does Ms. Lee send a letter to Mr. Mercier?
   (A) Mr. Mercier purchased more than $200.
   (B) Mr. Mercier wanted to enroll in the premium membership.
   (C) Ms. Lee received a report that Mr. Mercier was dissatisfied.
   (D) Ms. Lee wished to apologize for damaged items.

2. The word "renowned" in line 6 is closest in meaning to
   (A) famous
   (B) unknown
   (C) disliked
   (D) foreign

3. When did members begin receiving 10% discounts?
   (A) June 11
   (B) June 17
   (C) October 11
   (D) October 17

Unit 06 편지와 이메일

Part 7

Part 7에 등장하는 편지와 이메일은 회사 간의 거래, 회의나 사업 제안, 신문/잡지 구독이나 서비스 갱신, 물품 배송, 회사와 입사 지원자 간의 연락, 개인 간의 안부 편지 등 실생활의 다양한 주제들이 출제됩니다. 편지와 이메일은 Part 7에서 가장 많이 출제되는 유형이지만 문제 형식이 거의 정해져 있으므로 난이도는 낮습니다. 글을 쓴 목적, 수신인과 발신인, 요청 사항에 관한 질문이 대부분입니다.

문제유형

▶ **글의 목적을 묻는 유형**

Why was the letter written? 이 편지가 쓰여진 이유는?
What is the purpose of the e-mail? 이 이메일의 목적은?

▶ **세부 사항을 묻는 유형**

What is mentioned as a requirement for the job? 그 일자리의 요건으로 언급된 것은?
What is indicated about the event on March 19? 3월 19일의 행사에 관해 지적된 것은?

▶ **요청 사항을 묻는 유형**

What are customers asked to do? 고객들이 하도록 부탁받은 것은?
What did Sean most likely request? Sean이 요청했을 가능성이 가장 높은 것은?

풀이전략

▶ **편지의 발신인과 수신인을 확인해야 합니다.**

문제에 여러 명의 이름이 나올 경우 혼동할 수 있으므로 누가 누구에게 보내는 편지인지, 누가 누구에게 무엇을 요청하는지 등을 정확히 파악해야 합니다.

▶ **그 다음에는 편지를 쓰는 목적을 찾아야 합니다.**

편지의 목적이 나온 다음에는 첨부물, 변경 또는 요구 사항 등과 관련된 세부 사항이나 부가 내용들이 이어집니다. 세부 사항과 관련된 문제는 질문을 먼저 읽고 핵심어를 파악한 다음 지문을 읽으면서 핵심어나 핵심어를 변형한 어휘에 초점을 맞추어 단서를 찾아야 합니다.

▶ **편지의 목적에 대한 단서는 주로 지문의 앞부분에서 다음 표현들 뒤에 등장합니다.**

I'm writing to ~ / I'm pleased to announce ~ / This is to inform you that ~

▶ **요청 사항에 대한 단서는 주로 지문의 중간이나 끝부분에서 다음 표현들 뒤에 등장합니다.**

Please feel free to ~ / I look forward to ~ / I would appreciate it if you ~

Sample Test — 문제풀이전략을 적용해 기출 유형 예제를 풀어 보세요.

From: willsallus@aismail.com
To: ashweis@aismail.com

Dear Ashley:

Mr. Kraus and I will be returning a day early from our business trip to New York. The company's fifth anniversary project proposal should be finished and ready for presentation by the time we return on May 21st. Moreover, the representatives of Simglass Co. will be visiting us at our facility for a sales conference the next day.

Finally, I have received news from the board of directors that Mr. Kraus will be transferred to the marketing department as the managing director because of his successful negotiations with Fansteel Inc., last month. Therefore, I plan to host a small party for him in the Square Meeting Lounge at 6 P.M. on May 22nd. Please contact Dike Felipe for any assistance during my absence there.

Q. What is the reason for a party?
(A) Mr. Kraus finished the project.
(B) Mr. Kraus retired from his position.
(C) Mr. Kraus got a promotion.
(D) Mr. Kraus returned from his business trip to Fansteel Inc.

어휘 anniversary 기념일 proposal 제안(서) presentation 프레젠테이션, 발표 representative 대표, 담당자 board of directors 이사회 transfer 이동시키다, 전출시키다 negotiation 협상, 교섭 assistance 지원, 도움 absence 부재, 결석

문제분석

From: willsallus@aismail.com 발신: willsallus@aismail.com
To: ashweis@aismail.com 수신: ashweis@aismail.com

Dear Ashley: Ashley에게

Mr. Kraus and I will be returning a day early from our business trip to New York. The company's fifth anniversary project proposal should be finished and ready for presentation by the time we return on May 21st. Moreover, the representatives of Simglass Co. will be visiting us at our facility for a sales conference the next day.
Kraus 씨와 나는 뉴욕 출장에서 하루 일찍 도착할 예정입니다. 5월 21일에 우리가 돌아갈 무렵에 회사 창립 5주년 기념일 프로젝트 제안서가 완료되어 발표 준비가 되어 있어야 합니다. 그리고 Simglass 사의 대표들이 그 다음 날 영업 회의를 위해 우리 시설에 방문할 예정입니다.

Finally, I have received news from the board of directors that Mr. Kraus will be transferred to the marketing department as the managing director because of his successful negotiations with Fansteel Inc., last month. Therefore, I plan to host a small party for him in the Square Meeting Lounge at 6 P.M. on May 22nd. Please contact Dike Felipe for any assistance during my absence there.
마지막으로 나는 이사회에서 Kraus 씨가 지난달 Fansteel 사와의 성공적인 협상 때문에 전무이사로서 마케팅부로 전출될 것이라는 소식을 들었습니다. 그래서 나는 5월 22일 오후 6시에 Square Meeting Lounge에서 그를 위해 작은 파티를 열 계획입니다. 내가 그곳에 없는 동안 도움이 필요하면 Dike Felipe에게 연락하십시오.

> 3. party를 열려는 이유가 자세히 나와 있습니다.
>
> 2. 파티가 나온 부분을 찾았지만 이 문장만으로는 단서를 찾을 수 없으므로 앞뒤 문장을 살펴봅니다.

Q. What is the reason for a party? 파티를 여는 이유는?

(A) Mr. Kraus finished the project. Kraus 씨가 프로젝트를 끝냈다.
(B) Mr. Kraus retired from his position. Kraus 씨가 퇴직했다.
(C) Mr. Kraus got a promotion. Kraus 씨가 승진했다.
(D) Mr. Kraus returned from his business trip to Fansteel Inc.
   Kraus 씨가 Fansteel 사 출장에서 돌아왔다.

> 1. party에 대한 세부 사항을 묻고 있으므로 지문에서 party가 나온 부분을 빨리 찾아야 합니다.
>
> 4. Kraus 씨가 협상 성공 때문에 전무이사로 전출된다는 지문 내용을 got a promotion으로 바꾸어 표현한 (C)가 정답입니다.

해설 접속사 Therefore 앞에 파티를 여는 이유가 나온다. Mr. Kraus will be transferred to the marketing department as the managing director에서 Kraus 씨가 마케팅부 전무이사로 승진해 자리를 옮기는 것을 알 수 있으므로 (C)가 정답이다.

Practice

정답 및 해설 p.169

Question 1 refers to the following letter.

Dear family and friends,

I am writing to let you know that I have finally come home after taking a 77-day trip around the world. Thanks to Andrew's recommendations, I was able to learn and experience many amazing things during my travel. I regret that I was unable to attend his wedding last week. However, I am looking forward to seeing everyone at the upcoming reunion at Arisville next month and telling you my travel stories. I also plan to return to the Emerson Institute of Language Art and focus on my academics.

Sincerely,
George Burns

1. What is mentioned about Mr. Burns?
   (A) He is a student.
   (B) He is married.

Question 2 refers to the following letter.

Dear staff members,

Over the past 10 years, Giovanna Dyke has become an admired employee at Telkon Mobile. Although she had sought the position of a team supervisor, Mr. Wilson had hired her as a chief manager due to her impressive qualifications. After just a few months of her joining the company, she was promoted to the position of director of the service department.

2. What was Giovanna Dyke's first position at Telkon Mobile?
   (A) Team supervisor
   (B) Chief manager

어휘 **1** recommendation 추천, 권고 attend 참석하다 upcoming 다가오는, 오는 reunion 재회, 동창회 institute 연구소, 기관 academics 학업
2 admire 칭찬하다, 감탄하다 seek 추구하다 chief manager 관리책임자 impressive 인상적인, 놀라운 be promoted 승진하다

Questions 1-3 refer to the following letter.

Official Food Tasters

Reviewing foods and restaurants in the New York area!
www.officialfoodtastersgroup.com

August 9, Monday

Dear OFT members,

Last year, OFT members Eliza Ruth and Brian Limskin had the privilege of sampling food from Jimmie's, a small Italian restaurant in the city. They, of course, rated the restaurant with top marks, and their review greatly complimented the way the food at Jimmie's harmonizes with the design and feel of the restaurant. Currently, we do not have many members; however, one member, Ophilia Winsley, has reported that the owner of Jimmie's has opened another restaurant in the suburbs near the Cameron post office. This new restaurant opened last Wednesday, and ever since, the business has been booming. Thus far, we have not had the opportunity to properly review this second location; however, initial impressions and feedback from the customers seem to be good.

We are going to review the second Jimmie's and will send it to you through e-mail as soon as it is completed.

Yours sincerely,
Amelia Vesti
Editor

---

1 Why was this letter written?

(A) To offer a membership
(B) To inform members of a new restaurant
(C) To announce a promotion
(D) To make members review a restaurant

2 Who reported the second Jimmie's?

(A) Eliza Ruth
(B) Brian Limskin
(C) Ophilia Winsley
(D) Amelia Vesti

3 What is true about Official Food Tasters?

(A) They are a worldwide organization.
(B) They are made up of women.
(C) They sell products to famous restaurants.
(D) They have a few members.

Part 7

Unit 07 광고

Part 7에서 광고 유형은 매회 출제되는 유형입니다. 제품이나 서비스, 구인, 할인 행사, 집수리, 부동산 등 다양한 분야의 광고가 출제됩니다. 이러한 주제들은 실생활에서도 쉽게 접할 수 있는 내용이므로 대체로 내용 자체가 어렵지 않고, 항상 나오는 패턴이 일정하기 때문에 난이도가 낮습니다. 반복되는 지문, 문제, 보기의 틀을 익혀 두면 아무리 긴 지문이라도 어렵지 않게 풀 수 있습니다.

문제유형

▶ **광고의 목적과 대상을 묻는 질문**

What is being advertised? 광고하고 있는 것은?
What is the purpose of this advertisement? 이 광고의 목적은?

▶ **제품의 특징이나 장점을 묻는 질문**

What is stated as a feature of this product? 이 제품의 특징으로 기술된 것은?
What is the competitiveness of the service? 그 서비스의 경쟁력은 무엇인가?

▶ **구인 광고에서 세부 사항을 묻는 질문**

Who is advertising the position? 일자리를 광고하고 있는 사람은?
What is mentioned as a requirement for the job? 그 일자리의 요건으로 언급된 것은?
Who most likely would respond to the advertisement? 광고에 반응할 가능성이 가장 높은 사람은?
How can people apply for the position? 사람들이 그 직책에 지원할 수 있는 방법은?

풀이전략

▶ **제품 광고**

제품에 대한 여러 사항이 나열되므로 먼저 제목과 초반부에서 광고의 대상과 목적, 업종과 같은 기본 정보를 파악하고 나서 제품의 특징과 구입 방법, 할인 혜택 등에 대한 정보를 파악해야 합니다. 제품의 특징에 대한 NOT/TRUE 유형 문제가 많이 출제됩니다. 제품의 특징과 서비스, 혜택에 관련된 정보는 지문의 중간 정도에 나옵니다.

▶ **구인 광고**

어떤 직위에 사람이 필요하고, 담당 업무와 자격 요건이 무엇인지 파악해야 합니다. responsibilities, qualifications, requirement 등의 단어가 나오는 부분을 주의해 살펴봐야 합니다. 자격 요건에 관련된 세부 정보는 지문의 중간 정도에 나옵니다. 지원 방법에 관련된 세부 정보는 지문의 끝부분에 나옵니다.

Sample Test 문제풀이전략을 적용해 기출 유형 예제를 풀어 보세요.

12th Annual Track and Field Day at Bailey Junior High School

Bailey Junior High School invites all students and families to come and enjoy the 12th Annual Track and Field Day organized by the Student Committee and Faculty.

The campus is located between Yorkshire Street and Fairfield Street on Greenwood Avenue. The gates will be open from 5 A.M. to 5 P.M. on Thursday, May 18, and from 10 A.M. to 7 P.M. on Friday, May 19.

Thursday activities will include:
- 100-meter Relay Race
- Baseball Throws
- High Jumps
- Long Jumps

Friday activities will include:
- Potato-sack Races
- Three-legged Races
- Group Jump Rope
- Tug-of-war
- Water Balloon Toss
- And much, much more…

Snacks and drinks will be available at our individual food stands nearby.

Admission is $10 for adults and faculty and $5 for children and students.
Children age 4 and under are free!

Q. Where will this ad most likely be posted?

(A) In a sports magazine
(B) On a community information Web site
(C) In a business newspaper
(D) On an academic bulletin board

어휘 annual 연례의 track and field 육상 경기 student committee 학생회 faculty 교수진 relay race 이어달리기 high jump 높이뛰기 long jump 멀리뛰기 tug-of-war 줄다리기 individual 개별적인, 개인의 admission 입장료, 입장권 community 지역 사회, 공동체 academic 학교의

문제분석

12th Annual Track and Field Day at Bailey Junior High School
제12회 Bailey 중학교 연례 육상 경기의 날

Bailey Junior High School invites all students and families to come and enjoy the 12th Annual Track and Field Day organized by the Student Committee and Faculty.
Bailey 중학교는 전교생과 가족들을 초청하오니 오셔서 학생회와 교사진이 준비한 제12회 연례 육상 경기의 날을 즐기십시오.

The campus is located between Yorkshire Street and Fairfield Street on Greenwood Avenue. The gates will be open from 5 A.M. to 5 P.M. on Thursday, May 18, and from 10 A.M. to 7 P.M. on Friday, May 19.
캠퍼스는 Greenwood Avenue의 Yorkshire 가와 Fairfield 가 사이에 위치해 있습니다. 교문은 5월 18일 목요일 오전 5시부터 오후 5시까지, 또 5월 19일 금요일 오전 10시부터 오후 7시까지 개방할 예정입니다.

Thursday activities will include: 목요일 종목
- 100-meter Relay Race 100m 이어달리기
- Baseball Throws 야구공 던지기
- High Jumps 높이뛰기
- Long Jumps 멀리뛰기

Friday activities will include: 금요일 종목
- Potato-sack Races 감자 자루 경주
- Three-legged Races 이인삼각 경주
- Group Jump Rope 단체 줄넘기
- Tug-of-war 줄다리기
- Water Balloon Toss 물 풍선 던지기
- And much, much more… 기타 다수 종목

Snacks and drinks will be available at our individual food stands nearby.
간식과 음료수는 가까이 있는 개별 음식 스탠드에서 이용하실 수 있습니다.

Admission is $10 for adults and faculty and $5 for children and students. Children age 4 and under are free!
어른과 교사 입장료는 10달러이고 아이들과 학생 입장료는 5달러입니다. 4세 이하 어린이들은 무료입니다!

> 2. 학교에서 열리는 행사임을 알 수 있습니다.
>
> 3. 학생회와 교사진이 주최하는 행사임을 알 수 있습니다.

Q. Where will this ad most likely be posted? 이 광고가 게시되어 있을 가능성이 가장 높은 곳은?

(A) In a sports magazine 스포츠 잡지
(B) On a community information Web site 지역 사회 정보 웹사이트
(C) In a business newspaper 비즈니스 신문
(D) **On a academic bulletin board** 학교 게시판

> 1. 광고의 대상이나 목적, 장소에 관한 단서는 대개 지문의 첫머리에 나오므로 그 부분을 중점적으로 살펴봐야 합니다.
>
> 4. 학교에서 열리는 행사이고, 학생회와 교사진이 주최한다고 했으므로 광고가 붙은 곳은 교내임을 알 수 있으므로 정답입니다.

해설 ▶ 학교에서 열리는 연례 육상 경기의 날에 대해 광고하고 있으며 학부모와 학생들을 초청하고 있기 때문에 학생들과 학부모가 학교 행사에 대한 정보를 접할 수 있는 (D)가 정답이다.

Practice

정답 및 해설 p.172

Question 1 refers to the following advertisement.

The Pearl Spa

We are proud to announce Pearl Spa's opening this April! When your body is in need of restoration and relief from stress, look no further. From aromatherapy oil massages to steam saunas, our team of experts guarantees to ease your stiff muscles. Take the opportunity to refresh yourself with our exquisite baths. We will be offering discounts to our first 30 customers, so don't miss this opportunity!

1. What is the purpose of the advertisement?
   (A) To publicize a new product
   (B) To announce the new facility

Question 2 refers to the following advertisement.

To Meet Your Personal Needs!

When receiving your inquiry, we will contact you as soon as possible. Subsequently, we will gather information regarding your business goals to thoroughly understand your company. We will also request information about the purpose of the site, that is, whether you would like to sell products online or create an informational site, and learn more about your ideal audience.

2. What type of business is being advertised?
   (A) A Web site design firm
   (B) An online shopping mall

어휘 1 restoration 회복, 복구 relief 완화, 경감 aromatherapy 아로마 요법 steam 증기 stiff 뻣뻣한 refresh 상쾌하게 하다, 활력을 주다 exquisite 절묘한, 최고의 2 inquiry 문의 goal 목표 request 요청하다 ideal 이상적인 audience 독자, 시청자

Questions 1-2 refer to the following advertisement.

FOR SALE

I am clearing out some equipment lying around in the house because I need to reduce my stuff. Up for sale is an almost new Juggen 1000 keyboard. It is a couple of years old, but it hasn't seen much use. It is my only keyboard. It originally came with a mouse, but I won't be including it. Selling for $50 or best offer. I live near the Delaware County area. Local buyers only.

E-mail me, Rodney Barney, at seller51@fsem.org

---

1. What has been indicated about Mr. Barney's keyboard?
   (A) It has not been used often.
   (B) It is a brand-new product.
   (C) It will be sold with a chair.
   (D) It will only be sold for $50.

2. According to the advertisement, why is Mr. Barney selling his keyboard?
   (A) He has more than one keyboard.
   (B) He wants to purchase another model.
   (C) He needs to make space in his house.
   (D) He is saving money for a house.

Unit 08 공지

Part 7

공지는 Part 7에서 가장 흔히 볼 수 있는 유형입니다. 공지의 내용은 매우 다양합니다. 회사의 경우 사내 이슈가 나오고 지역사회의 경우 지역 행사나 공익에 관련된 내용이 등장합니다. 여러 사항을 포함하고 있는 공지 유형은 질문을 읽고 지문에서 구체적인 정보를 찾은 다음 보기에 있는 단어와 비교하면서 정답을 찾아야 합니다. 공지를 하는 목적, 공지의 대상, 공지에서 요청받은 일 등을 묻는 질문이 많습니다. 문제 형식이 거의 일정하므로 조금만 익숙해지면 쉽게 문제를 풀 수 있습니다.

문제유형

▶ **공지의 목적이나 주제, 출처, 대상을 묻는 질문**

What is the purpose of the notice? 이 공지의 목적은?
Who is the notice intended for? 이 공지의 대상은?
Where would the notice most likely be found? 이 공지를 보게 될 가능성이 가장 높은 곳은?

▶ **세부 사항을 묻는 질문**

What will probably happen on July 3? 7월 3일에 일어나게 될 일은?
What is indicated about the Queens Plaza? Queens Plaza에 대해 지적된 것은?
When will the winners be chosen? 우승자들이 선정되는 때는?

▶ **요청 사항을 묻는 질문**

What is Mr. White asked to do? White 씨가 하도록 부탁받는 것은?
How can the recipients respond to the request? 요청에 대해 수령인이 응답할 수 있는 방법은?
According to the notice, what should employees do? 공지에 의하면 직원들이 해야 하는 것은?

풀이전략

▶ **공지문의 구성 형식을 알고 있어야 합니다.**

공지는 일반적으로 첫머리에 글을 쓰는 목적과 대상을 언급하고 중간 부분에서 세부적인 정보를 제공하고 끝부분에서 요청이나 제안을 합니다. 이러한 구성 형식만 알고 있으면 정답의 단서를 찾을 곳을 쉽게 파악해 신속하게 문제를 풀 수 있습니다.

▶ **특정한 날짜와 시간에 주의해야 합니다.**

공지는 보통 행사와 회의에 관련된 내용이 많아서 보통 지문의 중간 부분에 날짜와 시간이 나오는데, 이와 관련된 문제가 자주 출제됩니다. 질문에 날짜가 보이면 지문에서 바로 찾아내어 표시해 두면 빨리 정답을 찾을 수 있습니다.

Sample Test　문제풀이전략을 적용해 기출 유형 예제를 풀어 보세요.

International Festival Day

On January 22, TRUST International High School will be opening the annual festival to all students, families, faculty, and neighborhood residents. Sponsored by the Flavors Foundation, it is a time to share and experience the diversity of different cultures and enjoy the beauty of tradition.

The festival will take place indoors at the Madison Building from 10 A.M. to 5 P.M. There will be dozens of performances, such as dances, songs, rituals, and skits, which will be displaying the cultures of different countries. A raffle ticket will be given to every visitor for giving them the chance to participate with the performers on the stage. Snacks and refreshments will also be available. If you wish to support the upcoming festival, voluntary donations are gladly accepted; please contact the main office for further information.

Q. What is the purpose of the festival?
(A) To gather donations for the future
(B) To sell a raffle ticket
(C) To watch a circus performance
(D) To learn different cultures

어휘 annual 연례의　faculty 교사진　neighborhood 이웃　resident 주민　sponsor 후원하다　diversity 다양성　tradition 전통　performance 공연　ritual 의식　skit 촌극　display 보여주다, 전시하다　raffle 경품 추첨　refreshment 다과, 음료　voluntary 자발적인　donation 기부(금)

문제분석

International Festival Day 국제 축제의 날

On January 22, TRUST International High School will be opening the annual festival to all students, families, faculty, and neighborhood residents. Sponsored by the Flavors Foundation, **it is a time to share and experience the diversity of different cultures** and enjoy the beauty of tradition.

1월 22일에 TRUST 국제고등학교는 전교생, 가족들, 교사진과 이웃 주민들을 대상으로 연례 축제를 열 예정입니다. Flavors 재단의 후원을 받는 본 행사는 여러 문화의 다양성을 나누고 체험하며 전통의 아름다움을 즐기는 시간입니다.

› 2. 축제의 목적을 말하고 있는 부분입니다.

The festival will take place indoors at the Madison Building from 10 A.M. to 5 P.M. There will be dozens of performances, such as dances, songs, rituals, and skits, which will be displaying the cultures of different countries. A raffle ticket will be given to every visitor for giving them the chance to participate with the performers on the stage. Snacks and refreshments will also be available. If you wish to support the upcoming festival, voluntary donations are gladly accepted; please contact the main office for further information.

축제는 오전 10시부터 오후 5시까지 Madison 빌딩의 실내에서 열릴 예정입니다. 춤, 노래, 의식, 촌극과 같은 수십 가지 공연이 펼쳐져 여러 나라의 문화를 선보일 것입니다. 무대 위의 공연자들과 함께 참여할 기회를 드리기 위해 모든 방문객에게 경품 추첨권을 드립니다. 간식과 음료도 제공될 것입니다. 곧 있을 축제를 지원하기를 원하신다면 자발적인 기부를 기쁘게 받겠습니다. 더 자세한 정보는 본관에 문의하시기 바랍니다.

Q. What is the purpose of the festival? 축제의 목적은?

(A) To gather donations for the future 장래를 위한 기부금을 모으기 위해
(B) To sell a raffle ticket 경품 추첨권을 팔기 위해
(C) To watch a circus performances 서커스 공연을 보기 위해
(D) **To learn different cultures** 여러 문화를 배우기 위해

› 1. 축제의 목적을 묻고 있으므로 지문의 도입부에서 단서를 찾아야 합니다.

› 3. 도입부에서 단서를 찾아 쉽게 정답을 고를 수 있습니다. '여러 문화의 다양성을 체험하다'라는 말이 '여러 문화를 배우다'라는 말로 바뀌었습니다.

해설 it is a time to share and experience the diversity of different cultures에서 축제가 여러 문화의 다양성을 나누고 체험하는 시간이라고 언급하고 있으므로 (D)가 정답이다. (A)와 (C)는 지문에 언급되지 않았고 raffle ticket은 모두에게 나눠주는 것이므로 (B)도 오답이다.

Practice

정답 및 해설 p.174

Question 1 refers to the following notice.

> **PUBLIC NOTICE TO ALL LOCALS OF NIS BUILDING**
>
> In response to this month's fire safety program, all resident companies and commercial shops are required to cooperate by permitting our security personnel to inspect fire alarms and safety devices installed in the facility next week. We will also perform a fire drill from 2 P.M. to 3 P.M. on Tuesday; therefore, do not be alarmed when you hear the announcement. Please be advised that all the elevators will be out of order during the fire drill. We apologize for the inconvenience and hope that everyone understands the safety precautions that need to be taken.

1. What is the purpose of the notice?
   (A) To invite people to a fire safety session
   (B) To make an announcement about a fire drill

Question 2 refers to the following notice.

> ***Carl's Home Appliance***
>
> Thank you for visiting Carl's Home Appliance. We provide our customers various useful items from furniture to kitchen tools. Please look at the product menu for our list of sales. A discount of 3% and other benefits will be given to all customers who register for a free membership. Click on the "Join" button now and we will provide all the purchased items without any delivery charge for a month. For further information, please feel free to call our service hotline at 555-2275.

2. Where is this notice most likely to appear?
   (A) At the entrance of Carl's Home Appliance building
   (B) On Carl's Home Appliance Web site

어휘 **1** commercial 상업적인 permit 허락하다 inspect 검사하다 device 장치 install 설치하다 facility 시설 drill 훈련 precaution 예방 조치 **2** home appliance 가정용품, 가전제품 discount 할인 register 등록하다

Questions 1-2 refer to the following notice.

Unfortunately, owing to unforeseen circumstances, we will be closing our retail store at 46 Underwood Street on November 10. We have been providing customers across the country with a place to come and enjoy indoor skating for over 30 years and we thank everyone who has enabled us to make these past years so enjoyable. Until our closing, we will be offering our products and services at reduced prices of up to 50%. Thank you very much.

1   What is the main purpose of the notice?
   (A) To offer a rent discount
   (B) To announce a change in store hours
   (C) To inform people about a store closing
   (D) To look for a new store location

2   What is indicated about the store?
   (A) It has only retail stores.
   (B) It has been closed for many years.
   (C) It will reopen later.
   (D) It offers a skating rink.

Part 7

Unit 09 회람

Part 7에서 회람 유형은 글을 쓴 목적과 회람을 받는 대상, 요청 사항에 관한 질문이 주를 이룹니다. 문제 유형이 거의 정해져 있으므로, 조금만 익숙해지면 점수를 따기 쉬워집니다. 주로 직원 환송회, 축하 파티, 인사이동, 회사 정책 변경, 사무실 이전 같은 내용들이 출제됩니다.

문제유형

▶ **글의 목적과 대상을 묻는 질문**

What does the memo mainly discuss? 회람이 주로 다루고 있는 것은?
What is the purpose of the memo? 회람의 목적은?
For whom is the memo most likely intended? 회람의 대상은?
What is being announced? 알리고 있는 것은?

▶ **요청 사항을 묻는 질문**

What are employees asked to do? 직원들이 하도록 부탁받는 것은?
What are hotel employees instructed to do? 호텔 직원들이 하도록 지시받는 것은?

▶ **세부 사항을 묻는 질문**

What is NOT suggested about the apartment? 아파트에 관해 암시되지 않은 것은?
Where does Greg Williams work? Greg Williams가 일하는 곳은?
What is indicated about Mr. Moon? Moon 씨에 대해 지적된 것은?

풀이전략

▶ **회람의 구성 형식을 알고 있어야 합니다.**

회람은 일반적으로 첫머리에 받는 사람과 보내는 사람, 글의 목적과 대상이 나오고 가운데 부분에서 세부적인 정보를 제공하고 마지막 부분에 문의하는 방법을 알리거나 요청이나 제안을 합니다. 이 구성만 알고 있으면 답의 단서를 어디서 찾을지 쉽게 파악하고 지문을 편하게 읽을 수 있습니다.

▶ **특정 날짜와 시간에 주의해야 합니다.**

회람은 보통 행사와 회의에 관련된 내용이 많아서 보통 지문의 중간 부분에 날짜와 시간이 나오는데, 이와 관련된 문제가 자주 출제됩니다. 질문에 날짜가 보이면 지문에서 바로 찾아 표시해 두면 빨리 답을 찾을 수 있습니다.

Sample Test

문제풀이전략을 적용해 기출 유형 예제를 풀어 보세요.

To: All team members
From: Jane Kang, Manager of Production Development
Date: March 19
Subject: Announcements

Dear colleagues:

I am pleased to announce that everyone who is working on developing our current video game project is invited to a casual dinner this Friday. On this occasion, I will also introduce our newest team member, Monty Osborn. As most of you might already know, Mr. Osborn greatly assisted us with script writing in our previous collaboration with TR Productions five months ago. Now, with seven years of experience, he will be responsible for 3D model art, such as preparing layouts, animation, and rendering.

I am convinced that Mr. Osborn will be a valuable asset to the team and I hope that you will be able to participate in this special dinner and use it as an opportunity to get to know your team members better. If you can attend, please inform Martha, my secretary, by March 25, so that we can make reservations at a restaurant. I am looking forward to seeing you all soon.

Sincerely,
Jane Kang

Q. What will Mr. Osborn be responsible for?
(A) Writing scripts for a film
(B) Designing computer graphics
(C) Preparing portfolios
(D) Taking photos of sculptures

어휘 announcement 알림, 공고 colleague 동료 casual 편한 occasion (특정한) 때, 행사 assist 돕다 script 대본 previous 이전의 collaboration 공동 작업 experience 경험 layout 레이아웃, 배치 rendering 렌더링, 완성 예상도 convince 설득하다 valuable 가치 있는 asset 자산 participate 참가하다 opportunity 기회 attend 참석하다 secretary 비서 reservation 예약

문제분석

To: All team members 수신: 모든 팀원
From: Jane Kang, Manager of Production Development 발신: Jane Kang, 생산 개발 과장
Date: March 19 날짜: 3월 19일
Subject: Announcements 제목: 알림

Dear colleagues: 동료 여러분께

I am pleased to announce that everyone who is working on developing our current video game project is invited to a casual dinner this Friday. On this occasion, I will also introduce our newest team member, Monty Osborn. As most of you might already know, Mr. Osborn greatly assisted us with script writing in our previous collaboration with TR Productions five months ago. Now, with seven years of experience, he will be responsible for 3D model art, such as preparing layouts, animation, and rendering.

우리의 현재 비디오 게임 프로젝트 개발을 진행하고 있는 모든 분을 이번 주 금요일 가벼운 저녁식사에 초대한다는 것을 알려드리게 되어 기쁩니다. 또한 이 자리에서 새 구성원인 Monty Osborn 씨를 소개할 예정입니다. 여러분 중의 대부분이 아마 아시다시피 Osborn 씨는 5개월 전 TR 프로덕션과 함께한 우리의 이전 공동 작업에서 우리의 대본 작성을 아주 많이 도와주었습니다. 이제 경력 7년차인 그는 레이아웃 준비, 애니메이션, 렌더링과 같은 3차원 모델 미술을 담당할 예정입니다.

I am convinced that Mr. Osborn will be a valuable asset to the team and I hope that you will be able to participate in this special dinner and use it as an opportunity to get to know your team members better. If you can attend, please inform Martha, my secretary, by March 25, so that we can make reservations at a restaurant. I am looking forward to seeing you all soon.

저는 Osborn 씨가 우리 팀에 아주 귀중한 자산이 될 것이라 확신하며 여러분이 이번 특별한 저녁식사에 참여해 여러분의 팀원들을 더 잘 알게 되는 기회로 활용할 수 있기를 바랍니다. 참석하실 수 있다면 우리가 식당을 예약할 수 있도록 3월 25일까지 제 비서인 Martha에게 알려주시기 바랍니다. 여러분 모두를 곧 만나기를 고대하고 있습니다.

Sincerely,
Jane Kang

Q. What will Mr. Osborn be responsible for? Osborn 씨가 담당하게 될 일은?

(A) Writing scripts for a film 영화의 대본 작성
(B) Designing computer graphics 컴퓨터 그래픽 디자인
(C) Preparing portfolios 포트폴리오 준비
(D) Taking photos of sculptures 조각품들의 사진 촬영

1. 세부 사항을 묻고 있습니다. 지문에서 Mr. Osborn이 나온 부분을 빨리 찾아야 합니다.
2. 질문에서 언급하는 이름이 있습니다. 앞뒤 문장을 읽어봅니다.
3. 비디오 게임 프로젝트 개발에 관여하는 사람임을 알 수 있습니다.
4. Mr Osborn이 맡게 될 구체적인 업무들을 제시하고 있습니다.
5. 3D model art를 담당한다고 했으므로 (B) 그래픽 디자인 업무가 정답임을 알 수 있습니다.

해설 지문 중간의 he will be responsible for 3D model art, such as preparing layouts, animation, and rendering에서 Osborn 씨가 컴퓨터 그래픽 디자인을 담당하게 된다는 것을 알 수 있으므로 (B)가 정답이다.

Practice

정답 및 해설 p.176

Question 1 refers to the following memo.

TO: All Pixapro employees
FROM: Julia Daring, Human Resource Management
RE: Pixapro Employee Survey

As you all may have heard by now, HRM will begin a survey for all Pixapro employees on May 10. The survey will be also accessible online. However, please note that the online survey will be available one day after its implementation. Simply visit www.pixapro.com and click on the "take survey" icon after logging into your personal account.

1 When can the survey be taken online?
(A) On May 10
(B) On May 11

Question 2 refers to the following memo.

To : All employees
From: Betty Miller, Manager, Technical Department
Re: Technical Inquiry

I would like to inform all employees of Vogatis Company that the Technical Department will be updating the main servers next week. Owing to their unavailability during this time, we advise that those who need specific equipment repair submit an inquiry to Ms. Rinas, our assistant manager. If you require urgent technical assistance, please contact Mr. Schutt on his mobile.

2 What are employees being asked to do?
(A) Call Mr. Schutt for urgent technical support
(B) Leave an inquiry at the Technical Department office

어휘 **1** human resource management 인사부 employee 직원 survey 설문조사 accessible 접속 가능한 note 주목하다 implementation 이행, 실행 account 계좌, 계정 **2** inquiry 문의 owing to ~ 때문에 unavailability 이용할 수 없음 specific 특정한 submit 제출하다 require 필요로 하다 urgent 긴급한 assistance 도움, 지원

Actual Test

정답 및 해설 p.177

Questions 1-4 refer to the following information.

Dear Northwest Airlines customers,

The mission of Northwest Airlines is dedication to the highest quality of customer service and we are very sorry for the inconvenience due to your flight's delay. --- [1] --- As soon as the weather gets better, we will resume operation. --- [2] --- We will distribute meal vouchers and coupons for a complimentary beverage at the front desk of Northwest Airlines in JFK Airport. --- [3] --- I apologize for the inconvenience you may have experienced. Customer service is our first priority and we look forward to serving you again. --- [4] ---

Vice president
Customer Relations
Northwest Airlines
Dallas, Texas 75235-1647

1 Why does the plane seem to be delayed?
(A) Because of the bad weather
(B) Because the pilot is sick
(C) Because of problems with the plane
(D) Because flight attendants are on strike

2 Why was the coupon given to customers?
(A) To notify the delay of the flight
(B) To apologize to customers
(C) To thank them for completing a survey
(D) To promote airline tickets

3 In which of the positions marked [1], [2], [3], and [4] does the following sentence best belong?
"You can use those coupons inside the airport."
(A) [1]
(B) [2]
(C) [3]
(D) [4]

Unit 10 안내문

Part 7

Part 7에서 안내문 유형은 광고문과 거의 같은 형태입니다. 글을 쓴 목적, 안내문이 게시된 장소와 안내문의 대상, 안내문의 세부 내용에 관한 질문이 주로 출제됩니다. 세부 내용에는 주의 사항, 절차, 제품 이용 방법, 회사 안내 등이 포함됩니다.

문제유형

▶ **글의 목적을 묻는 질문**

What is this information about? 이 안내문은 무엇에 관한 것인가?
What is the purpose of the information? 이 안내문의 목적은?

▶ **장소와 대상을 묻는 질문**

Where would the information most likely be found? 이 안내문이 발견될 가능성이 가장 높은 곳은?
Who will read this information? 이 안내문을 읽게 될 사람은?
For whom is the information intended? 이 안내문의 대상은?

▶ **세부 사항을 묻는 질문**

What type of products does the company sell? 회사가 팔고 있는 제품의 종류는?
What is mentioned about the company's facility? 회사의 설비에 관해 언급된 것은?
What is indicated about luggage? 짐에 대해 알 수 있는 것은?

▶ **요청 사항을 묻는 질문**

What are customers asked to do? 고객이 하도록 요청받는 것은?
What recommendation is made? 추천하는 것은?
What does Mr. Gonzales request? Gonzales 씨가 요청하는 것은?

풀이전략

▶ **목적이나 이유, 대상을 묻는 질문은 주로 지문의 앞부분에 단서가 나옵니다.**

반면에 안내문이 붙어 있는 위치에 관한 것은 전체를 다 읽고 추론을 통해 풀어야 하는 경우가 많습니다.

▶ **질문의 핵심어에 집중해야 합니다.**

안내문의 질문에는 대부분 고유명사나 특정한 날짜가 등장합니다. 이 부분을 지문에서 빨리 찾아 앞뒤 문장에서 단서를 빨리 파악해야 합니다.

Sample Test   문제풀이전략을 적용해 기출 유형 예제를 풀어 보세요.

Have you heard about CR101?

Ellasion Innovation Inc. will be launching CR101, a new universal remote control, which is integrated with LiveBay home appliances and Ellasion model devices. Once installation and connections are completed, the CR101 will enable residents to comfortably access their televisions, stereos, air conditioners, gas boilers, lamp stands, front door locks, washing machines, and electric stoves. Synchronizations will be arranged by trained technicians. If you wish to order this remote control, please visit your nearest Ellasion electrical outlet mall for more information or visit us at www.ellinnovate.com.

Q. Which of the following functions can be performed by the CR101?

(A) Operating refrigerator temperatures

(B) Automatic calling service for a technician

(C) Heating water for bathrooms and kitchen

(D) Timed operation of microwave ovens

어휘 launch 출시하다 universal 보편적인 integrate 통합하다 appliance 가전제품 installation 설치 resident 거주자 comfortably 편안하게 access 접근하다, 이용하다 synchronization 동기화

문제분석

Have you heard about CR101? CR101에 대해 들어보셨나요?

Ellasion Innovation Inc. will be launching CR101, a new universal remote control, which is integrated with LiveBay home appliances and Ellasion model devices. Once installation and connections are completed, the CR101 will enable residents to comfortably access their televisions, stereos, air conditioners, gas boilers, lamp stands, front door locks, washing machines, and electric stoves. Synchronizations will be arranged by trained technicians. If you wish to order this remote control, please visit your nearest Ellasion electrical outlet mall for more information or visit us at www.ellinnovate.com.

Ellasion Innovation은 LiveBay 가전제품과 Ellasion 모델 장비가 통합된 새로운 범용 원격 제어 장치인 CR101을 출시할 예정입니다. 일단 설치 및 연결이 끝나면 CR101은 거주자가 쉽게 텔레비전, 스테레오, 에어컨, 가스보일러, 스탠드 램프, 현관문 잠금장치, 세탁기와 전기레인지를 이용할 수 있게 합니다. 동기화는 숙련된 전문가에 의해 진행될 것입니다. 이 원격 제어 장치를 주문하기 원하시면 가장 가까운 Ellasion 전자 상가에 방문하셔서 더 많은 정보를 얻으시거나 저희 사이트 www.ellinnovate.com를 방문하시기 바랍니다.

2. 동사 enable에서 제품의 기능이 나올 것임을 예상할 수 있습니다.

1. 제품의 기능에 대해서 물어보고 있음을 빨리 파악하고 지문을 읽기 시작합니다.

Q. Which of the following functions can be performed by the CR101?
다음 중 CR101이 수행할 수 있는 기능은?

(A) Operating refrigerator temperatures 냉장고 온도 조절
(B) Automatic calling service for a technician 기술자를 위한 자동 전화 연결 서비스
(C) Heating water for bathrooms and kitchen 욕실과 주방의 온수 공급
(D) Timed heating for microwave ovens 전자레인지 예약 작동

3. 지문의 gas boilers의 기능을 다른 표현으로 바꾸어 쓴 (C)가 정답입니다.

해설 지문에 언급된 gas boilers로 미루어 난방을 가능하게 한다는 것을 알 수 있으므로 이를 바꾸어 표현한 (C)가 정답이다. 나머지 보기는 지문에서 언급되지 않았기 때문에 답이 될 수 없다.

Practice

정답 및 해설 p.178

Question 1 refers to the following information.

> Thank you for choosing the Barovo Health Center, a place to gather and enjoy exercising! Please feel free to use our extra programs and facilities, including our badminton courts, giant swimming pool, well-being snack bar, massage spa, and group aerobics. On your first membership admission, you will be offered a free gym introduction with our personal trainer. If you wish to receive a free training trial, please speak with our front desk staff and fill out a brief physical information form.

1. What needs to be arranged at the front desk?
   (A) Gym introductions
   (B) Complimentary trials

Question 2 refers to the following information.

> **Annual Winter Sale!**
> **Winter Wears at Low Prices!**
>
> It is finally time for the Braveaux Annual Winter Sale Event! All Braveaux stores will be launching a winter sale next week for all its customers. Huge discounts are being offered on winter wear, such as coats and jackets. The newly released duck-down jumper is also a popular item. It is designed with an easy zipper fit and packed with the best duck feathers to make you warm even in the coldest temperatures. Covered with quality Gore-Tex fabric and a removable hoodie, it is the ideal winter jumper for people seeking both warmth and fashion.

2. What is NOT stated about the jumper?
   (A) It can withstand the winter cold.
   (B) It has an elastic fit for any wearer.

어휘 **1** gather 모이다 extra 특별한 aerobics 에어로빅, 유산소 운동 admission 가입 free training 무료 체험 교육 brief 간단한 **2** launch 개시하다 discount 할인 duck-down 오리털 fit (옷이) 몸에 맞음 removable 제거할 수 있는 ideal 이상적인 seek 찾다, 추구하다

266

Questions 1-3 refer to the following information.

Grand Opening
Hamilton Dance School for the Gifted
Friday, February 22

10:00 A.M. Welcome Ceremony and Opening Remarks
Mayor John Oldman
Director Ivan Rueol

Each of the instructors of the school will give short speeches regarding their expectations for the future of the academy.

11:30 A.M.–12:30 P.M.
An open forum will be held where people's questions and concerns will be answered by Instructor Sylvia Ena.

12:30 P.M. Lunch and Refreshments
A buffet-style meal will be served by Rose Catering Services.

2:00 P.M. Performance from Instructors
Danny Revitt from the hit television show, Dance with Me, will perform a special dance with his dance partner, Rumi Rodrick.

3:00 P.M. Closing Ceremony
The Director will end the day with a toast to the success of the academy, followed by a short message to prospective students.

---

1 Who is the director of the school?
 (A) John Oldman
 (B) Ivan Rueol
 (C) Danny Revitt
 (D) Rumi Rodrick

2 What is implied about Silvia Ena?
 (A) She is a school graduate.
 (B) She is a news anchor.
 (C) She is a teacher at the school.
 (D) She is a prospective student.

3 According to the information, what did Danny Revitt do?
 (A) He has given a speech at school.
 (B) He was on a television dance show.
 (C) He previously owned the school.
 (D) He taught at the dance school.

Unit 11 기사

Part 7

기사문 유형은 지문의 길이가 상당히 길고 어휘의 수준이 높기 때문에 Part 7에서 가장 난이도가 높은 유형에 속합니다. 기사의 주제, 특성, 세부 내용, 내용 일치/불일치에 관한 질문이 주를 이룹니다. 회사의 합병, 제품 출시, 최근 경제 소식, 사업 실적, 사업 확장이나 행사, 지역 도로 공사 등의 내용이 자주 등장합니다.

문제유형

▶ **글의 주제와 목적을 묻는 질문**

What is this article mainly about? 이 기사의 주된 내용은?
What is the purpose of the article? 기사의 목적은?

▶ **세부 사항을 묻는 질문**

According to the article, how can people learn more about the product?
기사에 따르면, 사람들이 제품에 대해 더 알 수 있는 방법은?

What does Tiffany Salem say about the construction? Tiffany Salem이 건설에 대해 하는 말은?
What will happen after May 5? 5월 5일 이후에 일어날 일은?

▶ **내용 일치/불일치**

Which is NOT reported to be a reason for increased cruise travel?
유람선 여행이 증가하고 있는 이유로 보도되지 않는 것은?

What is NOT a feature of the product? 제품의 특징이 아닌 것은?
What is NOT stated in the article? 기사에서 언급되지 않는 것은?

풀이전략

▶ **기사 지문을 보지 말고 문제를 먼저 보면서 핵심어에 표시해야 합니다.**

핵심어를 미리 파악하지 않고 지문을 먼저 읽으면 읽었던 지문을 다시 읽어야 하는 경우가 생깁니다.

▶ **질문의 핵심어에 집중합니다.**

질문에 나오는 고유명사나 날짜가 등장하는 부분을 지문에서 찾아 앞뒤 문장을 파악해야 합니다.

▶ **기사문의 제목도 꼭 읽어야 합니다.**

기사 지문의 제목에서 대략적인 주제와 내용을 먼저 파악할 수 있으므로 제목을 반드시 확인해야 합니다.

Sample Test — 문제풀이전략을 적용해 기출 유형 예제를 풀어 보세요.

Trenton, July 8 - Last Friday, Enjoi Coffee, a popular café chain, opened a new store in Trenton, New Jersey. The store has been quite successful, conducting more business than their main stores.

Joshua Ling, founder of Enjoi Coffee, interviewed with us that this may pave the way for more local store locations in the near future. He expressed his interest in opening local stores, primarily near the Pennsylvanian cities of Philadelphia and Pittsburgh. He also thanked all the customers who enjoy having Enjoi coffee.

Mr. Ling originally opened the first branch located in New York, in March of 2000, in which cafés and similar outlets were neither well-known nor popular. Ever since, many new café stores have opened; however, none of them have experienced the success that Enjoi Coffee has.

Q. What is mentioned about Joshua Ling?
(A) He graduated a university in Pittsburgh.
(B) He has inherited the business from his father.
(C) He has only opened one store location.
(D) He is interested in opening stores locally.

어휘 / popular 인기 있는, 유명한 successful 성공적인 conduct 운영하다, 수행하다 founder 창업자 pave the way for ~을 위해 길을 닦다, ~을 용이하게 하다 express 표시하다 primarily 첫째로, 주로 similar 유사한 outlet 직판점, 판매 대리점

문제분석

> Trenton, July 8 - Last Friday, Enjoi Coffee, a popular café chain, opened a new store in Trenton, New Jersey. The store has been quite successful, conducting more business than their main stores.
> 7월 8일, Trenton – 지난주 금요일, 인기 카페 체인인 Enjoi Coffee가 New Jersey 주 Trenton에 새 매장을 열었다. 그 매장은 아주 성공적이어서 그 체인의 주요 매장들보다 장사가 더 잘되고 있다.
>
> Joshua Ling, founder of Enjoi Coffee, interviewed with us that this may pave the way for more local store locations in the near future. He expressed his interest in opening local stores, primarily near the Pennsylvanian cities of Philadelphia and Pittsburgh. He also thanked all the customers who enjoy having Enjoi coffee.
> Enjoi Coffee의 설립자, Joshua Ling은 인터뷰에서 이 매장이 가까운 미래에 더 많은 지역 매장들을 열기 위한 길을 닦는 것일 수도 있다고 말했다. 그는 주로 Pennsylvania 주의 도시들인 Philadelphia와 Pittsburgh 근처에 지역 매장들을 여는 것에 관심을 표시했다. 그는 또한 Enjoi 커피를 즐겨 마시는 모든 고객들에게 감사했다.
>
> Mr. Ling originally opened the first branch, located in New York, in March of 2000, in which cafés and similar outlets were neither well-known nor popular. Ever since, many new café stores have opened; however, none of them have experienced the success that Enjoi Coffee has.
> Ling 씨는 원래 2000년 3월, 뉴욕에 1호점을 열었는데, 그곳에서는 카페와 그와 유사한 직판점들이 유명하지도 인기가 있지도 않았다. 그 이후로 많은 새로운 카페 매장들이 문을 열었다. 하지만, 그곳들 중 아무 곳도 Enjoi Coffee가 거둔 성공을 거두지 못했다.

2. 지문에서 Joshua Ling이 등장하는 부분에 정답의 단서가 있습니다.

Q. **What is mentioned about Joshua Ling?** Joshua Ling에 관해 언급되는 것은?

(A) He graduated a university in Pittsburgh. 그는 피츠버그의 한 대학교를 졸업했다.
(B) He has inherited the business from his father. 그는 아버지로부터 사업을 물려받았다.
(C) He has only opened one store location. 그는 한 매장만을 열었다.
(D) **He is interested in opening stores locally.** 그는 지역마다 매장들을 여는 데 관심이 있다.

1. 문제에 고유명사 Joshua Ling이 제시되었습니다.

3. 둘째 단락의 He expressed his interest in opening local stores를 바꾸어 표현한 (D)가 정답이 됩니다.

해설 Joshua Ling이 언급된 두 번째 단락, He expressed his interest in opening local stores, primarily near the Pennsylvanian cities of Philadelphia and Pittsburgh.에서 펜실베이니아 주에 있는 도시들 근처에 지역 매장들을 여는 데 관심을 표시했다고 했으므로 (D)가 정답이다.

Practice

정답 및 해설 p.181

Question 1 refers to the following article.

Serexin Packaging Tech will be presenting its new PSI film at the upcoming annual Food Processing & Packaging Expo. Acknowledged by over 20 different countries, the customized food film is suitable for all types of products that require fresh food packaging. Its diversity in thickness permits superior flexibility and tear resistance, ideal for any wrapping machine. Besides its optimal permeability to water, steam, and gases, it enhances product appeal and preserves product freshness.

1 What is NOT mentioned as a feature of PSI film?
(A) It is resistant to tearing.
(B) It extends the expiry date of foods.

Question 2 refers to the following article.

Dengue fever is an infectious disease, which is known to cause severe pain in the eyes and head. Transmitted by the bite of a mosquito called *Aedes aegypti*, this disease causes patients to suffer from fever, headache, muscle and joint pain, and allergies. If it spread towards the lower body, it may also cause abdominal pain or vomiting. The classic dengue fever usually lasts about six to seven days, and the patient's temperature eventually drops. Though it is very common during rainy seasons in tropical regions, it is considered to be heading towards extinction.

2 What does this article say about dengue fever?
(A) It is contagious among people.
(B) It is no longer a threat.

어휘 **1** upcoming 다가오는 annual 연례의 acknowledge 인정하다 customized 맞춤형의 suitable 적합한 diversity 다양함 thickness 두께 permit 가능하게 하다, 허용하다 superior 뛰어난 flexibility 유연성 tear 찢어짐 resistance 저항력 wrapping 포장 besides 게다가, 이외에도 optimal 최적의 permeability 투과성 steam 수증기 enhance 개선하다 appeal 매력 freshness 신선함 **2** fever 열병 infectious disease 전염병 severe 심한 pain 통증 transmit (병을) 옮기다 mosquito 모기 muscle 근육 spread 퍼지다 abdominal 복부의 vomit 구토하다 temperature 체온 eventually 결국, 마침내 common 흔한 tropical 열대의 consider 간주하다, 여기다 extinction 소멸, 멸종

Unit 11 : 기사

Questions 1-3 refer to the following e-mail.

To: Harry Pratt, Director of advertising department
From: Kris Jenner, Vice President
Subject: Jessica Simpson
Date: May 12

Dear Harry,

I heard that your department has won several new clients this month. --- [1] --- I would like you to consider Jessica Simpson for an advertising assistant position on your team. --- [2] --- She has been an intern in my office for the last six months, and she is organized, efficient and extremely competent. --- [3] --- She follows directions well and has worked both independently and with groups. The feedback on her contributions has been very positive. Ms. Simpson completed her degree in business this year and I'm aware that she is interested in pursuing her career in advertising here. I would be happy to provide you with more information. --- [4] --- If you have any questions about her, please do not hesitate to contact me.

Sincerely,

Kris Jenner

Vice President

Passion Associates

---

1 What is the purpose of the e-mail?

(A) To describe a change in hiring policies.
(B) To make a recommendation.
(C) To request a report on new clients.
(D) To propose a meeting agenda.

2 What does the e-mail indicate about Ms. Jenner?

(A) She recently started a business.
(B) She would like to join Harry's team.
(C) She will be promoted.
(D) She has worked with Ms. Simpson for half a year.

3 In which of the positions marked [1], [2], [3], and [4] does the following sentence best belong?
"Congratulations and I believe you are in need of additional staff."

(A) [1]
(B) [2]
(C) [3]
(D) [4]

Part 7

Unit 12 송장과 양식

Part 7의 송장과 양식은 다소 쉬운 유형에 해당합니다. 양식에 기재되어 있는 숫자와 날짜 등이 중요하며 양식의 작성 목적과 용도, 회사의 종류와 제품, 수치와 날짜, 시간, 금액 등을 주로 묻습니다. 제품 주문서, TV 프로그램, 채널, 방영 시간, 여행 일정, 멤버 가입 신청서, 고객 평가서, 요금 청구서 등의 내용이 자주 등장합니다.

문제유형

▶ **목적과 업종을 묻는 질문**

What is the purpose of the form? 양식의 목적은?
What is WSJ? WSJ는 무엇인가?

▶ **세부 사항을 묻는 질문**

How much will Mr. Watson pay? Watson 씨가 내야 하는 금액은?
What is indicated about the form? 양식에 관해 지적된 것은?
When do Ms. Rose want to leave for Busan? Rose 씨가 부산으로 떠나기를 원하는 때는?

▶ **내용 일치/불일치**

What is NOT listed as a method of donation? 기부 방식으로 나열되지 않는 것은?
Who does NOT have an appointment in the afternoon? 오후에 약속이 없는 사람은?
What is NOT mentioned as a way to purchase bus tickets? 버스표를 구입하는 방법으로 언급되지 않는 것은?

풀이전략

▶ **제목과 보낸 사람의 업종, 표에 기재된 제품에 집중해야 합니다.**

양식의 목적이나 용도는 주로 제목이나 지문의 초반부에 단서가 나옵니다. 업종과 제품은 표에 기재된 품목을 통해 추론할 수 있습니다.

▶ **구체적인 날짜나 수치 등에 유의해야 합니다.**

날짜나 수치에 관한 문제는 반드시 1문항은 출제되므로 지문의 숫자에 집중하는 연습을 미리 해 두어야 합니다.

▶ **예외적인 사항에 주의해야 합니다.**

예외 사항이 있으면 표나 양식의 하단에 따로 명시하는 경우가 많으므로 이 부분을 반드시 놓치지 않도록 해야 합니다.

Sample Test   문제풀이전략을 적용해 기출 유형 예제를 풀어 보세요.

RECEIPT

Date: 28 August

Received from: Hyun-Sung Lee
The sum of: $ 370

For rent at   Avalon Apartments
                     No. 14 6B Street
                     Binh Hung, District 9

For the period from 1 September to 30 September.

The next monthly payment is due no later than   3 October.

Received by: Harry C. Floyd
Signature: *Harry C. Floyd*

Q. When was the money received?
   (A) On August 28
   (B) On September 1
   (C) On September 31
   (D) On October 3

어휘 sum 총액 rent 임대, 집세 period 기간 payment 지급, 납부 due 지불해야 하는 no later than 늦어도 ~까지

문제분석

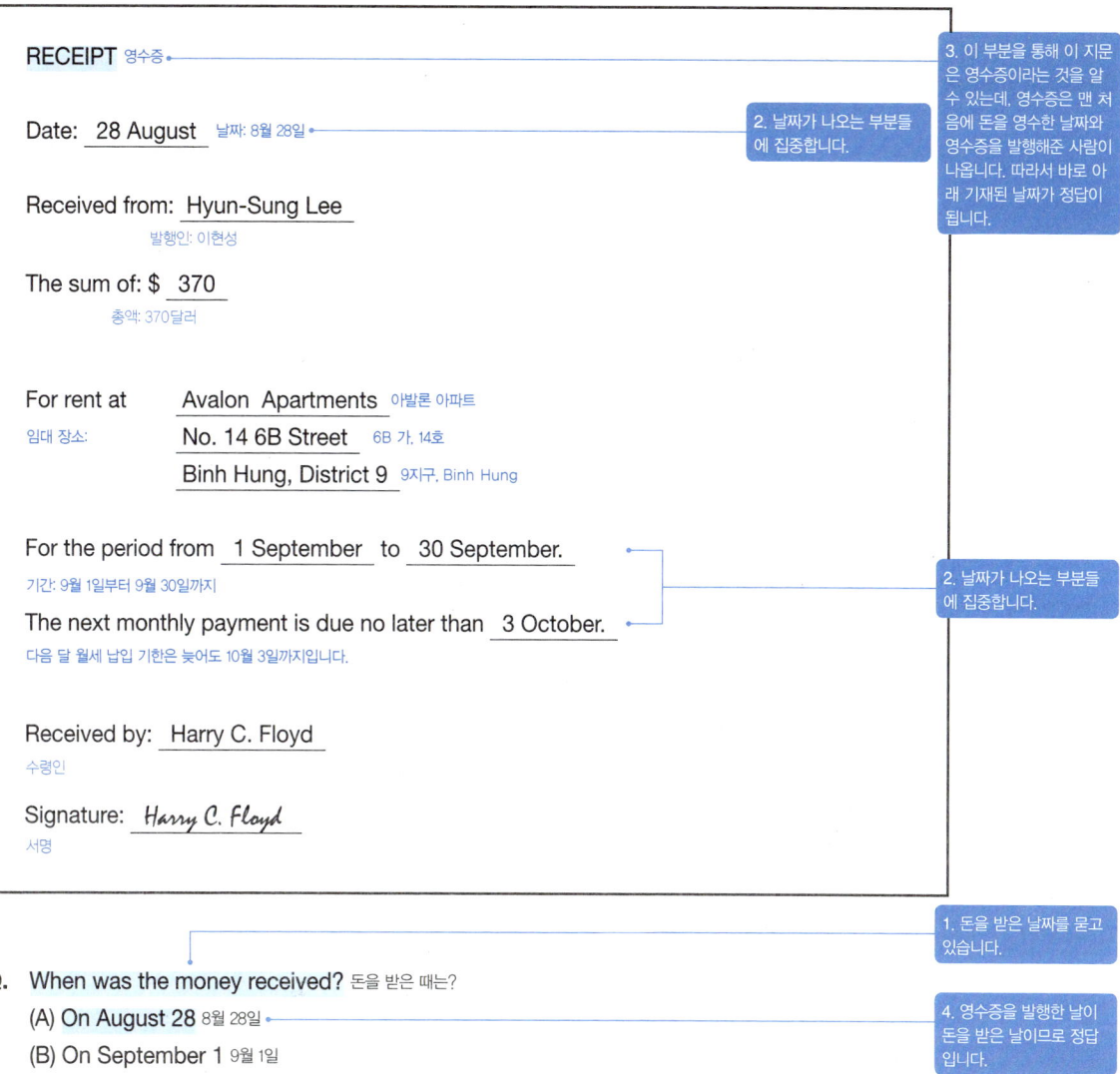

Q. When was the money received? 돈을 받은 때는?
 (A) On August 28 8월 28일
 (B) On September 1 9월 1일
 (C) On September 30 9월 30일
 (D) On October 3 10월 3일

해설 지문 상단에 RECEIPT라고 되어 있어 영수증임을 알 수 있고, 날짜가 28 August와 함께 발행인과 총액이 기재되어 있으므로 돈을 받은 때가 (A)임을 알 수 있다. (B)와 (C)는 임대 기간이며(For the period from 1 September to 30 September.), (D)는 다음 달 월세 납입 기한(The next monthly payment is due no later than 3 October.)이다.

Practice

정답 및 해설 p.184

Question 1 refers to the following invoice.

Intelox Inc. 3334 North Dackson Street Wichita, Kansas 67203				
Invoice Number	2144		Invoice Date	May 22
Balance Due	$1300.00		Payment Due	June 21
Billed to:	Joseph Levinson 8015 North Elmwood Avenue Kansas City, Missouri 64119			
Catalog No.	Product Name	Qty.	Unit Price	Total
122	23-in LED Monitor VH8-P	2	139.99	279.98
554	AG3620-UR Desktop PC	1	882.25	882.25
81	G500 Wireless Mouse	1	57.18	57.18
107	Elite Keyboard RZ03-U1	1	113.00	113.00
Subtotal				$1332.41
Shipping and Handling				70.00
Total Purchasing				$1402.41
Frequent-customer Bonus Discount				−102.41

1 What is suggested by the invoice?

(A) That delivery is free of cost

(B) That repeat customers are rewarded

Question 2 refers to the following invoice.

KEST Supermarkets
Delivery Invoice

Quantity	Item Name	Item Price	Total
3	Honey Nut Cereals	3.98	$11.94
7	Corned Beef Hash	22.46	$157.22
5	Ranch Style Beans	33.19	$165.95
2	Roast Ground Coffee	6.98	$13.96

2 Which product is the most expensive?

(A) Corned Beef Hash

(B) Ranch Style Beans

어휘 **1** invoice 청구서, 송장 balance due 미납 금액 payment due 지급 기한 qty. 수량 (quantity) unit price 단위 가격 subtotal 소계 shipping and handling 발송 및 취급 frequent-customer 단골 고객 **2** delivery 배송 honey 꿀 nut 견과류 hash 해시 (삶아서 잘게 썬 고기 요리)

276

Questions 1-3 refer to the following online form.

http://www.bankofamericangold.com/apply/form

American Gold Online Application Form

Please take a moment to fill in the following fields.
After completing the form, click the "Save and continue to Payment Options section" arrow at the bottom-right corner of the screen.

Personal information:

Name:	Emily Richards
Organization:	Kansas State University
Address:	705 Hickory Circle, Kansas City, KS 64101
E-mail:	erichards@kansu.edu

Select one:
◎ I am at least 18 years of age.
● I am below 18 years of age and will require the permission of a parent.

Select your account type:
◎ Premium $100
◎ Basic Plus $70
◎ Basic $40
● Free $0

Select a card type (optional):
◎ Credit Card $10
● Debit Card $10
None

→ Click

---

1 Why did Ms. Richards complete the form?

(A) To apply for a graduate school
(B) To sign up for a bank account
(C) To enter a countrywide contest
(D) To renew a membership

2 How much will Ms. Richards probably be charged?

(A) $10
(B) $40
(C) $70
(D) $100

3 Who most likely is Ms. Richards?

(A) A college professor
(B) A bank employee
(C) A university student
(D) A faculty

Part 7

Unit 13 초대장

Part 7의 초대장은 난이도가 다소 낮은 유형입니다. 초대장에 있는 행사의 날짜나 장소 등이 중요하며 행사의 종류, 행사의 주체, 초대를 받는 대상, 행사 일정, 행사 빈도 등을 묻습니다. 창립 기념식, 국제 페스티벌, 입학식, 졸업식, 연례 총회, 영화, 연극 등의 내용이 자주 등장합니다.

문제유형

▶ 행사의 주체와 대상을 묻는 질문

What foundation is hosting this conference? 이 총회를 주최하는 재단은?
Who is this invitation for? 이 초대장을 받는 대상은?

▶ 세부 사항을 묻는 질문

When will Ms. Diaz's latest film be shown? Diaz의 최신 영화가 상영되는 때는?
What should Mr. Park do if he wants to buy tickets? Park 씨가 표를 사려면 해야 하는 것은?
When does the event close on the last day? 마지막 날 행사는 언제 끝나는가?

▶ 내용 일치/불일치

What is NOT covered by the $200 fee? 200달러 수업료에 포함되지 않는 것은?
What does the invitation NOT offer to guests? 초대장에서 손님들에게 제공하지 않는 것은?

풀이전략

▶ 행사의 종류와 주최자는 대개 지문의 첫머리에 단서가 있습니다.

제목이나 제목 아래의 1~2행에서 문제 해결의 단서를 찾을 수 있습니다.

▶ 구체적인 날짜나 시각 등에 유의해야 합니다.

날짜나 시각에 관한 문제는 반드시 1문항이 출제되므로 지문의 숫자에 민감해지는 연습을 미리 해 두어야 합니다.

▶ 요청 사항이나 추가 정보에 유의해야 합니다.

요청 사항이나 추가 정보는 대개 지문의 맨 아래에 따로 나오므로 이 부분을 반드시 놓치지 말아야 합니다.

Sample Test — 문제풀이전략을 적용해 기출 유형 예제를 풀어 보세요.

As a valuable member of the Presley Group, you are pleasantly asked to join our 20th anniversary celebration.

Friday, December 29
The Pacific Hall of Holly's Hotel
31 River Drive
Somton City

6:30 P.M. Opening Speech
Remarks by the CEO, John Gradula

7:00 P.M. Banquet
Appetizers, a main entree, beverages, and dessert

8:00 P.M. Awards Ceremony
A ceremony to acknowledge the best employee of the year

There will be an orchestra performance during the dinner.
All donations made by our members in the event are to be used for improving the working environment.

Please make sure to contact Lindsay at extension #133 to confirm your attendance by Friday, December 22.

Q. What must guests do prior to attending the event?

(A) Call Lindsay's office
(B) Reserve a flight
(C) Arrange an interview
(D) Purchase tickets

어휘 valuable 가치 있는, 소중한 opening speech 개회사 remark 발언, 논평 banquet 연회 appetizer 전채 요리, 애피타이저 entrée 앙트레, 주요리 acknowledge 인정하다, 감사를 표하다 donation 기부금 working environment 근무 환경 extension 내선, 구내전화 confirm 확인해 주다 attendance 참석

문제분석

As a valuable member of the Presley Group, you are pleasantly asked to join our 20th anniversary celebration. Presley 그룹의 소중한 회원인 귀하를 저희 20주년 기념일 축하 행사에 기쁘게 초대합니다.

Friday, December 29 12월 29일, 금요일
The Pacific Hall of Holly's Hotel Holly's 호텔, Pacific Hall
31 River Drive 31 River Drive
Somton City Somton 시

6:30 P.M. Opening Speech 오후 6시 30분, 개회사
Remarks by the CEO, John Gradula 최고경영자 John Gradula의 짧은 연설

7:00 P.M. Banquet 오후 7시, 연회
Appetizers, a main entrée, beverages, and dessert 애피타이저, 주요리, 음료, 디저트

8:00 P.M. Awards Ceremony 오후 8시, 시상식
A ceremony to acknowledge the best employee of the year
올해의 최고 직원을 인정하는 예식

There will be an orchestra performance during the dinner.
저녁 식사 동안 오케스트라 공연이 있을 예정입니다.

All donations made by our members in the event are to be used for improving the working environment.
행사에서 회원들이 내시는 모든 기부금은 근무 환경을 개선하는 데 사용될 것입니다.

Please make sure to contact Lindsay at extension #133 to confirm your attendance by Friday, December 22.
반드시 12월 22일, 금요일까지 내선 133번으로 Lindsay에게 연락하셔서 귀하의 참석 여부를 확인해 주시기 바랍니다.

> 2. 마지막 부분에 요청 사항의 내용이 나오고 있습니다. 행사 참석 여부를 확인해 주는 전화를 달라고 요청하고 있습니다.
>
> 1. 손님들에게 요청하는 사항을 묻고 있습니다. 보통 요청 사항은 지문의 끝부분에 나옵니다.
>
> 3. 지문의 contact를 call로 바꾸어 표현한 (A)가 정답이 됩니다.

Q. What must guests do prior to attending the event? 손님들이 행사에 참석하기 전에 해야만 하는 것은?
 (A) Call Lindsay's office Lindsay의 사무실로 전화한다.
 (B) Reserve a flight 항공편을 예약한다.
 (C) Arrange an interview 인터뷰를 주선한다.
 (D) Purchase tickets 표를 구입한다.

해설 지문은 12월 29일에 있을 20주년 기념일 축하 행사 초대장임을 알 수 있는데, 맨 끝을 보면 12월 22일까지 Lindsay에게 전화로 참석 여부를 확인해 달라고 했으므로 (A)가 정답이다.

Practice

Question 1 refers to the following invitation.

> This winter season, we invite everyone to visit the Payton Hill Ski Resort. Starting on January 27, our recreation facility will be giving a 25% discount on all rental ski equipment. Furthermore, all customers making room reservations at our resort hotel before January 22 will be given an opportunity to win a free hot air balloon experience over Payton Hill.

1. What will happen on January 27?
   (A) A hot air balloon trip will be awarded to raffle winners.
   (B) Ski equipment will be rented at a discount.

Question 2 refers to the following invitation.

> Everyone should experience the excitement and love for baseball that resonates in the stadium. Now, with the Golden Cat's "Give the Chance" program, we will be extending the ball game experience to non-profit organizations around Virginia. We are personally inviting you to participate in this program. Our goal is to welcome as many youth programs and charitable organizations as possible to Centennial Field throughout the season. This is a great opportunity to bring Golden Cat fans together and this will surely be an experience that nobody will ever forget!

2. What is the purpose of this invitation?
   (A) To collect charity money from fans for non-profit organizations
   (B) To help share the baseball experience with non-profit organizations

---

어휘 **1** invite 초대하다 facility 시설 equipment 장비 furthermore 또한, 더구나 opportunity 기회 hot air balloon 열기구 **2** resonate 울려 퍼지다 extend 확장하다 non-profit organization 비영리 단체 personally 개인적으로 goal 목표 charitable organization 자선 단체 surely 확실히

Questions 1-2 refer to the following invitation.

All residents are welcome to attend the top bestseller Bob Santon's book signing event at the community center.

Please come and join him in celebrating the publication of his new book, *The Lost City*.

In addition to meeting the author, a representative of the publisher, Jake Samson, will give a short talk and distribute vouchers to all the participants.

Wednesday, October 8

1 P.M.–4 P.M.

Newport Community Center

An admission fee is not required, and refreshments will be prepared during the event. Also, there will be a photo time with Bob Santon at the end of the function.

Please arrive on time to minimize the interruption.

1   What will be celebrated at the event?
(A) A product launch
(B) A promotion
(C) A publication
(D) A marriage

2   Who most likely is Jake Samson?
(A) A celebrity
(B) A writer
(C) A CEO
(D) A chef

Part 7

Unit 14 편지·이메일 연계 지문

Part 7의 연계 문제를 풀기 위해서는 양쪽 지문에서 정보를 종합해 정답을 찾아야 합니다. 즉 첫째 지문의 정보와 둘째 지문의 정보 중에서 서로 관련된 정보를 파악해 종합적인 결론을 도출해야 합니다. 편지·이메일 연계 지문은 일반적으로 쉽게 접할 수 있는 내용이 나오므로 다소 쉬운 지문에 해당합니다. 다음과 같은 내용이 자주 등장합니다.
- [이메일] 예약과 입금 안내+[편지] 청구서 오류 사과
- [이메일] 인턴 프로그램 안내+[이메일] 일정이 맞지 않음을 알리고 양해를 구함
- [이메일] 제품 불만 항의+[이메일] 사과와 교환 약속

편지·이메일 연계 지문은 Part 7에서 가장 많이 출제되고 있는 유형입니다.

문제유형

▶ **글의 목적을 묻는 질문**

What is the purpose of the first letter? 첫째 편지의 목적은?
Why did Mr. Haistrom write an e-mail? Haistrom 씨가 이메일을 쓴 이유는?
Why was the e-mail sent? 이메일을 보낸 이유는?

▶ **구체적인 정보를 묻는 질문**

When will the car repair shop begin their work? 자동차 수리점은 언제 일을 시작하는가?
What is attached to the e-mail? 이메일에 첨부된 것은?
What is indicated about Mr. Bapat? Bapat 씨에 대해 지적된 것은?

▶ **해야 할 일과 대상을 묻는 질문**

What should employees do? 직원들이 해야 하는 것은?
Who should be contacted for more information? 더 많은 정보를 얻기 위해 연락해야 할 대상은?
What is Ms. Cane asked to do? Cane 씨가 하도록 부탁받는 것은?

풀이전략

▶ **지문을 읽으면서 이름이 나오는 부분에 집중해야 합니다.**

편지, 이메일 연계 지문에는 이름이 많이 언급되고, 그에 따른 문제가 꼭 출제됩니다.

▶ **두 지문에 연계된 문제가 하나 이상 출제됩니다.**

두 지문을 모두 비교해야 풀 수 있는 문제가 있는데, 보통 둘째 지문에서 질문의 내용이 나오고 첫째 지문에서 보기의 내용이 나오는 경우가 많습니다.

Sample Test

문제풀이전략을 적용해 기출 유형 예제를 풀어 보세요.

To: rlyons@netsop.com
From: silverwoods@hotels.com
Date: November 11
Subject: Reservation confirmation

Dear Mr. Lyons,

Thank you for choosing Silverwoods Hotel for your upcoming stay. Your reservation includes a complimentary ticket to the grand opening of Silverwoods Museum, which is opening on November 24.

Should you wish to cancel your reservation, please do so at least two days prior to your arrival date to avoid charges for late cancellation.

As per your request, we have also reserved a seat for you at the Silverwoods Technology Conference. Please feel free to contact us at www.silverwoodshotel.com for any requests that you may have during your stay here with us.

Silverwoods Hotel

To: Silverwoods Hotels
From: Lyons
Date: November 16

Dear Silverwoods Hotel,

Although I currently have a Deluxe Single Room reserved, I will need to make a slight alteration to this reservation. My friend, who was originally not planning on coming, has decided to come with me at the last minute. Therefore, I would like to upgrade my current room type to a Suite.

Please contact me if there is any additional information that you would need to successfully make this change to the reservation.

Thank you in advance for your assistance.

Sincerely,
Richard Lyons

Q. What is suggested about Mr. Lyons?

(A) He will be attending a local conference.
(B) He stays at the hotel often.
(C) He needs to cancel his reservation.
(D) He will help with the museum opening.

어휘 upcoming 다가오는 stay 체류 complimentary ticket 무료 입장권 cancel 취소하다 prior to ~ 이전에 arrival 도착 avoid 피하다 charge 요금, 수수료 slight 약간의 alteration 변경 originally 원래는 at the last minute 마지막 순간에 additional 추가적인 assistance 도움

문제분석

To: rlyons@netsop.com
From: silverwoods@hotels.com
Date: November 11
Subject: Reservation confirmation

Dear Mr. Lyons,

Thank you for choosing Silverwoods Hotel for your upcoming stay. Your reservation includes a complimentary ticket to the grand opening of Silverwoods Museum, which is opening on November 24.

Should you wish to cancel your reservation, please do so at least two days prior to your arrival date to avoid charges for late cancellation.

As per your request, we have also reserved a seat for you at the Silverwoods Technology Conference. Please feel free to contact us at www.silverwoodshotel.com for any requests that you may have during your stay here with us.

Silverwoods Hotel

> 2. 편지를 받는 사람이 문제에 언급된 Mr. Lyons 임을 알 수 있습니다.

> 3. 정답의 단서가 나와 있습니다. 호텔에서 콘퍼런스의 자리를 예약해 주었음을 알 수 있습니다.

To: Silverwoods Hotel
From: Lyons
Date: November 16

Dear Silverwoods Hotel,

Although I currently have a Deluxe Single Room reserved, I will need to make a slight alteration to this reservation. My friend, who was originally not planning on coming, has decided to come with me at the last minute. Therefore, I would like to upgrade my current room type to a Suite.

Please contact me if there is any additional information that you would need to successfully make this change to the reservation.

Thank you in advance for your assistance.

Sincerely,
Richard Lyons

Q. What is suggested about Mr. Lyons? Lyons 씨에 관해 암시되는 것은?

(A) He will be attending a local conference. 지역 콘퍼런스에 참석할 것이다.
(B) He stays at the hotel often. 호텔에 자주 머문다.
(C) He needs to cancel his reservation. 예약을 취소해야 한다.
(D) He will help with the museum opening. 박물관 개장을 도울 것이다.

1. 질문에서 Mr. Lyons라는 사람 이름이 나왔음을 파악합니다.

4. 콘퍼런스 예약에 관한 내용이 지문에 나오므로 (A)가 정답입니다.

해설 Lyons 씨에 관하여 알 수 있는 것을 묻는 문제이므로 보기와 지문의 내용을 대조해 보아야 한다. 첫 지문 셋째 문단의 As per your request, we have also reserved a seat for you at the Silverwoods Technology Conference.에서 Lyons 씨의 요청으로 호텔 측에서 콘퍼런스장에 자리를 예약해 두었다고 했으므로 Lyons 씨는 콘퍼런스 참석차 호텔에 묵는 것임을 알 수 있다. 따라서 (A)가 정답이다.

Questions 1-5 refer to the following two e-mails.

From: Carter Long <carter609@mandi.com>
To: Customer Service <customerservice@Alpha.com>
Date: March 12
Subject: Sound problem

I purchased a new television set from your company on February 17 and have been using it with great joy ever since. However, during the last couple of days, I have been experiencing a strange problem while using this television. When I start the television, occasionally, a buzzing sound emanates from the back of the television. It only lasts for a couple of seconds, but it is quite annoying.

Before sending you this e-mail, I have tried to fix this problem by myself. I referred the user manual and even your Web site to determine any solutions to this problem. I have attempted to reset all the settings and reconnected my cable modem; however, neither of these things resolved the problem. I have contacted my cable company and they have assured me that the sound is not being caused by the modem, but by the television. I have the receipt of purchase and the television can still be returned, but I have grown attached to the television, and therefore, I would rather not return it. Is there anything that I can do to fix this strange sound problem?

Your customer,
Carter Long

From: Customer Service ⟨customerservice@Alpha.com⟩
To: Carter Long ⟨carter609@mandi.com⟩
Date: March 13
Subject: RE: Sound problem

Dear Mr. Long:

It sounds like your problem must be quite annoying! Please do not worry; we are here to help. After considering the steps that you have taken to attempt to alleviate this strange sound, there appears to be a malfunction with the motherboard. Since you have stated that you would rather not return or exchange your product, we recommend another solution. We have many authorized repair shops across the country, and you can take your television set to one of these stores where one of the many highly trained specialists will be able to look at the problem. The fee for this, of course, would be handled by us, as long as you get it repaired at one of our authorized shops. Please carefully retain the receipt that you receive from the repair shop and send it to us to receive reimbursement for the repairs.

Sincerely,

Alexis Silverman
Customer Service

1. When did Carter Long purchase the television set?
   (A) A day ago
   (B) A week ago
   (C) A month ago
   (D) A year ago

2. What most likely is Alpha.com?
   (A) Movie rental service
   (B) An electronics seller
   (C) A cable company
   (D) A movie studio

3. According to the second e-mail, what should Carter Long do next?
   (A) Take the product to a repair shop
   (B) Return the product
   (C) Reset the television settings
   (D) Purchase a new cable modem

4. According to the first e-mail, when does the strange sound occur?
   (A) When he listens to music
   (B) When he turns on the television
   (C) When he turns off the television
   (D) When he changes channels

5. Why does Carter Long NOT want to return his product?
   (A) It is not a serious enough problem.
   (B) The shipping fees are too expensive.
   (C) He has misplaced the receipt.
   (D) He likes the television despite the problem.

Unit 15 광고 연계 지문

Part 7

광고의 경우에는 내용이 그렇게 많지 않고 그에 따른 연계 지문의 형태도 이메일 같은 쉬운 유형이 출제되므로 난이도는 낮은 편입니다. 보통 첫째 지문에는 제품이나 서비스 광고가 나오고 둘째 지문에는 그 광고에 대한 질문이나 항의, 서비스에 대한 감사 등의 내용이 나옵니다. 다음과 같은 내용이 자주 등장합니다.
- [광고+기사] 부동산 광고+새로 이전하는 회사에 관한 기사
- [광고+이메일] 서비스 광고+서비스 신청에 감사하는 이메일 (가장 자주 출제되는 유형)
- [광고+양식] 제품에 대한 광고+주문 양식

문제유형

▶ **광고의 목적과 대상을 묻는 질문**

What is the purpose of the advertisement? 광고의 목적은?
For whom is the advertisement intended? 광고의 대상은?

▶ **세부 사항을 묻는 질문**

Where is Mr. Bush's company located? Bush 씨의 회사가 위치한 곳은?
What does Mr. Ochoa offer to do? Ochoa 씨가 제안하는 것은?
What is suggested about Ms. Pineda? Pineda 씨에 대해 알 수 있는 것은?

▶ **내용 일치/불일치**

What is NOT mentioned in the advertisement about Lewison Ltd.? Lewison 사의 광고에 언급되지 않는 것은?
What is true about ADD Corporation? ADD 사에 관해 사실인 것은?

풀이전략

▶ **제목부터 읽고 어떤 광고인지 파악해야 합니다.**

제목이나 제목 아래의 1~2행에서 단서를 찾을 수 있습니다.

▶ **문제의 핵심어만 표시해야 합니다.**

문제에서 중요한 부분만 표시하고, 지문을 읽으면서 그 핵심어가 나오면 문제로 돌아가서 그때 보기까지 같이 읽으면서 정답을 찾는 것이 더 효율적입니다.

▶ **두 지문에 연계된 문제가 하나 이상 출제됩니다.**

두 지문을 모두 비교해야 풀 수 있는 문제가 있는데, 보통 두 번째 지문에서 질문의 내용이 나오고 첫 번째 지문에서 보기의 내용이 나오는 경우가 많습니다. 첫 번째 지문에 있는 숫자나 이름과 두 번째 지문에서 언급된 숫자나 이름을 연관시켜 정답을 찾아야 합니다. 특히 숫자나 날짜, 금액 등에 유의해야 합니다.

| Sample Test | 문제풀이전략을 적용해 기출 유형 예제를 풀어 보세요. |

Startrek Airlines

Choose Startrek Airlines for your next trip!

Let the top airline, Startrek Airlines serve you on your next vacation or journey. Our international flight tickets cost up to 15% less than other airlines. More surprisingly, our domestic flights are 20% cheaper than the flights of our competitors! In addition, if you wish to reserve accommodations, we offer discounted deals at our partner hotels.

To arrange your flight schedule or ask questions, please call us at 646-555-9311 or visit our Web site at www.startrekairlines.com. Thank you.

* e-mail *
To: James Harrison<jharrison@gmail.com>
From: Anthony Naim<Anaim@startrekairlines.com>
Date: 5 July
Subject: Re: My itinerary

Dear Mr. Harrison,

This is to confirm your ticket reservation for Tuesday, 11 July at 7:00 A.M. Your destination is Paris from La Guardia airport in New York. You must go to Gate 12, where there is a sign indicating the location of our airline, at least 20 minutes before departure.

Our records also indicate that you have requested our hotel reservation service. Therefore, we have made reservations for you based on your itinerary through 13 July.

Thank you again for choosing Startrek Airlines. If you have any further questions, feel free to contact me.

Best regards,

Anthony Naim
General Manager, Startrek Airlines

Q. What is suggested about Mr. Harrison?

(A) He is working for an airline company.
(B) He got a discounted rate on a hotel reservation.
(C) He is using Startrek for the first time.
(D) He will leave in the afternoon.

어휘 serve 섬기다, 응대하다 journey 여행 surprisingly 놀랍게도 domestic flight 국내선 항공편 competitor 경쟁사 in addition 게다가 reserve 예약하다 accommodation 숙박 시설 deal 거래, 대우 arrange 계획하다, 정하다 destination 목적지, 도착지 departure 출발 indicate 나타내다 itinerary 여행 일정

Startrek Airlines

Choose Startrek Airlines for your next trip!

Let the top airline, Startrek Airlines serve you on your next vacation or journey. Our international flight tickets cost up to 15% less than other airlines. More surprisingly, our domestic flights are 20% cheaper than the flights of our competitors! In addition, if you wish to reserve accommodations, we offer discounted deals at our partner hotels.

To arrange your flight schedule or ask questions, please call us at 646-555-9311 or visit our Web site at www.startrekairlines.com. Thank you.

---

* e-mail *

To: James Harrison<jharrison@gmail.com>
From: Anthony Naim<Anaim@startrekairlines.com>
Date: 5 July
Subject: Re: My itinerary

Dear Mr. Harrison,

This is to confirm your ticket reservation for Tuesday, 11 July at 7:00 A.M. Your destination is Paris from La Guardia airport in New York. You must go to Gate 12, where there is a sign indicating the location of our airline, at least 20 minutes before departure.

Our records also indicate that you have requested our hotel reservation service. Therefore, we have made reservations for you based on your itinerary through 13 July.

Thank you again for choosing Startrek Airlines. If you have any further questions, feel free to contact me.

Best regards,

Anthony Naim
General Manager, Startrek Airlines

Q. What is suggested about Mr. Harrison? Harrison 씨에 관해 암시되는 것은?

(A) He is working for an airline company. 그는 항공사에서 일한다.
(B) He got a discounted rate on a hotel reservation. 그는 할인가를 적용받아 호텔 예약을 했다.
(C) He is using Startrek for the first time. 그는 Startrek을 처음 이용하고 있다.
(D) He will leave in the afternoon. 그는 오후에 떠날 것이다.

1. Harrison이라는 이름이 언급되어 있으므로 지문에서 이름이 언급된 부분을 찾아 어떤 인물인지 먼저 파악해야 합니다.

6. 할인된 가격으로 호텔 예약을 했음을 알 수 있으므로 (B)가 정답입니다.

해설 첫째 광고 지문의 if you wish to reserve accommodations, we offer a discounted deals at our partner hotels에서 항공사에 호텔 예약을 원하는 경우 제휴 호텔들에서 할인된 가격을 제공한다고 했으며, 항공사 직원이 고객에게 보낸 둘째 이메일 지문에서는 you have requested our hotel reservation service. Therefore, we have made reservations for you에서 고객이 호텔 예약 서비스를 요청해 예약을 해주었다는 내용이 언급되어 있으므로 고객인 Harrison 씨는 할인된 가격으로 호텔 예약을 했음을 알 수 있다.

Actual Test

Questions 1-5 refer to the following advertisement and order form.

Tees To You

Custom T-shirts for all occasions!
30 Wellington Way, Manhattan, NY
215-010-6849

Owner: Washington Davy
We offer custom-made T-shirts and other apparel
at prices that are lower than our competitors!
Great gifts for the holidays!

- Choose from our catalog of 100+ designs or send us a design of your own!

- We provide our own delivery services, thereby keeping prices down by not employing third-party delivery companies.

- Orders can be paid for by check or credit card. (Sorry, no cash orders!)

- Delivery requires 4-5 days of processing before being shipped. Customers will receive their orders within 2 business days of being shipped.

Order Date: Tuesday, December 3		**Shipping Date:** Monday, December 9	
Customer Information **Name:** Robert Sputen **Address:** 899 Saint Mary Avenue, Voorhees, NJ 13072 **Phone:** 315-557-8667		**Deliver to** **Name:** Kimberly Peace **Address:** 1632 Cherry Ridge Drive, Fairport, NY 14450	
Item Number	Description	Quantity	Price
32SG	Long-sleeve knitted sweater	2	$30 each
Message: Surprise! Happy Holidays. Thanks for the help with baby-sitting the kids. You were an excellent baby-sitter!		**Delivery Cost:**	$5
Payment Method: Credit Card		**Total Cost:**	$65

1. What does Mr. Davy's company provide to customers in New York?
   (A) Discounted designer clothes
   (B) Personalized clothing
   (C) Clothes for babies and children
   (D) Materials for sewing

2. What does the advertisement mention about delivery?
   (A) It takes 4-5 days for delivery.
   (B) It is available on weekends.
   (C) It is free for orders of two or more.
   (D) It accepts payments through checks.

3. What does the order form indicate about Robert Sputen?
   (A) He works with Kimberly Peace.
   (B) He has young children.
   (C) He received a gift from the company.
   (D) He resides in New York State.

4. What is true about Kimberly Peace?
   (A) She paid for the order with a credit card.
   (B) She is seeking another job.
   (C) She worked for Robert Sputen.
   (D) She is an employee of the company.

5. When will the order probably be received?
   (A) December 3
   (B) December 9
   (C) December 11
   (D) December 15

Unit 16 알림 연계 지문

Part 7

회람의 경우에는 내용이 그렇게 많지 않고 그에 따른 연계 지문의 형태도 양식이나 이메일 같은 쉬운 유형이 출제되므로 난이도는 낮은 편입니다. 주로 제품 주문에 관하여 사람들에게 알리는 내용이 출제됩니다.
- [회람+양식] 사무실 비품 교체 신청+비품 교체 신청서
- [회람+이메일] 주문 방법 변경에 관한 알림+주문 확인

문제유형

▶ **회람의 목적과 대상을 묻는 질문**

Why was the memo written? 회람을 작성한 이유는?
What is the purpose of the memo? 회람의 목적은?
For whom is the memo intended? 회람을 받는 대상은?

▶ **세부 사항을 묻는 질문**

Where will the event take place? 행사가 열리게 될 장소는?
Why should employees go to the conference room? 직원들이 회의실에 가야 하는 이유는?

▶ **내용 일치/불일치**

What is NOT suggested about Hurst Trucking? Hurst 운송에 대해 암시되지 않은 것은?
What is true about Mr. Anderson? Anderson 씨에 관해 사실인 것은?

풀이전략

▶ **발신자, 수신자, 제목을 확인해야 합니다.**

From: / To: / Subject 부분이 정답의 단서가 되는 경우도 있습니다.

▶ **문제의 핵심어만 표시해 두어야 합니다.**

모든 문제의 보기를 읽는 것은 도움이 되지 않습니다. 본문을 읽을 때 기억에서 쉽게 사라지기 때문입니다. 질문에서 중요한 핵심어에 표시한 후에 지문을 읽어야 합니다. 지문에서 그 핵심어가 나오면 문제로 돌아가 그때 보기를 함께 읽으며 정답을 찾는 것이 더 효율적입니다.

▶ **두 지문이 연계된 문제가 한 개 이상 출제됩니다.**

두 지문을 모두 비교해야 풀 수 있는 문제가 있는데, 보통 둘째 지문에서 질문의 내용이 나오고 첫째 지문에서 보기의 내용이 나오는 경우가 많습니다. 특히 숫자나 날짜, 금액 등에 유의해야 합니다.

Sample Test   문제풀이전략을 적용해 기출 유형 예제를 풀어 보세요.

Newly Released DVDs

CONTACT: Russell Hoyt at (646) 493-9022

Happy Days in Berlin **by Jackie Lee**
In this memoir, the director Jackie Lee reminisces about his youth in Berlin.

Unbelievable Powers **by Jonathan Hawkins**
In 2045, the Earth is endangered by the invasion of aliens from the Andromeda Galaxy.

Bad Boys **by Mark Leplarn**
The best actors in the comedy industry will make you laugh through the entire time.

Dreams Knocked Down **by Jennifer Kawasaki**
In this film, the Asian-American director describes the hardship that foreigners may undergo.

Coming Up In Charlottesville

Sunday, September 25

Our well-known event, the Charlottesville Film Fair, will be held at city hall in a few weeks! Top U.S. directors including Jonathan Hawkins, Jackie Lee, and Jennifer Kawasaki who have been invited to the fair will grace the occasion. The directors' short Q&A session, led by Chris Yeadon, will follow clips of movie highlights. The celebrities will also talk about what motivated them to start working on their pieces, which were released last month. There will be autograph signings on DVDs of their films at the end of the event. Please e-mail cyeadon@charlottesville.org with any inquiries.

Q. What DVD will NOT be signed at the event?

(A) Dreams Knocked Down
(B) Bad Boys
(C) Unbelievable Powers
(D) Happy Days in Berlin

문제분석

Newly Released DVDs 새로 발매된 DVD

CONTACT: Russell Hoyt at (646) 493-9022 연락처: Russel Hoyt, (646) 493-9022

Happy Days in Berlin **by Jackie Lee** 베를린에서의 행복한 날들, 감독: Jackie Lee
In this memoir, the director Jackie Lee reminisces about his youth in Berlin.
이 회고록에서 감독 Jackie Lee는 베를린에서의 유년 시절을 추억한다.

Unbelievable Powers **by Jonathan Hawkins** 믿을 수 없는 능력, 감독: Jonathan Hawkins
In 2045, the Earth is endangered by the invasion of aliens from the Andromeda Galaxy.
2045년에 지구는 안드로메다 은하계에서 온 외계인들의 침략으로 위기에 처한다.

Bad Boys **by Mark Leplarn** 나쁜 소년들, 감독: Mark Leplarn
The best actors in the comedy industry will make you laugh through the entire time. 코미디 업계의 최고 배우들이 상영 시간 내내 당신을 웃게 만들 것이다.

Dreams Knocked Down **by Jennifer Kawasaki** 나가떨어진 꿈, 감독: Jennifer Kawasaki
In this film, the Asian-American director describes the hardship that foreigners may undergo. 이 영화에서는 아시아계 미국인 감독이 외국인들이 겪을 수 있는 어려움을 묘사한다.

> 4. 감독들의 이름과 작품이 나와 있습니다.

Coming Up In Charlottesville Charlottesville에서 열립니다

Sunday, September 25 9월 25일, 일요일

Our well-known event, the Charlottesville Film Fair, will be held at city hall in a few weeks! Top U.S. directors including **Jonathan Hawkins, Jackie Lee, and Jennifer Kawasaki who have been invited to the fair** will grace the occasion. The directors' short Q&A session, led by Chris Yeadon, will follow clips of movie highlights. The celebrities will also talk about what motivated them to start working on their pieces, which were released last month. **There will be autograph signings on DVDs** of their films at the end of the event. Please e-mail cyeadon@charlottesville.org with any inquiries.

우리의 유명한 행사인 Charlottesville 영화 축제가 몇 주 후 시청에서 열릴 것입니다! Jonathan Hawkins, Jackie Lee, Jennifer Kawasaki를 포함한 미국 최고의 감독들이 자리를 빛내 줄 것입니다. Chris Yeadon이 이끄는 감독들의 짧은 질의응답 시간이 영화의 하이라이트 장면 상영 후에 있을 것입니다. 그 유명 인사들은 지난달에 개봉된 자신들의 작품을 만들기 시작하게 된 동기가 무엇이었는지에 대해서도 이야기할 것입니다. 행사 마지막에는 그들이 만든 영화의 DVD 사인회도 있을 것입니다. 문의 사항이 있으시면 cyeadon@charlottesville.org로 이메일을 보내 주세요.

> 3. 행사에 초청된 감독들의 이름이 나열되어 있어 이들이 사인회를 열 것임을 알 수 있습니다.

> 2. 행사에서 영화 DVD 사인회가 있습니다.

Unit 16 : 알림 연계 지문

Q. What DVD will NOT be signed at the event? 행사에서 사인되지 않을 DVD는?

(A) Dreams Knocked Down
(B) Bad Boys
(C) Unbelievable Powers
(D) Happy Days in Berlin

1. 행사에서 사인을 받을 수 없는 DVD가 무엇인지 묻고 있습니다.

5. 초대되지 않은 감독 Mark Leplarn의 작품이라서 사인을 받을 수 없으므로 정답입니다.

해설 첫째 지문은 새로 출시된 영화 DVD의 목록을 보여 주고 있으며, 각 영화마다 감독 이름이 언급되어 있다. 둘째 지문은 영화 축제 행사 안내인데, 첫머리에 참석하는 감독들(Jonathan Hawkins, Jackie Lee, and Jennifer Kawasaki)이 언급되어 있고 후반부에는 이들이 만든 영화의 DVD 사인회가 있을 것이라고 했으므로 행사에 참석하지 않은 감독 Mark Leplarn의 작품 Bad Boys는 사인을 받지 않는다는 것을 알 수 있다. 따라서 (B)가 정답이다.

Questions 1-5 refer to the following advertisement and e-mails.

WowFashion
Sales Associates Positions

WowFashion is now opening another store at Brooklyn Mate mall and seeking sales associates. We started the first store in Manhattan in the summer of 2014. WowFashion today is an internationally known fashion retailer with shops in over 15 countries around the world. We require professionalism, high energy and team spirit. WowFashion will put you into the heart of the action and the heart of its growth.

The job of a sales associate involves selling, restocking and merchandising. The sales associate is responsible for greeting and assisting customers as well as maintaining the appearance of the store and the merchandise. The sales associate must be friendly and energetic as well as swift to ensure customer satisfaction. Excellent customer service is our goal and the Sales Associates are our means of achieving it.

Requirements:
- Flexible schedule/open availability especially over the weekends
- Previous retail experience a plus
- Passion for fashion!
Our company requires professionalism, imagination, high energy and team spirit. Sounds like you? Then Apply today!

Please submit a copy of your updated resume by e-mail at kevinlee7@wowfashion.com by Oct. 31

Oct. 27, 2017

Dear Mr. Kevin Lee,

I am writing to apply for the position of a sales associate advertised on your website. I am interested in fashion and have always been visiting your website. I have enclosed a copy of my resume, including references. I have been working for SwaggingFashon since you opened your first store in Manhattan. I'm passionate for fashion and I won an employee of the year award last year. I would be happy to speak with you more about the position in person. I can travel to your office for an interview at any time. Also I have a favor to ask you. As you know, I'm currently working for SwaggingFashion and I'd like you to finish the interview within an hour. I look forward to hearing from you. Thank you.

Brad Hawn

Dear Brad Hawn,

As a result of your application for the position of sales associate, I would like to invite you to attend an interview on Nov 1, at 9 AM at our office in Brooklyn, NY. You will have an interview with the department manager, Edward Lee. The interview will be completed within an hour as you requested. Please bring three references to the interview. If the date or time of the interview is inconvenient, please contact me by phone (212-555-2418) or email (hrmanager2@wowfashion.com) in order to arrange another appointment. We look forward to seeing you.

Best regards,

Kevin Lee
Personnel Director, HR Department
5 Beard Street, Brooklyn, NY 11231
212-555-2579
hrmanager2@wowfashion.com

1. What area of the store positions are being advertised?
   (A) Sales
   (B) Maintenance
   (C) Cashier
   (D) Retailer

2. What is NOT true about WowFashion?
   (A) It first opened a shop in Manhattan.
   (B) It specializes in children's clothing.
   (C) It has been in business for 3 years.
   (D) There are many other WowFashion stores around the world.

3. How long has Mr. Hawn worked for SwaggingFashion?
   (A) For six months
   (B) For a year
   (C) For two years
   (D) For three years

4. In the first e-mail, the word "favor" in line 6 is closest in meaning to
   (A) kindness
   (B) request
   (C) support
   (D) reputation

5. According to the e-mails, how long will the interview last?
   (A) One day
   (B) Two hours
   (C) Over an hour
   (D) Less than an hour

Part 7

Unit 17 기사 연계 지문

기사 연계 지문은 내용이 많고 단어나 상황이 어렵기 때문에 난이도가 가장 높은 편입니다. 보통 첫 지문에 기사가 나오고 둘째 지문에 이메일, 편지, 표지판, 웹사이트 등 다양한 종류의 글이 등장하는 것이 특징입니다. 다음과 같은 지문 구성으로 많이 출제됩니다.
- [기사+이메일] 신제품 출시 기사+판매 담당자의 판매 장려 이메일
- [기사+편지] 호텔의 장단점에 대한 기사+단점을 개선했음을 알리는 편지
- [기사+표지판] 유명인의 이름을 딴 공원 개장에 대한 기사+지도
- [기사+웹사이트] 대학교 옆으로 이전해 온 시설에 대한 기사+시설 입장료

문제유형

▶ 기사의 목적과 출처를 묻는 질문

Why was the article written? 기사를 쓴 이유는?
What is the purpose of the article? 기사의 목적은?
Where would the article most likely appear? 기사가 실릴 가능성이 가장 높은 곳은?

▶ 세부 사항을 묻는 질문

Who is Mr. Tadashi? Tadashi 씨는 누구인가?
What is indicated about Hyun Export Company? Hyun Export 사에 관해 지적되는 것은?
What is stated about the Manzoni family? Manzoni 가족에 대해 진술되는 것은?

▶ 내용 일치/불일치

What is NOT mentioned as a benefit of building the new facility? 새 시설을 건축하는 것의 이점으로 언급되지 않는 것은?
What is true about Ms. Patel? Patel 씨에 관해 사실인 것은?

풀이전략

▶ 사람의 이름과 지명에 주의해야 합니다.

지문에 사람 이름과 지명이 상당히 많이 등장하고 그 고유명사들이 문제와 보기에 그대로 나오기 때문에 기사를 읽으면서 미리 표시해 두어야 해당 부분을 찾기가 쉬워집니다.

▶ 두 지문에 연계된 문제가 한 개 이상 출제됩니다.

두 지문을 모두 비교해야 풀 수 있는 문제가 있는데, 보통 둘째 지문에서 질문의 내용이 나오고 첫째 지문에서 보기의 내용이 나오는 경우가 많습니다.

| Sample Test | 문제풀이전략을 적용해 기출 유형 예제를 풀어 보세요. |

The Melin Corporation Newsletter
21 March

As you may all know, Jason Milder is leaving us and returning to peaceful rural life in Maryfield as of next month. Mr. Milder has raised the stock price of Melin Corp by 50% since last year. This superstar of Melin started as a part-time employee at our Brooklyn branch. He was finally promoted to development director of headquarters in Springfield five years ago and became the best employee in our company's history.

Along with being responsible for the surprising rise in our stock price, Mr. Milder has been acknowledged for his effort in simplifying the designs of our products. Our corporation was awarded the Best Design of the Century prize due to Mr. Milder's enthusiastic work. Please wish him luck with his retirement.

Dear Jason,

It's been a long time since we worked together in Brooklyn. I still remember the kindness and respect you showed me. However, I recently heard that you will soon leave Melin Corp. I wanted to congratulate you on your honorable retirement.

By the way, do you know which department I am currently working in? You will be surprised. A few days ago, I was promoted to General Manager of the Design Department in Jamestown.

I am planning on visiting your town in April since I have a conference in the area. I hope we can look back on our 22 years in Melin together. Please get back to me by e-mail before you leave!

Sincerely,
Jefferson Brown

Q. To what city will Mr. Brown most likely travel in April?
(A) Jamestown
(B) Brooklyn
(C) Maryfield
(D) Springfield

어휘 corporation 주식회사 peaceful 평화로운, 평온한 rural 시골의 as of ~부터 stock price 주가 branch 지점 promote 승진하다 headquarters 본사 acknowledge 인정하다 enthusiastic 열심인 retirement 은퇴 respect 존경 department 부서 general manager 부장 conference 회의

문제분석

The Melin Corporation Newsletter Melin 사 사보

21 March 3월 21일

As you may all know, Jason Milder is leaving us and **returning to peaceful rural life in Maryfield as of next month.** Mr. Milder has raised the stock price of Melin Corp by 50% since last year. This superstar of Melin started as a part-time employee at our Brooklyn branch. He was finally promoted to development director of headquarters in Springfield five years ago and became the best employee in our company's history.

여러분 모두 아시겠지만, Jason Milder가 우리 곁을 떠나 다음 달부터 Maryfield에서 평화로운 시골 생활로 돌아갈 것입니다. Milder 씨는 지난해부터 Melin 사의 주가를 50퍼센트까지 올렸습니다. Melin의 이 슈퍼스타는 Brooklyn 지사에서 비정규직 직원으로 출발했습니다. 그는 5년 전에 마침내 Springfield에 있는 본사의 개발 책임자로 승진했고, 우리 회사 역사상 가장 훌륭한 직원이 되었습니다.

Along with being responsible for the surprising rise in our stock price, Mr. Milder has been acknowledged for his effort in simplifying the designs of our products. Our corporation was awarded the Best Design of the Century prize due to Mr. Milder's enthusiastic work. Please wish him luck with his retirement.

우리 주가의 놀라운 상승을 담당한 것과 더불어, Milder 씨는 우리 제품의 디자인을 단순화시킨 데 있어서 그의 노력을 인정받았습니다. Milder 씨의 열정적인 노력으로 인해 우리 회사는 금세기 최고의 디자인 상을 받았습니다. 그의 은퇴에 행운을 빌어 주시기 바랍니다.

> 2. 질문의 April보다 1개월 앞선 시점임을 알 수 있습니다.
>
> 3. next month가 있으므로 질문의 April과 관련 있는 부분입니다.

Dear Jason, Jason에게,

It's been a long time since we worked together in Brooklyn. I still remember the kindness and respect you showed me. However, I recently heard that you will soon leave Melin Corp. I wanted to congratulate you on your honorable retirement.

우리가 Brooklyn에서 함께 일한 지 오랜 시간이 흘렀네요. 저는 당신이 제게 보여 준 친절과 배려를 여전히 기억하고 있습니다. 하지만, 최근에 당신이 곧 Melin 사를 떠나게 된다는 소식을 들었습니다. 당신의 명예로운 은퇴를 축하드리고 싶었습니다.

By the way, do you know which department I am currently working in? You will be surprised. A few days ago, I was promoted to General Manager of the Design Department in Jamestown.

그런데, 제가 현재 어느 부서에서 일하고 있는지 아시나요? 놀라실 거예요. 며칠 전에 제가 Jamestown에 있는 디자인부의 총괄 매니저로 승진했습니다.

I am planning on visiting your town in April since I have a conference in the area. I hope we can look back on our 22 years in Melin together. Please get back to me by e-mail before you leave!

당신이 사는 도시에서 총회가 있어서 4월에 그곳에 방문할 계획입니다. 우리가 Melin에서 함께한 22년을 되돌아볼 수 있기를 바랍니다. 떠나시기 전에 이메일로 답장해 주시기 바랍니다!

Sincerely,
Jefferson Brown

> 4. April에 Jason이 있는 곳으로 방문할 계획이라고 나와 있습니다.

Q. To what city will Mr. Brown most likely travel in April?

Brown 씨가 4월에 여행할 가능성이 가장 높은 도시는?

(A) Jamestown
(B) Brooklyn
(C) Maryfield
(D) Springfield

> 1. 사람 이름과 날짜가 있으므로 지문에서 이 고유 명사가 있는 부분을 집중하면서 읽습니다.

> 5. April에 방문할 곳이 Jason이 있는 Maryfield 임을 첫째 지문에서 찾을 수 있으므로 정답입니다.

해설 질문의 핵심어는 what city, Mr. Brown, travel, in April이다. Brown 씨가 쓴 둘째 지문에서 4월이 언급된 부분인 I am planning on visiting your town in April since I have a conference in the area.에서 그가 총회 참석차 4월에 Jason이 사는 도시를 방문하겠다고 했으며, 첫째 지문의 Jason Milder is leaving us and returning to peaceful rural life in Maryfield as of next month.에서 Jason이 회사를 떠나 Maryfield로 돌아갈 것이라고 했으므로 Brown 씨가 방문할 도시는 Maryfield임을 알 수 있다.

Questions 1-5 refer to the following article and letters.

Jan. 21, 2018 San Francisco Times

The 'Seablue House' is a restaurant situated in the heart of Monterey, California. As you enter the place, you are welcomed by a magnificent setting, a delightful marriage of antique cut stones and the luxuries of modernity. Sitting in any table, you have a wonderful view of the Del Monte Beach. For those who do not book a table and are waiting, there is a cozy lounge with aged leather armchairs.

The menu offers a wide variety of mouth-watering starters. White asparagus by a mousseline sauce is the menu you must taste. The main course consists of a risotto with scallop cooked in cream and a cassolette of coley with mussels, which will really thrill you.

All the products are fresh and the dishes have the warmth of home-made food. The chefs take great care in selecting the best quality ingredients.

The owner and hostess, a middle-aged charming woman, is always around willing to exchange some kind words with all her clients. I highly recommend going to the Seablue House.

by
columnist Linda Lopez

To: Howard Anderson, Fresh Veg <handerson@Freshveg.com>
From: Louis Cruz, Seablue House <louis@seablue.com>
Date: Jan 28
Subject: Vegetable Order

We would like to place an additional order for asparagus. We need at least 2 cartons of white asparagus by next week. More and more customers are looking for white asparagus menu after an article was published in San Francisco Times last week.

I know spring is the best season for fresh asparagus. I'm afraid you'll have enough white asparagus. If there is any problem to meet the demand, please get back to me as soon as possible. Thank you.

To: Louis Cruz, Seablue House <louis@seablue.com>
From: Howard Anderson, Fresh Veg <handerson@Freshveg.com>
Date: Jan 29
Subject: Vegetable Order

As always, We truly appreciate your business. We greatly value your trust and confidence and sincerely appreciate your loyalty to our business. Unfortunately, we could not ship all 2 cartons of white asparagus you requested since it's not the best season for it. However we do have canned white asparagus. If you want canned one, we can send it right away. We can also send green or violet asparagus instead. I believe you can get white one in about two or three weeks without difficulty because crops are harvested from late Feb. Why don't you check your inventory first? Please let me know what you prefer. Thank you.

Howard Anderson
Fresh Veg

1. What is the article about?
   (A) The relocation of a business
   (B) A local restaurant
   (C) An upcoming grand opening
   (D) A retirement of the president

2. In the article, the word "setting" in paragraph 1, line 2 is closest in meaning to
   (A) stage
   (B) environment
   (C) music
   (D) beach

3. What has affected the increase of white asparagus order?
   (A) A change in shipping methods
   (B) Opening of a branch
   (C) A newspaper article
   (D) An increase in number of restaurants

4. What does Mr. Anderson suggest that Mr. Cruz do?
   (A) Check the inventory
   (B) Order canned food
   (C) Doing business with another supplier
   (D) Visit an asparagus farm

5. What is NOT true about the order?
   (A) Mr. Cruz wants to buy white asparagus.
   (B) This is the first time Mr. Cruz ordered food from Fresh Veg.
   (C) Fresh Veg has canned white asparagus in stock.
   (D) Mr. Anderson wants Mr. Cruz to call him back.

Unit 18 기타 연계 지문

Part 7

기타 연계 지문에서는 웹 페이지, 고객 설문 조사, 프로그램 목록, 송장, 보증서 같은 양식이 주로 등장하며 다음과 같은 지문 구성으로 많이 출제됩니다.
- [웹 페이지+이메일] 저자 사인회의 일정을 알리는 웹 페이지+사인회 일정을 문의하는 이메일 (가장 흔한 형식)
- [웹 페이지+웹 페이지] 부동산 검색 웹 페이지+검색 결과 웹 페이지
- [계약서+고객 설문 조사] 가구 대여 서비스 계약서+서비스가 좋았다는 내용의 고객 평가서

문제유형

▶ **목적과 주체를 묻는 질문**

What is the purpose of the survey? 설문 조사의 목적은?
What kind of business is IAT Corporation? IAT 사의 업종은?

▶ **세부 사항을 묻는 질문**

According to the search results, when is the property available? 검색 결과에 따르면 부동산을 이용할 수 있는 때는?
What is Mr. Ryu's job? 류 씨의 직업은?
What is suggested by the invoice? 송장에서 암시되는 것은?

풀이전략

▶ **지문을 읽을 때 고유명사와 숫자에 집중해야 합니다.**

기타 연계 지문은 주로 양식 형태이며 회사와 사람 이름이나 금액, 날짜에 관한 질문이 많이 출제됩니다.

▶ **문제의 핵심어만 표시해 두어야 합니다.**

모든 문제의 보기를 읽는 것은 도움이 되지 않습니다. 지문을 읽을 때 기억에서 쉽게 사라지기 때문입니다. 질문에서 중요한 핵심어에 표시한 후에 지문을 읽어야 합니다. 지문에서 그 핵심어가 나오면 문제로 돌아가 그때 보기를 함께 읽으며 정답을 찾는 것이 더 효율적입니다.

▶ **두 지문에 연계된 문제가 한 개 이상 출제됩니다.**

두 지문을 모두 비교해야 풀 수 있는 문제가 있는데, 보통 둘째 지문에 질문의 내용이 나오고 첫째 지문에 보기의 내용이 나오는 경우가 많습니다.

Sample Test

문제풀이전략을 적용해 기출 유형 예제를 풀어 보세요.

MOBILITY TELECOMMUNICATIONS

All representatives assisting customers over the phone are expected to do so using the following script. This script will enable you to address customers' questions and concerns more appropriately.

Monthly offers are also posted on the Web site and representatives should check for them at the beginning of every month. Ensure that you outline the details and benefits to customers who call.

Opening: Hello and thank you for calling Mobility Telecommunications. My name is _____, and I will be assisting you. What is your reason for calling today?

Verify Customer Information: May I have a full name and the billing address on your account?

Feedback Request: We greatly value your feedback. If you would take a moment of your time to complete a customer satisfaction survey on our Web site, it would benefit us in providing the best possible service to you, our customer. Customers who complete surveys are eligible to receive a 20% discount on their next bill.

Closing: Thank you for your call, and as always, we appreciate your patronage. We hope that we were able to provide some assistance to you.

MOBILITY TELECOMMUNICATIONS

Account Number: 7984568-1532
Bill for April 26 – May 26

Account Holder:
Priya Patel

Billing Address:
89A County Line Rd, Denver, CO 80012

Monthly Statement Summary

Mobility Digital Cable	$24.99
Mobility Internet	$34.99
Mobility Digital Voice	$19.99
In-home Repair Service	$19.95
Total Monthly Amount	$99.92
Discount	-$19.98
Total Amount Due	$79.94
Payment Method	Credit Card

Q. What did Ms. Patel do before her bill was issued?

(A) She applied for a credit card.

(B) She completed an online survey.

(C) She paid a late fee.

(D) She changed an existing service.

어휘 representative 담당 직원 script 대본 enable 할 수 있게 하다 address 다루다, 처리하다 concern 관심사 appropriately 적절하게 post 게시하다 outline ~의 요점을 말하다 detail 세부 사항 benefit 혜택 assist 돕다 verify 확인하다 billing address 청구지 주소 account 계정 greatly 매우 value 소중하게 여기다 customer satisfaction 고객 만족 be eligible to ~할 자격이 있는 patronage 단골 거래, 애용

MOBILITY TELECOMMUNICATIONS MOBILITY 통신

All representatives assisting customers over the phone are expected to do so using the following script. This script will enable you to address customers' questions and concerns more appropriately.

전화상으로 고객들을 지원하는 모든 상담원들은 다음 대본을 이용하여 안내하시면 되겠습니다. 이 대본은 여러분이 고객의 질문과 관심사를 더 적절히 처리할 수 있도록 해줄 것입니다.

Monthly offers are also posted on the Web site and representatives should check for them at the beginning of every month. Ensure that you outline the details and benefits to customers who call.

월간 제안 상품도 웹사이트상에 게시되어 있으므로 상담원들은 매월 초 그것들을 확인해야 합니다. 여러분은 반드시 전화하는 고객들에게 세부 정보와 혜택들을 설명해 주어야 합니다.

Opening: Hello and thank you for calling Mobility Telecommunications. My name is _____, and I will be assisting you. What is your reason for calling today?

시작: 안녕하세요, Mobility 통신에 전화해 주셔서 감사합니다. 제 이름은 _____이며, 제가 고객님을 도와드릴 것입니다. 오늘 무엇 때문에 전화하셨나요?

Verify Customer Information: May I have a full name and the billing address on your account?

고객 정보 확인: 제가 고객님의 계정의 성명과 청구서 발송 주소를 알 수 있을까요?

Feedback Request: We greatly value your feedback. If you would take a moment of your time to complete a customer satisfaction survey on our Web site, it would benefit us in providing the best possible service to you, our customer. **Customers who complete surveys are eligible to receive a 20% discount on their next bill.**

> 4. 요금 할인을 받은 이유가 나와 있습니다.

의견 요청: 저희는 고객님의 의견을 정말 소중히 생각합니다. 저희 웹사이트 상에서 고객 만족 설문을 작성할 시간을 내주시면, 저희가 고객님께 가능한 한 최상의 서비스를 제공하는 데 도움이 될 것입니다. 설문을 작성하신 고객들에게는 다음 청구 시에 20퍼센트 할인을 받을 자격이 주어집니다.

Closing: Thank you for your call, and as always, we appreciate your patronage. We hope that we were able to provide some assistance to you.

마무리: 전화해 주셔서 감사합니다. 그리고 언제나처럼 애용해 주시는 것을 감사드립니다. 저희가 도움이 되었기를 바랍니다.

MOBILITY TELECOMMUNICATIONS MOBILITY 통신

Account Number: 7984568-1532 계정 번호: 7984568-1532
Bill for April 26–May 26 청구 기간 4월 26일 – 5월 26일

Monthly Statement Summary
월간 내역 요약

Mobility Digital Cable $24.99
Mobility 디지털 케이블
Mobility Internet $34.99
Mobility 인터넷
Mobility Digital Voice $19.99
Mobility 디지털 음성
In-home Repair Service $19.95
가정 방문 수리 서비스
Total Monthly Amount $99.92
월간 총합계

Discount .... –$19.98
할인
Total Amount Due....................... $79.94
납부금 총합계
Payment Method.................Credit Card
결제 방식   신용 카드

Account Holder: 계정 보유자
Priya Patel

Billing Address: 청구서 발송 주소
89A County Line Rd, Denver, CO 80012

> 2. Patel 씨에게 발행된 청구서임을 알 수 있습니다.
> 3. 요금 할인을 받았음을 알 수 있습니다.

Q. What did Ms. Patel do before her bill was issued? Patel 씨가 자신의 청구서가 발송되기 전에 한 일은?
(A) She applied for a credit card. 신용 카드를 신청했다.
(B) She completed an online survey. 온라인 설문을 작성했다.
(C) She paid a late fee. 연체료를 지불했다.
(D) She changed an existing service. 기존 서비스를 변경했다.

> 1. Patel이 언급된 부분을 먼저 찾고, 청구서의 특이한 점을 찾아야 합니다.
> 5. 청구서의 할인된 금액은 설문 조사에 응했기 때문임을 알 수 있으므로 정답은 (B)가 됩니다.

해설 양쪽 지문을 모두 고려해야 하는 문제로, 첫째 지문의 Customers who complete surveys are eligible to receive a 20% discount on their next bill.에서 설문을 작성한 고객들은 다음 청구 시에 20퍼센트 할인을 받을 것이라고 했는데, Patel 씨가 받은 청구서인 둘째 지문에서 월간 총합계(Total Monthly Amount) 99.92달러 중 할인(Discount)이 19.98달러이므로 Patel 씨가 온라인 설문을 작성해 할인을 받았음을 알 수 있다. 따라서 (B)가 정답이다.

Questions 1-5 refer to the following letters and employee handbook

To: Emily Lake <emily2@gmail.com>
From: Thomas Perez <Perezpersonnel@jacob.com>
Date: October 25
Subject: Job offer

Dear Ms. Emily Lake:

We are pleased to offer you employment at Jacob Electronics. We feel that your skills and background will be valuable assets to our team. Your starting date will be November 1 and you will be working under the direct supervision of the territory manager.

The enclosed employee handbook outlines the compensation, medical and retirement benefits that our company offers. If you choose to accept this offer, please sign the second copy of this letter in the space provided and return it to us. A stamped, self-addressed envelope is enclosed for your convenience. We look forward to welcoming you as a new employee at Jacob Electronics.

Sincerely,

Thomas Perez
Personnel Director

To: Thomas Perez <Perezpersonnel@jacob.com>
From: Emily Lake <emily2@gmail.com>
Date: October 26
Subject: Job offer

Dear Mr. Thomas Perez,

I'm very pleased to accept your offer of employment for the position of sales associate. I really enjoyed interviewing with Mr. Brandon Woods and look forward to working under his guidance. I have examined the employee handbook you sent to me and fully accept the job offer.

However, I have concerns about my starting day. The project I'm in charge of at my current work has not finished yet. My manager wants me to finish the task before I leave. I think it will take about two weeks. Would it be possible for me to begin work on November 14 instead? Please let me as soon as possible.

Thank you and I look forward to being an employee of Jacob Electronics.

Sincerely,

Emily Lake

Emily Lake
Thermo Fisher Scientific,
New Jersey, 07676
(847) 305-8325

Jacob Electronics
215 West 5th Street
New York, NY 10013
(212) 555-8753

1. When does Ms. Emily Lake want to start work?
   (A) On October 25
   (B) On October 26
   (C) On November 1
   (D) On November 14

2. What is the purpose of the second letter?
   (A) To request an interview
   (B) To accept a job offer
   (C) To apply for a job
   (D) To inquire about the employee handbook

3. What is Brandon Woods' position at Jacob Electronics?
   (A) Secretary
   (B) Sales Associate
   (C) Director of Human Resources
   (D) Territory manager

4. Why is Ms. Emily Lake unable to start work on November 1?
   (A) She hasn't finished a task at her current job
   (B) She has no intention to retire.
   (C) The office is being renovated.
   (D) She doesn't like the working conditions.

5. Where is Jacob Electronics located?
   (A) In New York
   (B) In New Jersey
   (C) In San Francisco
   (D) In Chicago

Unit 19 고득점을 위한 독해 연습

단일 지문

Questions 1-3 refer to the following article.

Atlanta, Georgia
May 1
Atlanta News
Geoff Deiner

Avalon Industries, currently one of the largest firms in the country, has announced plans to sell off parts of its large business. This news comes as a shock to many.

It is also reported that the company head, Henry Dostan, will step down from his current position because of health reasons. Many worry that the company will not remain sustainable. Mr. Dostan is credited with not only saving the company but also guiding it to become a world leader in electronics.

Unfortunately, Mr. Dostan was not present at the press conference, but recently appointed Vice President Rio Franz was, and he was available to answer many questions that people had about the reasons for selling parts of the business. When asked if the company was headed towards a similar path as that of rival company GoodTech (who filed for bankruptcy last year), he stated that Avalon Industries was "simply cutting down unnecessary spending to create more high-quality products."

Many reports are stating that Rio Franz may be the first in line for the company's succession, but the company has yet to release an official statement regarding the matter.

1. What is the topic of the article?
   (A) A company is downsizing.
   (B) A company has been sued.
   (C) A company has gone out of business.
   (D) A company bought a rival company.

2. What did Rio Franz mention as a reason for the company selling parts of its business?
   (A) The company is being merged by a rival company.
   (B) The company wishes to minimize the costs.
   (C) The company is in danger of bankruptcy.
   (D) The company's product is not selling well.

3. What is indicated about Rio Franz?
   (A) He is retiring due to health concerns.
   (B) He attended a press conference.
   (C) He has worked in the company for many years.
   (D) He has officially been announced as the next company president.

Questions 1-3 refer to the following letter and invitation.

Wildwood
121 Lakeside Street
Eastern, NJ
Phone: 862-555-1674 Fax: 494-555-4186

January 9

Mrs. Linn Rummings
Meadow Apartments, Apt 32A
Eastern, NJ 18633

Dear Mrs. Rummings:

We cordially invite you to join us in celebrating the retirement of our office manager, Mr. Umbridge. Mr. Umbridge has been a part of the Wildwood family for a long time and has worked hard during his tenure. He first assumed his current position 23 years ago, after being transferred from another office. We, here at Wildwood, would like to thank Mr. Umbridge for providing us with numerous professional development opportunities. We have sincerely enjoyed working with him throughout the years and have always appreciated his support. Although Mr. Umbridge will retire only on the first of next month, the retirement ceremony will be held on January 31 at Olivia's Winery. The company president will also attend this ceremony.

Moreover, this ceremony is being held unbeknownst to Mr. Umbridge, so please do not tell him. If you would like to come to the celebration, please reply to this letter.
Thank you and we hope to see you on that special day!

Sincerely,

James Turner
Wildwood Offices

Dear Mr. Turner:

I received your letter about Mr. Umbridge's retirement. However, owing to a conflicting schedule that day, I regret to inform you that I will not be able to attend the ceremony. Unfortunately, my relatives from out of town will be coming to visit me the same day. I have heard that his colleagues are throwing a small party the day before the ceremony. I will probably be there for this party, though I certainly wish I could attend both events. Once again, I apologize about not being able to make it to the ceremony.

Sincerely,

Linn Rummings

1. What is the purpose of the letter?
   (A) To invite a coworker to a ceremony
   (B) To state a notice of tenure
   (C) To reserve a restaurant
   (D) To ask for driving directions

2. When will Mr. Umbridge retire?
   (A) January 9
   (B) January 30
   (C) January 31
   (D) February 1

3. What is true about the retirement ceremony?
   (A) It coincides with Linn's birthday party.
   (B) It will be at Wildwood Offices.
   (C) Only his office workers will attend.
   (D) It is a surprise party.

4. What should Mrs. Rummings do if she wishes to attend?
   (A) Confirm attendance through a letter
   (B) Meet at a restaurant
   (C) Speak with Mr. Umbridge
   (D) Call or send a fax to the office

5. What is suggested about Mrs. Rummings?
   (A) She is the president of a company.
   (B) She has another appointment.
   (C) She is 23 years old.
   (D) She is being transferred to another office.

Questions 1-5 refer to the following article, expense report and e-mail.

Jan. 3

CES - International Consumer Electronics Show - is one of the world's largest trade fairs which is held every January in Las Vegas. Internationally renowned manufacturers in the electronics industry showcase here annually the latest products and a growing number of people from around the world are visiting Vegas. Visitors can find out here in depth and comprehensive information on the latest developments, trends and products.

CES 2018 will be another record breaking show, with more than four thousand companies exhibiting across 200,000 net square meters of show floor space – the largest show in CES history. We expect the show to highlight major breakthroughs in the way of transportation, smart connections and future technologies.

The CES International Consumer Electronics Show will take place for 4 days this year.

Travel Expense report

Name: Allen Herman   Employee ID: M15101200
E-mail: allenh@jkelectronics.com   Approved by James White

Date	Description	Amount	Memo
Jan. 25	Accommodation	$ 150	
Jan. 25	Meals (Lunch & Dinner)	$ 100	With clients
Jan. 26	Accommodation	$ 150	
Jan. 26	Meals (Lunch & Dinner)	$ 115	With clients
Jan. 27	Rental Car (For 3days)	$ 430	
Jan. 27	Fuel (For 3days)	$ 85	

Signature: *Allen Herman*   Date: Jan. 31

I certify that I have paid out these amounts for new smartphone model J8 promotion related activities. Please reimburse me for the expenses as soon as possible.

To: Allen Herman <allenh@jkelectronics.com>
From: Amanda White <amandaw@jkelectronics.com>
Date: Feb 2
Subject: Business expenses

Dear Mr. Allen Herman,

I'm writing to acknowledge your travel expense report. As you know, receipts are required for all expenses spent over the amount of $5. Thank you and your marketing team members for contributing to raising awareness of our company. Receipts should be attached to the Travel Expense Report, and arranged in the order that they are listed on that report. Original, itemized receipts must be submitted for reimbursement:

Original itemized receipts showing what was purchased must be attached to the Travel Expense Report form. If the receipt does not show that the amount was paid in full, proof of payment must also be attached. (such as a credit card slip or statement) Please note that proof of payment alone is not sufficient. There must be an itemized list of items purchased.

Also, there must be a complete description of why the expenditure was a business expense.

If you have further questions about it, please contact me directly. Thank you.

Sincerely,

Amanda White

1. What is NOT suggested about CES?
   (A) It is held annually in Las Vegas.
   (B) People from all over the world participate in the show.
   (C) CES 2018 will be the largest ever.
   (D) It takes place for a week.

2. In the article, the word "showcase" in paragraph 1, line 3 is closest in meaning to
   (A) display
   (B) introduce
   (C) sell
   (D) purchase

3. When was the CES 2018 held?
   (A) In early February
   (B) In late January
   (C) In early September
   (D) In late October

4. _____ is the highest price Mr. Herman spent during his business trip?
   (A) Accommodation
   (B) Meals
   (C) Rental Car
   (D) Fuel

5. In which department most likely does Mr. Herman work?
   (A) Accounting
   (B) Sales
   (C) Marketing
   (D) Personnel

Final Test

READING TEST

In the Reading Test, you will read a variety of texts and answer several different types of reading comprehension questions. The entire Reading test will last 75 minutes. There are three parts, and directions are given for each part. You are encouraged to answer as many questions as possible within the time allowed. You must mark your answers on the separate answer sheet. Do not write your answers in the test book.

PART 5

Directions: A word or phrase is missing in each of the sentences below. Four answer choices are given below each sentence. Select the best answer to complete the sentence. Then mark the letter (A), (B), (C), or (D) on your answer sheet.

101. In a press conference earlier this morning, GLT Motors ------- its plan to expand its sales network across Asia, particularly in India.
    (A) is announced
    (B) would announce
    (C) announced
    (D) announces

102. The advertisement showed various internship ------- for undergraduates.
    (A) opens
    (B) opened
    (C) opening
    (D) openings

103. Sortabiz Travel offers ------- rates for hotels, transfers, and package tours at prices lower than those charged by other agencies.
    (A) reflective
    (B) competitive
    (C) protective
    (D) excessive

104. A journalist from Nations Magazine suggested that Mr. Forrest was one of ------- most influential politicians last year.
    (A) its
    (B) some
    (C) the
    (D) much

105. At TOPS Supermarkets, we offer a service to deliver your purchased groceries to your homes for an additional ------- of $10.
    (A) bill
    (B) invoice
    (C) charge
    (D) estimate

106. The laboratory is recognized as a center of ------- in research and teaching.
    (A) excel
    (B) excelled
    (C) excellent
    (D) excellence

107 As a result of the crash, the traffic surveillance team is ------- investigating the cause of the accident.
(A) evenly
(B) currently
(C) randomly
(D) meagerly

108 In addition to the standard transport containers, Zinno Shipping has special containers for the transport of ------- goods.
(A) perish
(B) perishes
(C) perishable
(D) perishables

109 Labels are attached on the panels ------- each section to allow shoppers to find their groceries more easily.
(A) beyond
(B) until
(C) above
(D) onto

110 The Endikas Corporation manufactures affordable sports clothing, ------- accessories for athletes.
(A) to start with
(B) as well as
(C) moreover
(D) similarly

111 The book, "How to Be a Trainee" was highly ------- by interns for its thorough introduction to career success.
(A) regarded
(B) regarding
(C) regards
(D) to regards

112 The TOSCA steel factory ------- tour groups on Wednesdays and Thursdays from 10:30 A.M. to 5:30 P.M.
(A) waits
(B) belongs
(C) welcomes
(D) remains

113 Conveyor belts were ------- placed to help speed up the loading process for delivery.
(A) strategic
(B) strategies
(C) strategized
(D) strategically

114 Students of Holgen Academy are meeting ------- at the Chandel Library to prepare for the upcoming final exam.
(A) more
(B) usually
(C) together
(D) highly

115 The IDM Guard Company has developed a network security software program ------- protects computer users from the risk of valuable data theft.
(A) that
(B) still
(C) so
(D) how

116 Garbage from independent houses must be put in specified garbage bags and placed in ------- areas for disposal.
(A) designated
(B) designation
(C) designating
(D) designates

GO ON TO THE NEXT PAGE

117. Mr. McKnight will be unavailable for ------- on May 13 due to his business conference in Montreal.
    (A) reputation
    (B) confidence
    (C) potential
    (D) consultation

118. Economic analyst, Gerry Ford ------- that the prices of commodities have been increasing rapidly since last year.
    (A) have noted
    (B) noting
    (C) being noted
    (D) noted

119. Due ------- to weather-related disasters, the amount of insured losses over the last four years exceeded $308 billion.
    (A) largely
    (B) large
    (C) largeness
    (D) larger

120. At NXI University, ------- offer educational opportunities to students all around the world.
    (A) we
    (B) our
    (C) us
    (D) ours

121. Mr. Oscar Johnson, a successful tailor, has established more than 10 branches of his tailor shops ------- the country.
    (A) throughout
    (B) opposite
    (C) during
    (D) besides

122. Myology expert, Dr. Sandoval stated that women who ------- wear high heels have shortened the calf muscles.
    (A) regular
    (B) regularly
    (C) regularity
    (D) regulars

123. Those who have not yet ------- a training presentation are expected to register for the last presentation this Friday.
    (A) employed
    (B) attended
    (C) participated
    (D) responded

124. The ------- waters of many Southeast Asian countries have some of the world's richest ecosystems.
    (A) coasts
    (B) coastal
    (C) coaster
    (D) coastlines

125. Applicants must submit a portfolio ------- several samples of their own work before the interview.
    (A) through
    (B) with
    (C) along
    (D) like

126. ------- IRS Electronics releases its new refrigerator, the prices of older models will eventually decrease
    (A) Whether
    (B) When
    (C) Immediately
    (D) Afterward

127 The manufacturers of the Alvimopan have suspended all studies of the drug until data can be further ------- and approved.
(A) supervised
(B) required
(C) analyzed
(D) vacated

128 Last month Medieport Inc. stated that it ------- to sell its 2.6 percent holding in Tecoz Corp. within 3 years.
(A) initiates
(B) previews
(C) intends
(D) considers

129 One of Mr. Daniels' most ------- achievements is his campaign for providing the best services in the airport terminal.
(A) noteworthy
(B) satisfied
(C) perceptive
(D) united

130 ------- who are wishing to apply for the student exchange program must finish their registration before January 10.
(A) Whoever
(B) Another
(C) Those
(D) Each

PART 6

Directions: Read the texts on the following pages. A word or phrase is missing in some of the sentences. Four answer choices are given below each of these sentences. Select the best answer to complete the text. Then mark the letter (A), (B), (C), or (D) on your answer sheet.

Questions 131-134 refer to the following press release.

For immediate release

18 July - FlashTech Inc. announced the appointment of Barbara Ivory as the new chief investment officer, as initially recommended by the --- 131. --- chief executive officer, Isaac Underwood.

Apart from her mutual connection with the company's ex-CEO, Ms. Ivory's impressive work experience has provided great interest to company officials. Before --- 132. --- FlashTech, her duty as chief sales manager at Quake Electronics was credited as superb, as was her service in various other roles, such as those in marketing research and product development.

She --- 133. --- her career as a part-time worker in the Telizen Post Financial Group. "We are lucky to have Ms. Ivory with us and we trust that her experience will be invaluable to our future." said Stanley Blythe, FlashTech's CEO. --- 134. ---.

---

131 (A) nearest
(B) former
(C) alternate
(D) potential

132 (A) joining
(B) founding
(C) promoting
(D) completing

133 (A) to begin
(B) begins
(C) began
(D) will begin

NEW

134 (A) Investors of the FlashTech are also positive to the announcement.
(B) The new CEO plans to take a vacation after his retirement.
(C) Everybody believes Issac Underwood will be the best CEO in the history.
(D) All full-time workers work 8 hours a day.

Questions 135-138 refer to the following letter.

Murray-Jones Real Estate
69 Lincoln Pl
Irvington, NJ 07111

December 15

Ms. Stella Lambert
119 Magnolia Ave.
Jersey City, NJ 07306

Dear Ms. Lambert,

My partner, Emmett Jones said to me that you had spoken with him about your plans to transfer to Irvington. --- 135. --- also mentioned that you were looking for something special due to particular requirements in your profession. I have previously assisted other individuals in similar situations, therefore I understand how difficult it may be when someone is --- 136. --- a sizeable workshop. Luckily, we were able to find a very spacious loft, which is extensible, in accordance with the specifications you made with regard to your large equipment, as you can see in the enclosed photographs.
Please inform me whether you think this room would be --- 137. --- enough for you.
We could subsequently discuss further details, and possibly arrange a mutually convenient time to visit the property, if you wish.
I will look forward to hearing from you. --- 138. ---.

Sincerely,
Ricky Murray

---

135 (A) He
(B) She
(C) We
(D) They

136 (A) selling
(B) seeking
(C) cleaning
(D) renovating

137 (A) warm
(B) close
(C) quiet
(D) big

NEW
138 (A) The real estate agent we send to you is highly qualified.
(B) You may contact me on 351-555-0943.
(C) The price of property in the region will rise considerably.
(D) Please send me the invoice as soon as possible.

GO ON TO THE NEXT PAGE

Questions 139-142 refer to the following memo.

To: Workers and Inspectors
From: David Keanes, Product Manager
Date: February 11
Subject: Spinex 5

I am writing to let you know that we --- 139. --- some unexpected complaints from our customers concerning the door seal on our new Spinex 5 washing machine. --- 140. ---.
Regarding this issue, I would like to remind our workers to ensure that the door seal is
--- 141. --- installed during assembly.
In addition, inspectors are required to double-check these --- 142. --- and confirm that there are no problems with the product prior to shipping.
If you wish to know more information about the Spinex 5 washing machine complaints or have any questions, please contact me on 555-2829. Thank you for your continued dedication to the company.

139 (A) have received
(B) will receive
(C) receiving
(D) receive

NEW
140 (A) Almost every household is equipped with a washing machine.
(B) Spinex 5 washing machine is our latest model.
(C) The majority of these messages indicate that the customers were dissatisfied with the inability to close the door because of a faulty seal.
(D) Customers are excited to see a new model.

141 (A) rapidly
(B) properly
(C) comfortably
(D) certainly

142 (A) payments
(B) vehicles
(C) schedules
(D) parts

Questions 143-146 refer to the following article.

Birmingham, England, 10 April - One of England's leading manufacturers of innovative electronic devices, Broswick Industries, has announced the --- 143. --- of Mr. Arnold Gilbert.
Previously Broswick Industries' sales director in London, Mr. Gilbert will now be serving in the Birmingham office as global managing director.
Mr. Gilbert mentioned plans that he hopes he will increase the sales quota by 10%.
--- 144. ---, he will be preparing to develop new products and improve customer services.
He also wishes to expand Broswick Industries by establishing new export markets in North America and Asia, while --- 145. --- stronger sales with the existing customer base in the United Kingdom. --- 146. ---.

143 (A) hiring
(B) preference
(C) promotion
(D) extension

144 (A) Nevertheless
(B) Rather
(C) As requested
(D) In particular

145 (A) maintain
(B) maintaining
(C) maintains
(D) maintenance

NEW

146 (A) Many other companies plan to build new factories in the area.
(B) Critics predict that other regions of Europe will also become new markets for Broswick products.
(C) Citizens expect more employment opportunities in the area.
(D) After months of deliberation, Mr. Gilbert decided to accept the proposal.

PART 7

Directions: In this part, you will read a selection of texts, such as magazine and newspaper articles, letters, and advertisements. Each text is followed by several questions. Select the best answer for each question and mark the letter (A), (B), (C), or (D) on your answer sheet.

Questions 147-148 refer to the following calendar.

Reservations for Room 104, April 22-26					
	Monday, Apr. 22	Tuesday, Apr. 23	Wednesday, Apr. 24	Thursday, Apr. 25	Friday, Apr. 26
9:00 A.M.	Global Economics Course A			Global Economics Course B	
11:00 A.M.		Multicultural Communication Exercise			Environmental Safety Seminar
1:00 P.M.	Lecture by Mr. Harley Logner on Entrepreneurship		Lecture by Dr. Gavin Heinrich on Socialization		
3:00 P.M.		Learning Health and Modern Medicine			Biochemistry Lab Workshop
5:00 P.M.				Voluntary Service Club Meeting	
7:00 P.M.	Study Group Session 1		Study Group Session 2		Study Group Session 3

147 Where is Room 104 most likely located?
(A) In a community center
(B) In a business company
(C) In a university building
(D) In a science institution

148 What event is scheduled on the same day as Learning Health and Modern Medicine?
(A) Environmental Safety Seminar
(B) Biochemistry Lab Workshop
(C) Voluntary Service Club Meeting
(D) Multicultural Communication Exercise

Questions 149-150 refer to the following e-mail.

To: All employees <employees@neolab.com>
From: Tierra Ashmore <tashmore@neolab.com>
Subject: Information
Date: July 20

To all employees at NeoLab Manufacturing Inc.:

I am writing to inform you of a temporary halt in the assembly line. The recent weather has caused much damage to the factory in sector C, and we are preparing to take this opportunity to renovate the facility.

Fortunately, we are ahead of the production schedule and have received no new orders. Moreover, due to these events, the board has graciously decided to grant a 1-week break to all employees in every department, starting next month.

The date of issue for paychecks will be the same as usual; however, employees in each department are required to work in weekly interval schedules.

Therefore, please submit the details of the week you would like to take off to Nigel Perrin by next week.

Sincerely,

Tierra Ashmore
General Manager

149 Why did Ms. Ashmore send the e-mail?

(A) To clarify a machine replacement
(B) To confirm a new payroll date
(C) To introduce a new production manager
(D) To announce a paid vacation

150 What are employees asked to do?

(A) Work during the next weekend
(B) Send a desired vacation schedule
(C) Check their new working hours
(D) Decline orders from customers

Questions 151-153 refer to the following letter.

November 6

Cherlyn Cecil

4710 Centennial Lane

Ellicott City, MD 21094

Dear Ms. Cecil,

Thank you for your continued visits to the Bellatio Club & Spa. I would like to inform you that the expiration date for your club membership is approaching very soon. To renew your status, just visit us online at www.bellatioclub.com/member and fill out a short application form. Your registration number is 182938.

Once completed, we will send you your new transaction card. The card will have the same account number as before, but with a new pin code.

If you have any questions, or want to receive more information, please call us, and our front desk receptionists will be happy to assist you.

Sincerely,

Jayson Calderon

Jayson Calderon

Membership Coordinator

662-555-5013

---

151 Why was the letter sent to Ms. Cecil?

(A) To invite her to join a club

(B) To notify her of an order completion

(C) To suggest a membership extension

(D) To inquire about a credit card status

152 What information appears in the letter?

(A) A pin code

(B) A contact number

(C) An account number

(D) An expiry date

153 What is Ms. Cecil instructed to do?

(A) Visit the Web site

(B) Call Jayson Calderon

(C) Attach a registration form

(D) Submit a payment for transaction

Questions 154-155 refer to the following receipt.

The Dublin Corner
28 Mary Ann Street

Newnan, GA 30265

770-555-6831

Customer: Nathan Hill	Sept. 17
At Your Service: Rianna Torres	14:26:18

Description

7 Guides To Healthy Exercise	$2.00
The Sound of Love Falling	$3.50
Tales of the Chinese Tradition	$3.50
Subtotal	$9.00
Tax 7%	$0.63
Total due	$9.63
Amount tendered	$10.00
Change	$0.37

Reminder of Policy

Customers are permitted to rent a maximum of six items at a time. All items must be returned within 48 hours from the date of lease. Customers will be fully charged for any damaged or lost merchandise. Overdue fees equal to the value of the relevant item(s) will be issued upon late returns.

154 What type of business is the Dublin Corner?
(A) A local bookstore
(B) A video rental shop
(C) A fitness center
(D) A language institution

155 What is true about the policy?
(A) A minimum of six items can be borrowed.
(B) Items are to be returned within 2 days.
(C) Lost items are charged at double the cost.
(D) Overdue fines are issued the next day.

GO ON TO THE NEXT PAGE

Questions 156-158 refer to the following letter.

May 25
Naomi Dumas
1903 Sevier St.
Nashville, TN 37205

Dear Ms. Dumas,

Thank you for your recent inquiry regarding our business. I'm glad to hear that you are considering our services, and understand that you would like further information.

Keynote Academy has been instructing various individuals in a musical education for more than 10 years. Those interested in music, both gifted and inexperienced, young and old, have been coming to our facility to learn and practice their desired instruments with our team of 20 skilled musicians.

Keynote Academy specifically offers the following services.

- We teach courses that cover the basics of musical theory and composition.
- We have programs for one-on-one tutoring and group activities.
- We provide advanced practice sessions and a variety of musical pieces.

If you wish to receive details of prices or have a further consultation, please feel free to contact us at 615-555-4688, or visit our website at www.keynote.academy.edu

Sincerely,

Roselina Velasco
Head Instructor
Keynote Academy

---

156 Why was the letter written?
(A) To arrange a consulting schedule
(B) To recommend a job opening
(C) To plan an academic system
(D) To provide information regarding services

157 According to the letter, what does Keynote Academy NOT provide?
(A) Group-oriented programs
(B) Classes for beginners
(C) Free musical instruments
(D) Several types of instruments

158 What is suggested about Keynote Academy?
(A) It has a competitive price.
(B) It sponsors talented students.
(C) It offers private lessons.
(D) It consists of a few instructors.

Questions 159-161 refer to the following letter.

Vancouver View Magazine

January 21

Deshawn Quiroz
66 SW Marine Dr
Vancouver, BC
V6T 1Z4

Dear Mr. Quiroz,

We would like to give you heads-up information on our newly released TMP edition, which is enclosed in this mail package. This special edition allows you to have access to a list of the latest reviews of popular local restaurants, entertainment venues, sports facilities and clothes shops. It will also include raffle tickets for the chance to win free prizes, such as cosmetics or a vacation overseas.

To show you our appreciation of your extended support, we offer this month's issue to you free of charge. If you decide to continue receiving service next month, your monthly bill will increase by only $7.50.

We are also promoting a referral program. If any of your friends or family members subscribe to our magazine on the basis of your recommendation, we will give you an extra issue for free!

For more information, please check our Web site at www.vviewmagazine.ca, or if you have any questions or concerns, call us on 405-555-4722.

Sincerely,

Isaac Gough
Isaac Gough
Customer Care Representative

---

159 What is the purpose of the letter?

(A) To explain a new service to a client
(B) To inform a customer that a bill must be paid
(C) To commemorate a special event
(D) To advertise a television subscription

160 What might be included in the TMP edition of the Vancouver View Magazine?

(A) Reviews of a nearby bistro
(B) Raffle tickets to win a trip to Canada
(C) Discount coupons for clothes shops
(D) Listings of upcoming local events

161 What will happen if Mr. Quiroz chooses to continue receiving the magazine?

(A) He will receive a free issue.
(B) His family will be entitled to a discount.
(C) The costs will be added to his bill.
(D) The price of each product will increase.

GO ON TO THE NEXT PAGE

Questions 162-165 refer to the following article.

London, December 3 – Ethan Warner, who is a business journalist from Bizilliant, a non-governmental research organization, had the opportunity to interview a couple of interesting people.

45-year-old Sebastian Lynch is a freelance travel critic. Mr. Lynch's daily routine consists of sleeping in luxurious hotels and eating in fancy restaurants, but he also spends a lot of time managing his travel review Web site. "It's surprising to see how many people want to know about the quality of services in certain locations. That's why I go ahead and enjoy it, and then write a full review, taking every single detail into account, such as testing the softness of slippers and wi-fi strengths, as well as assessing the cleanness of facilities." he said. Although Mr. Lynch's occupation does not come with a high salary, he is more than satisfied and takes pleasure in his work.

Despite her young age, 22-year-old Kate Summers is a self-employed on-site photographer. She recently began her business by taking wedding and portrait photos upon request, and sending them to her clients. She mentioned that she is pleased with her career, saying, "It's not a profitable job, but the places that I go to and the people I meet are what makes the experience more exciting. I can't get enough of it."

These two individuals have very distinct similarities. One thing they both have in common is doing what they love to do, regardless of their low income. Bizilliant general manager Jack Randall stated how more people prefer doing their dream job than a job that brings money. "Living with a job that will make you happy will bring benefit in the long run," he said. More than 1,000 people from a wide variety of occupations in London responded to a survey conducted by Bizilliant, with statistics showing more workers preferred to work happily than to work because of good pay.

162 What is the purpose of the article?
(A) To explain how to start a new business
(B) To analyze recent job tendencies
(C) To report the benefits of self-employment
(D) To focus on a certain age group

163 What is NOT indicated about the two interviewed individuals?
(A) They are quickly promoted.
(B) They are both self-employed.
(C) They belong to different age groups.
(D) They are both low-paid workers.

164 Who works as a manager?
(A) Ethan Warner
(B) Kate Summers
(C) Sebastian Lynch
(D) Jack Randall

165 According to the article, what is true about the survey?
(A) It was released on December 3.
(B) It was conducted by the government.
(C) Fewer than 1,000 people responded to it.
(D) It was taken by people with different jobs.

Questions 166-169 refer to the following memo.

From: Emma Stevens, Executive Secretary
To: All employees
Subject: Training Workshop
Date: August 8

As you all know by now, the Nurplex Co. training workshop will take place next Monday, August 12. Due to much concern and interest from the committee, the board has also decided to attend the workshop. Furthermore, since additional preparation is needed along with a larger space, the workshop will now be held in room 315 of the Crestview Convention Center instead of the Conference Hall in our office building. The remainder of the event, including the schedule outlined in my July 29 memo, remains unchanged.

Since the results of last month's worker performance assessment were surprisingly unsatisfactory, the committee has decided to make this a mandatory event. Therefore, all Nurplex Co. employees are required to attend. In addition, our company president, Mr. Charlie Watkins, will be presenting the opening speech in the morning, so everyone is requested to be on time. Light snacks and refreshments will be available. Please remember that employee identification cards will be inspected by a security guard at the main door. If you have any questions, please contact me at my office on extension 559, or leave a message.

166 Why was the memo sent?
(A) To remind employees of an office relocation plan
(B) To request a time change for a business dinner party
(C) To report a new location for an event
(D) To warn of an upcoming spot inspection

167 What is indicated about Ms. Stevens?
(A) She is the president of Nurplex Company.
(B) She conducted a performance assessment.
(C) She sent a previous memo about an event.
(D) She will be presenting an opening speech.

168 The word "mandatory" in paragraph 2, line 2, is closest in meaning to
(A) compulsory
(B) unessential
(C) spontaneous
(D) annual

169 What are attendees requested to do?
(A) Do not be late at the event
(B) Prepare light snacks and refreshments
(C) Show identification at a parking booth
(D) Call Mr. Watkins' office on extension 559

GO ON TO THE NEXT PAGE

Questions 170-171 refer to the text message chain.

Cara Montana 10:02
Hi, Joe. Did you hear that a new electronics store is opening tomorrow?

Eddy Johnson 10:02
Yes, it's called Great Buy, right?

Cara Montana 10:03
Would you like to go there with me tomorrow? They are having a big opening sale tomorrow.

Eddy Johnson 10:03
Oh, really? What time do you want to go?

Cara Montana 10:03
It will open at 11. So how about 10:30? Too early?

Eddy Johnson 10:04
Let's say 10:45. I will drive and pick you up.

Cara Montana 10:04
Thanks. Are you going to buy something?

Eddy Johnson 10:05
I need to buy a new cell phone. My cell phone LED is broken. I have been using this for three years.

Cara Montana 10:06
Oh, I can help you choose a right one for you. I need to drop by a grocery store to get something to eat now. See you tomorrow.

NEW

170 At 10:05 A.M. what does Mr. Johnson most likely mean when he writes, "I have been using this for three years"?

(A) He likes his cellular phone.
(B) It's time to get a new cell phone.
(C) It's too early to replace his cell phone.
(D) He had no choice but to use it.

171 What will Ms. Montana most likely do next?

(A) Ask help from sales person
(B) Purchase a new mobile phone
(C) Go to a grocery store
(D) Pick Johnson up to the electronics store

Questions 172-175 refer to the following article.

2018 Summer Music Festival in Vancouver

More than 10,000 people are expected to attend the 10th annual Summer Music Festival from July 15 to 16 scheduled to be held on the weekend at Stanley park. Last year, the festival began with a dazzling show featuring over 20 popular singers. --- [1] ---

The festival is free and open to the public. There will be fantastic music and dance performances. Meals and snacks will be available for purchase. Complimentary parking is available around the park, and shuttle buses will transport guests to and from the heart of the town center at no charge. --- [2] ---

The festival hours are 3 p.m. to 8 p.m. on Saturday. The world-renowned singer-songwriter, Jennifer Bent will start the performance at 3 p.m. on the main stage. On Sunday the festival will run from 1p.m. to 10p.m. Those planning to attend should arrive early for the best seating. --- [3] --- You can enjoy the performance by the popular guitarist Steve Bell. More information is available on the website atwww.stanleypark.ca --- [4] ---

172 What is the purpose of the article?
(A) To provide an overview of a local event
(B) To describe the popularity of a local musician
(C) To announce the grand opening of the national park
(D) To publicize musicians from Canada

173 For what will guests be charged?
(A) Priority Seating
(B) Shuttle bus rides
(C) Parking
(D) Food

174 What is indicated about Mr. Bell?
(A) He is a popular singer-songwriter.
(B) He will be at Stanley park on July 16.
(C) He has been a resident of Vancouver for ten years.
(D) He will not be available this year's event.

175 In which of the positions marked [1], [2], [3], and [4] does the following sentence best belong?
"This year, the festival features more than 30 musicians from across the country."
(A) [1]
(B) [2]
(C) [3]
(D) [4]

Questions 176-180 refer to the following advertisement and e-mails.

From: customerservice@widetechelectronics.com
To: TomRobins@ymail.com
Date: March 4
Subject: Order number 140325

Dear Mr. Robins,

Thank you for your purchase of a laptop computer and a document scanner for a total of $810. Your new widescreen and lightweight laptop computer will come fully equipped with an operating system(OS), 6GB RAM, and two USB cables. As a special bonus for spending over $800, you will also receive a complimentary carrying case.

Your purchase is scheduled to be delivered on March 15, but please be aware that you are eligible for our express shipping offer. For only $6, you can receive your purchase 5 days earlier, on March 10. In order for you to receive this upgrade offer, you must reply on or before March 7. Please be reminded that this offer will be invalid after March 7.

Thank you again for shopping with Widetech Electronics.

Sincerely,

Paris Anderson
Customer Service

From: TomRobins@ymail.com
To: customerservice@widetechelectroincs.com
Date: March 6
Subject: Re: Order number 140325

Dear Ms. Anderson,

Please upgrade my shipping to the express option and charge it to my credit card.

In addition, I will be moving within the next two weeks and would like the items shipped to my office. The correct address is specified in the "bill to" section on my order form. Please disregard the "ship to" information that I filled out in the form. Thank you.

Tom Robins

176 What is one reason the first e-mail was sent?
(A) To place a new order
(B) To change the contracts of a shipment
(C) To report a shipping delay
(D) To present a limited-time offer

177 According to the first e-mail, why will Mr. Robins receive a free item?
(A) He spent over a stated amount.
(B) He made a purchase before March 6.
(C) He opened a business account.
(D) He is a frequent customer.

178 What is NOT included with the shipment?
(A) A document scanner
(B) An operating system
(C) A screen protector
(D) A carrying case

179 When will Mr. Robins most likely receive his order?
(A) On March 5
(B) On March 6
(C) On March 10
(D) On March 15

180 What does Mr. Robins mention in his e-mail?
(A) He would prefer to upgrade the laptop computer.
(B) He wants the shipment sent to a different address.
(C) He would like to cancel two items.
(D) He is moving to an overseas location.

GO ON TO THE NEXT PAGE

Questions 181-185 refer to the following e-mails.

From: joshua.hilton@tdextrade.org
To: interns@tdxtrade.org
Date: February 11, 10:50 A.M.
Subject: Chris Gardner

Dear TD X-Trade interns,

As intern stockbrokers of TD X-Trade, you are recommended to attend an upcoming seminar with Chris Gardner, who is a top-level pension fund manager of a multi-million dollar brokerage firm.

The seminar will take place on March 4 from 1 to 6 P.M. at the Glide Memorial Conference Center, 1687 Willis Avenue, one block from the Winborne Hotel. Since Mr. Gardner is a close acquaintance of Mr. Witter, chairman of TD X-Trade, the registration fee of $200 will be covered by the administration offices for this limited event.

Although this is a voluntary event, interns should take advantage of this rare opportunity, as Mr. Gardner will be providing valuable tips on investment plans, financial management, and finding new methods in earning commission from trade deals at the scheduled seminar. A book of Mr. Gardner, *Rise Above*, valued at $40, will also be handed out to attendees free of charge.

The Glide Memorial Conference Center has an auditorium with 300 seats, in addition to a well-designed business and recreation facility, and is also equipped with complimentary Internet access. The Center has also offered a discounted parking price of $4.00 per vehicle, and a free shuttle service from Malvern train station will be available.

Please do not hesitate to contact me or the other event coordinator, Thomas Carey, at 386-555-8819, for more information.

Joshua Hilton

From: thomas.carey@tdxtrade.org
To: interns@tdxtrade.org
Date: February 11, 1:14 P.M.
Subject: Re: Chris Gardner

Dear TD X-Trade interns,

There was some inaccurate information in Joshua Hilton's e-mail from earlier this morning. The scheduled seminar will be on March 5 not 4. We apologize for this error and hope it won't create any confusion in the future.

Thank you for your understanding!

Thomas Carey

---

181 What is the purpose of the first e-mail?
(A) To promote a stock investment plan
(B) To advertise a new conference center
(C) To introduce a company chairman
(D) To invite participation at an educational event

182 How much is the original cost of the scheduled seminar?
(A) Free of charge
(B) $4.00
(C) $40.00
(D) $200.00

183 What is revealed about the Glide Memorial Conference Center?
(A) It can accommodate only 200 people.
(B) It provides free Internet services.
(C) It is located near the bus station.
(D) It does not charge parking fees.

184 Why was the second e-mail sent?
(A) To receive feedback
(B) To support a claim
(C) To correct an error
(D) To answer a question

185 Who sent the second e-mail?
(A) An event coordinator
(B) An executive officer
(C) A shuttle bus driver
(D) A building manager

Questions 186-190 refer to the following Web article, e-mail and list.

Tech Economics, San Francisco
Sep, 25

In today's offices, color copiers are absolutely necessary for any industry. Whether you need to print a photo or scan multiple documents, they are extremely useful for many different projects. Premium models are equipped with special features like stapling and hole punching capabilities to make workplace document production easy.

When deciding on the perfect color copier printer for your office, first consider how it will primarily be used. Businesses that produce high volumes of color documents, such as brochures, marketing materials or reports, will find it important to purchase a photocopier with a high resolution. Generally, 1,200 x 1,200 dpi (dots per inch) is considered very good color quality. Another characteristic you want to take note of is the toner yield, which indicates how many color images you can produce before having to change toner cartridges.

Considering all these things, the new models Kanon K-3515, JPC J-2000 and HPY Officejet X-30 can be the best pick for small and medium sized offices. These will all come into market next month.

A photocopier is a necessary part of today's busy workspace. Every office relies heavily on multitasking and needs a copy machine that can handle a variety projects. With the right photocopier, you can increase your efficiency and produce high quality images that make your company stand apart from the rest.

To: Maria Lopez
From: Dorothy Clark
Date: September 28
Subject: New Color Copier

Dear Ms. Maria Lopez,

As part of our equipment updates here at Johnny AD World, I strongly suggest the purchase of a color photocopier next month. I'd like to propose that we purchase an Officejet X-30 model from HPY. This equipment was introduced in Tech Economics, San Francisco. K-3515 model can also be a great choice, but this model doesn't have automatic stapling function.

As you know, our Marketing team has been using the outdated Officejet X-10 model for over 5 years. We can save the company some money but it's not competitive in the long run because employees waste too much time on copying, stapling and punching.

Let me know what you think about my suggestion. I will be in Fukuoka next week for a convention, but perhaps we can meet before then to discuss this in more detail. If you approve, I'd like to place an order with HPY as soon as the model becomes available.

Thank you.
Dorothy Clark

	K-3515	J-1500	X-10	X-30
Automatic paper sorting	V	V	V	V
Automatic binding	V	V		V
Automatic stapling				V
Automatic hole punching	V			V

186 Where would the article most likely appear?
 (A) In a design magazine
 (B) In a travel journal
 (C) In a financial newspaper
 (D) In a technology business magazine

187 What is inferred about the X-30?
 (A) It is the most expensive model in the market.
 (B) It can be purchased online.
 (C) It is not yet available in stores.
 (D) Discount is offered for limited time.

188 What is the purpose of the e-mail?
 (A) To suggest a product purchase
 (B) To compare magazine articles
 (C) To request maintenance service for a faulty product
 (D) To raise a fund to buy computers

189 When does Dorothy Clark want to buy the X-30 model?
 (A) In August
 (B) In September
 (C) In October
 (D) In December

190 Why does Ms. Clark recommend buying a new copier model?
 (A) It looks great.
 (B) It is inexpensive.
 (C) It will save time.
 (D) It has appeared in a magazine.

GO ON TO THE NEXT PAGE

Questions 191-195 refer to the following e-mails and list.

To: The Lux Office Building tenants
From: Ms. Anna Gray, Topcare Inc.
Date: March 15

Topcare Inc. is pleased to announce that we have assumed the management of the Lux office building beginning April 1. We will be responsible for the physical management of the property, including regular maintenance and emergency repairs.

❖ Maintenance - We will be in charge of performing preventative property maintenance to keep the property functioning in top condition. For example, we must hire someone to, check for leaks, landscape, shovel snow and remove trash. This maintenance aims to keep current tenants happy and attract new tenants.

❖ Repairs - when there is an issue, we will attend to it ourselves or must hire someone to attend to it. We have a large network of reliable plumbers, electricians, carpenters and other contractors.

We are looking forward to working with you.
Thank you.

Sincerely yours,
Anna Gray, Topcare

Below is the list of important contacts in our company. Tenants now can call whenever they need help.

Legal Department
Administrative Assistant, Mr. Pat Wescon <pwescon@topcare.com>

Building Maintenance
Facilities manager, Ms. Janice Faris <jfaris@topcare.com>
(For problems with telephone lines and internet access, please contact Mr. Zack Bardon of Wirenotch & Cable directly at bardon@wirenotch.com)

Technical support
Technical support manager, Ms. Anna Gray <anna2@topcare.com>

Topcare Inc.
908-277-2405

From: Susan Lohan <slohan@smart.com>
To: Janice Faris <jfaris@topcare.com>
Date: April 2
Subject: Lock installation

My name is Susan Lohan and I work at Smart Consulting. We are located on the fifth floor of the Lux Office Building. We would like to add an additional lock to the front door of our office in order to increase security. We will need five copies of the new key and the original. I would appreciate it if you could send me an estimate of the cost by the end of the month.

Sincerely,

Susan Lohan

---

191 What kind of business is Topcare Inc?
(A) A property management company
(B) A hardware supplier
(C) A real estate agency
(D) A construction company

192 What is indicated in the memo?
(A) The Lux office building is seeking new tenants.
(B) Telephone lines are being repaired.
(C) Topcare Inc. will hire new staff.
(D) Various individuals may be contacted for assistance.

193 To what office did Ms. Lohan write the e-mail?
(A) Legal Department
(B) Building Maintenance
(C) Technical Support
(D) General management

194 What is the purpose of Ms. Lohan's e-mail?
(A) To report a lost key
(B) To check the cost of installing locks
(C) To seek advice on office security
(D) To request information on leasing an office

195 In the memo, the word "assumed" in paragraph 1, line 1 is the closest in meaning to
(A) contacted
(B) supposed
(C) taken over
(D) decided

Questions 196-200 refer to the following advertisement, price list, and e-mail.

Haevichi Hotel & Resort - Overlooking the ocean, Haevichi Hotel combines the luxury of a resort with all the services to meet your business needs. In addition to four conference rooms for large meetings, the Ruby and Emerald halls offer the perfect solution for small groups of up to thirty people. Haevichi Hotel has both a formal dining room and a more casual cafe. All rooms are wired for Internet access, and have fax machines and coffee makers. Guests can also take advantage of the indoor and outdoor swimming pool.

For reservations or information, contact Johnlee@haevichihotel.com or call 212-780-8656.

Meeting room price list

ROOM	HALF DAY RATE	FULL DAY RATE	EQUIPMENT IN SITU IN EACH ROOM
GOLD	$ 450	$ 980	Internet, Fax and Coffee maker
SILVER	$ 450	$ 900	Internet, Fax and Coffee maker
DIAMOND	$ 400	$ 800	Internet, Fax and Coffee maker
SAPPHIRE	$ 350	$ 700	Internet, Fax and Coffee maker
RUBY	$ 250	$ 500	Internet, Fax, Coffee maker, Projector and Screen
EMERALD	$ 200	$ 400	Internet, Fax and Coffee maker

※ Please make a deposit of 50% of the total amount of your reservation.

TO: David Martin dmartin@yoondesign.com
FROM: John Lee Johnlee@haevichihotel.com
DATE: Aug 2, 2018
SUBJECT: Reservation

Dear Mr. Martin,

Thank you for your reservation for Aug 13. After paying the remainder, you can use the requested meeting room all day long on the designated date. It is the only venue equipped with overhead projector and screen.

As indicated in the price list, there is equipment in situ in each room. Please let us know what additional equipment you will need for your presentation so that we can prepare for you in advance.

In addition, to discuss the luncheon for your group, you should contact our catering manager Katherine Kim, at 212-780-8600. extension 132.

Sincerely,

John Lee
Reservations Manager, Haevichi Hotel & Resort

196 For whom is the advertisement most likely intended?
(A) Families
(B) Hotel managers
(C) Students
(D) Business professionals

197 What is NOT mentioned as a feature of the Haevichi Hotel & Resort?
(A) An exercise center
(B) Restaurants
(C) An indoor pool
(D) In-room fax machine

198 What is suggested about Mr. Martin?
(A) He is a company president.
(B) He has stayed at the Haevichi Hotel & Resort.
(C) He is responsible for a presentation.
(D) He received a discounted rate for the meeting space.

199 What is true about the meeting?
(A) Payment for the catering service has been made.
(B) No more than thirty people will attend.
(C) Participants will receive a discount on hotel rooms.
(D) Complimentary meal will be provided during the break.

200 What is the total amount of deposit David Martin has made?
(A) $ 200
(B) $ 250
(C) $ 400
(D) $ 450

메모

메모